UNDERSTANDING LITERACY AND DISADVANTAGE

SAGE was founded in 1965 by Sara Miller McCune to support the dissemination of useable knowledge by publishing innovative and high-quality research and teaching content. Today, we publish over 900 journals, including those of more than 400 learned societies, more than 800 new books per year, and a growing range of library products including archives, data, case studies, reports, and video. SAGE remains majority-owned by our founder, and after Sara's lifetime will become owned by a charitable trust that secures our continued independence.

Los Angeles | London | New Delhi | Singapore | Washington DC

DEBRA MYHILL, ANNABEL WATSON, RUTH NEWMAN AND CLARE DOWDALL

UNDERSTANDING LITERACY AND DISADVANTAGE

A SAGE Publishing Company
1 Oliver's Yard
55 City Road
London EC1Y 1SP

SAGE Publications Inc.
2455 Teller Road
Thousand Oaks, California 91320

SAGE Publications India Pvt Ltd
B 1/I 1 Mohan Cooperative Industrial Area
Mathura Road
New Delhi 110 044

SAGE Publications Asia-Pacific Pte Ltd
3 Church Street
#10-04 Samsung Hub
Singapore 049483

Library of Congress Control Number: 2022935314

British Library Cataloguing in Publication Data

**A catalogue record for this book is available from the
British Library**

Editor: Amy Thornton
Senior project editor: Chris Marke
Project management: TNQ Technologies
Marketing manager: Lorna Patkai
Cover design: Wendy Scott
Typeset by: TNQ Technologies
Printed in the UK

ISBN: 978-1-5297-8040-6
ISBN: 978-1-5297-8039-0 (pbk)

At SAGE we take sustainability seriously. Most of our products are printed in the UK using FSC papers and
boards. When we print overseas we ensure sustainable papers are used as measured by the PREPS grading
system. We undertake an annual audit to monitor our sustainability.

CONTENTS

ABOUT THE AUTHORS

Debra Myhill is Professor of Education at the University of Exeter. Her interests are in the teaching and research of language and literacy. Debra is the Director of the Centre for Research in Writing. She is committed to the bringing together of teaching, teacher education and research so that children and young people's experience of literacy learning enables them to be confident, articulate citizens of the future.

Clare Dowdall is Lecturer in Education (Language and Literacy) at the University of Exeter. Clare has an active interest in all aspects of literacy education and sits on the Executive Council of the United Kingdom Literary Association (UKLA), with responsibility for convening the UKLA Research Sub-Committee. Clare's current research focuses on children's writing and text production in a variety of school-based and informal contexts.

Ruth Newman is Associate Professor of Language Education at the University of Exeter. Ruth's research interests focus on the role of talk in the teaching of language and literacy, including the role of dialogic metatalk in the development of metalinguistic understanding and writing. Ruth is a member of the *Centre for Research in Writing* and teaches primarily on the Secondary English PGCE programme and MA Language and Literacy.

Annabel Watson is a Senior Lecturer in Language Education, Programme Director for Exeter School Direct initial teacher training courses and leads the Exeter Secondary English PGCE. Annabel's research interests focus primarily on the teaching of writing. She is a member of the Graduate School of Education's Centre for Research in Writing and has been part of a team conducting research which investigates the potential that a contextualised and rhetorical approach to teaching grammar might have for improving students' writing ability and metalinguistic understanding.

INTRODUCTION

A recognition of the powerful link between a child's social background and their educational outcomes is not new, despite the current political and media attention afforded to it. Indeed, a concern about the educational gap between the socially privileged and the socially disadvantaged is more than a hundred years old, at least. The first significant report on English teaching, the Newbolt Report (1921), saw the subject of English as a way of addressing this gap. And yet, the difference in educational attainment for students from socially disadvantaged circumstances remains one of the most stubbornly persistent phenomena of the British education system.

The consequence of this gap is far-reaching for those it affects, not least in terms of social mobility and life chances. The Social Mobility Commission (2020a, pp. 35–36) draws attention to the fact that at the end of Key Stage 2, 51% of disadvantaged students achieve the expected standard in writing, reading and mathematics, compared with 71% of all other students; 25% of disadvantaged students achieve a good pass in English and Maths GCSE, compared with 50% of all other students. These differences in educational outcomes play out into differing life opportunities: students from disadvantaged backgrounds are 'less likely to attend university than those from wealthier backgrounds growing up in the same area. Across local authorities, education gaps between sons from poor and wealthy families explain, on average, around 80% of the gap in adult earnings between them' (SMC, 2020b, p. 6).

Because of this, successive recent governments have recognised the need to break the link between home background, educational outcomes and life opportunities (for example, Ofsted, 2013; House of Commons Education Committee, 2014, 2021; Department for Education, 2015), and efforts to 'close the gap' in educational outcomes are now a priority focus for schools and for initial teacher education.

In the light of this, this book focuses on literacy and subject English and its importance in enabling students to access educational and life opportunities. The book sets out to provide a thorough understanding of the complex relationships between literacy achievement and social background, evidenced by research. It will challenge deficit discourses about students from socially disadvantaged backgrounds which suggest that their educational success is predetermined by their background and emphasise instead the transformative power of a high-quality literacy education. The first chapter will review and explore what research tells us about the relationship between social disadvantage and educational outcomes in general; and subsequent chapters will each take one aspect of literacy, examining the research in that area and offering practical strategies and guidance for that aspect of English teaching which support the aims of achievement for all.

The book is founded upon four key messages which resonate through each chapter:

1. Addressing disadvantage through literacy requires high-quality teaching, first and foremost: there are no quick fixes and no simple solutions or silver bullets;

2. Addressing disadvantage through literacy necessitates the avoidance of deficit descriptions of disadvantaged students and low expectations of what they can achieve;

3. Addressing disadvantage through literacy is achieved through a challenging, diverse and inclusive English curriculum within a rich literacy environment;

4. Addressing disadvantage through literacy is underpinned by acknowledging, valuing and drawing on students' backgrounds and experiences and getting to know each student as a unique individual.

1

UNDERSTANDING THE RELATIONSHIP BETWEEN SOCIAL DISADVANTAGE AND EDUCATIONAL OUTCOMES

INTRODUCTION

A concern about discrepancies in educational outcomes between children from different social backgrounds is not new and can be traced back to the first major national report on the teaching of English – the Newbolt Report (1921). Newbolt observed that more privileged communities maintained 'schools and universities for the special treatment of their own sons and daughters' (p. 6) and recommended educating students from different backgrounds together as 'the way to bridge the social chasms which divide us' (p. 6). Some 30 years later, Floud et al. (1957) drew specific attention to the educational outcomes of working-class children, arguing that 'the education, attitudes and ambitions of parents were reflected in the examination performance of children' (p. 144). The same points were made in the 1960s by Douglas et al. (1968) who found that children from 'economically or culturally deprived homes… seemed to be saddled with a cumulative series of educational handicaps' (p. 3). Halsey et al.'s seminal study (1980) of the educational outcomes of students from different social classes found that middle- and upper-class students were significantly more likely to stay at school until age 16; to continue in education post-16; and to go to university. At the same time, new reports were highlighting new disparities in educational outcomes for students from ethnic minority groups (the Rampton Report, 1981; the Swann Report, 1985) and lower achievement by girls (Deem, 1980; Askew and Ross, 1988). More recently, research has drawn attention to the lower attainment of students in care (O'Higgins et al., 2015) and students with disabilities (Chatzitheochari and Platt, 2018). In a nutshell, students in the English education system who differ in some way from the mainstream majority seem predisposed to lower educational outcomes. And of these differences, as highlighted in the recent government report (House of Commons Education Committee, 2021), the outcomes for white working-class students have been stubbornly resistant to improvement.

UNDERSTANDING THE CONCEPT OF SOCIAL DISADVANTAGE

Before looking more closely at the data and explanations about social disadvantage, it is important to address some of the problems of language used and definitions of social disadvantage. Even in the opening paragraph, the quotations have used the expressions 'culturally deprived' and 'educational handicaps', which to modern ears seem inappropriate. The term 'working-class' is itself contested, with some feeling that it is a demeaning term. Vincent et al. (2008) note that for some, the term is 'a disrespectful, disreputable phrase' (p. 62), but others choose to use it because they see it as a positive group identity marker, and it avoids 'a denial of working-class experiences, based on the false assumption that the viewpoints and perceptions of the middle classes are universal' (p. 63). Similarly, the phrase 'ethnic minority' or acronyms such as BAME (Black and Minority Ethnic) can be reductionist, failing to recognise that students from the same ethnic backgrounds may also be different from each other in 'socio-economic status, religion and gender, amongst others' (Stevenson et al., 2019, p. 45). It is all too easy to unwittingly generate deficit discourses about students from different groups, with the result that the lower educational outcomes are positioned as a problem within the group, rather than as a societal problem.

Even the word 'disadvantage' is itself a contested term in the context of educational outcomes (Smit, 2012; Gazeley, 2019; Lampert et al., forthcoming). There is a strong argument that the standard educational discourse around disadvantage represents deficit thinking which can lead to stereotypical or biased attitudes towards socially disadvantaged students. In other words, a deficit discourse of disadvantage can sustain and reproduce the very inequality it sets out to address. A Dutch review of European research, for example, found that 'disadvantaged students are the target of more implicit negative attitudes as compared to advantaged students' (Geven et al., 2018, p. 35). The parallel debate about disability has relevance here: is the appropriate adjective for people with disability 'disabled' or 'differently abled', and for people from less advantaged backgrounds, 'disadvantaged' or 'differently advantaged'? Children and young people in school are conscious of being labelled 'disadvantaged', and this risks defining them, rather than a way to channel appropriate support. On the other hand, not to name it 'disadvantage' risks ignoring it or papering over the issue with euphemisms. Francis (2017) maintains that the use of the word 'disadvantage' 'forces schools to attend to materially benefitting those pupils from low SES backgrounds' (p. 100), and Bibby et al. (2017) argue that it is important to talk explicitly about disadvantage because the new generation of teachers may not 'have been exposed to a more economic, historical, spatialised or sociological account of the individual circumstances that present in their classrooms' (p. 198). With this in mind, we use the term 'social disadvantage' in this book to acknowledge and address the way children and young people from different backgrounds are differentially positioned within our educational system, and in using the term we hope to challenge both deficit discourses and social stereotyping.

There is a related definitional challenge in the research: the concept of social disadvantage in studies drawing attention to gaps in educational outcomes is explained and measured in different ways. Hartley and Platt note that 'social advantage and disadvantage are catch-all terms with no established definition' (2016, p. v), and, recognising that 'definitions of disadvantage vary across the literature', Crenna-Jennings suggests we should think about social disadvantage from three perspectives: 'income poverty... a lack of social and cultural capital... control over decisions that affect life outcomes' (Crenna-Jennings, 2018, p. 4). Similarly, Elliot Major (2020) highlights the multi-faceted nature of disadvantage, including poverty, instability, inequality and unemployment, and thus the corresponding complexity of addressing it. In some studies, the term 'socio-economic status' (SES) is used, rather than social disadvantage. For example, Strand (2021) measured SES by also considering parental occupation, parents' educational qualifications and family income. As Early et al. (2020) note, SES is a multi-dimensional construct.

Nonetheless, in England, the dominant way of defining social disadvantage is economic, focusing on financial poverty. The Education Endowment Foundation (EEF), which has a mandate to commission studies that attempt to close the gap in educational outcomes attributable to social disadvantage, sees its role as breaking the connection between family financial circumstances and student attainment. In its 2018 report on the attainment gap, it states 'This report uses the broad term "disadvantage" to refer to those children and young people who face particular challenges because of the economic circumstances they face when growing up' (EEF, 2018a, p. 1). In practice, this means that the significant majority of studies and government reports in England use Free School Meals (FSMs) status or Pupil Premium (PP) status as the proxy measure for social disadvantage (see, for example: Cassen and Kingdon, 2007; Ofsted, 2013, 2016; House of Commons Education Committee, 2014, 2021; Andrews et al., 2016; Classick et al., 2021). Elliot Major (2020) draws attention to the limitations of using FSM as a proxy for 'white working class', not least because FSM is a binary measure, which does not 'reflect the gradations of disadvantage and advantage across pupil populations' (p. 2). The limitations of the FSM measure is acknowledged in many of the reports, but because they are data which are available for all state schools, it is easy to access and use for large-scale statistical analysis. The House of Commons Education Committee Report (HCEC, 2021, pp. 11–17) provides an excellent analysis of some of the challenges of defining social disadvantage and is well worth further reading.

In this book, however, we will be looking at social disadvantage from a broader perspective, drawing on Crenna-Jennings (2018) and Strand (2021) and considering not simply economic disadvantage, but also social and cultural differences, and parental education and support. The Ofsted report, *Unknown Children* (2016) argued that some schools had a too narrow view of disadvantage as economic, and that 'the most effective schools and settings visited had a much wider definition of disadvantage' which recognised 'the unique circumstances surrounding an individual child, group of children or family' (p. 10). It is also important to acknowledge that students are often socially disadvantaged by circumstances over which they have little control, and which frequently serve to perpetuate the advantage of other groups.

DIFFERENCES IN EDUCATIONAL OUTCOMES LINKED TO SOCIAL DISADVANTAGE

The effects of social disadvantage on life chances are pernicious and long-lasting. For example, children from families classed as disadvantaged have a shorter life expectancy and are more likely to suffer from health problems, including mental health issues (BMA, 2017). They are less likely to find graduate employment (Morrison, 2019), and they are also more likely to be unemployed and less likely to earn the same salaries in professional and managerial employment compared with their more socially advantaged peers (Friedman et al., 2017). Our principal interest here, however, is with the relationships between social disadvantage and educational outcomes in school: indeed, some of the deep-rooted inequalities in relation to later health and employment are themselves attributable to lower educational outcomes. Educational attainment is not simply about securing good examination results, but also about how those results shape and influence future life chances.

Gillborn and Mirza's study (2000) of inequalities in educational outcomes provides one of the most comprehensive analyses, considering the different outcomes of ethnic minority students, working-class students and girls, when compared with more advantaged groups. In terms of ethnicity, they avoid simply comparing the group of ethnic minority students with white British students and look instead at specific ethnic groups. They found significant differences according to the ethnic group: Indian students achieved more highly than white British students, while African-Caribbean, Pakistani and Bangladeshi pupils are markedly less likely to attain five higher grade GCSEs than their white British counterparts (p. 12). Equally important, they point out that these national level data are not consistent across regional local authorities, where some nationally low-achieving groups do very well. For example, in some local authorities, Pakistani students outperformed white British students. They also found 'a strong direct association between social class background and success in education: put simply, the higher a child's social class, the greater are their attainments on average' (p. 18) and draw attention to the interaction between ethnicity and social class in attainment patterns. In other words, you can be doubly disadvantaged by being both working-class and from an ethnic minority group. Nonetheless, their data lead them to conclude that 'social class factors do not override the influence of ethnic inequality: when comparing pupils with similar class backgrounds there are still marked inequalities of attainment between different ethnic groups' (p. 21). They also highlight that while there had been steadily rising examination results for all groups, the gaps in attainment between groups were not narrowing and indeed were growing wider for Black, Bangladeshi and Pakistani students.

This study remains important because it provides a nuanced and critical analysis of the data: it does find a link between social disadvantage, in terms of ethnicity and social class, and educational outcomes. But it also highlights *within-group* differences, with some ethnic groups achieving above average, and regional differences which do not reflect national patterns. Crucially, they remind us not to simplistically attribute these gaps to home or social backgrounds and caution against the assumption that 'all (or most) of the reason for differences in attainment lie outside the school' (Gillborn and Mirza, 2000, p. 19). Instead, they note that ways of working in school may contribute to or exacerbate these differential outcomes for different groups: for example, the setting processes used, the quality of teaching and teacher expectations.

REFLECTION POINT

Read Gillborn and Mirza's report *'Educational Inequality: Mapping Race, Class and Gender'* (2000). Although some of the data patterns have altered since 2000, the way this report avoids simplistic reading of the data and looks at within-group as well as between-group differences remains highly relevant. In practice, this is a reminder that national data point to patterns, but these patterns may not be applicable to individual students you teach.

Since 2000, as political consciousness of the gaps in educational outcomes has grown, there have been a succession of reports analysing school test and examination results to monitor these differences and implement strategies intended to close the gap. Ofsted's *Unseen Children* report (2013) notes that at Key Stage 2 the gap between children with FSMs and their better-off peers had narrowed by 8 percentage points. Like Gillborn and Mirza (2000), they also found different outcomes for different ethnic groups: Indian and Chinese students were achieving higher than average; Bangladeshi and Black African at or above average; and only Pakistani and Black students attained below the average (Ofsted, 2013, p. 25). The GCSE results in 2019 point to similar patterns, with Chinese, Asian and Mixed groups attaining above the average and Black groups attaining below (DfE, 2020). As awareness of the risks of broad generalisations spread across large ethnic groups, research is increasingly examining outcomes in more granular detail: for example, identifying the lower educational outcomes of Gypsy/Roma students.

White British students are, of course, the ethnic majority in England and it is typically their performance against which other groups are compared. However, Ofsted highlighted the interaction of class and ethnicity, finding that white British students from disadvantaged backgrounds were 'consistently the lowest performing of all of the main ethnic groups and gaps in attainment to other groups have widened over time' (Ofsted, 2013, p. 29). While being white might be an educational advantage, being white and working-class is less so. More recently, this has been the source of increasing attention, partly because some of the gaps in ethnic minority attainment have been narrowing and partly because the group of white working-class students is numerically large and thus affecting the futures of many students. The House of Commons Education Committee report (HCEC, 2021) refers to white working-class students as the 'forgotten', and their analysis indicates that white students with FSM are less likely to achieve the Development Goals for 4- to 5-year-olds and less likely to access higher education than the average for all students with FSM. They also attain less well at GCSE, as measured by Attainment 8 score, than other peers with FSM (p. 3). A more rigorous study (Strand, 2021) which uses more complex measures to determine social disadvantage and analyses the statistics using regression modelling comes to a similar conclusion. The report observes that, nationally, ethnic minority students are more likely to be socially disadvantaged than the white British majority, but nonetheless:

> the overwhelming picture is that ethnic minority groups have higher educational achievement at age 16 than White British students of the same sex and SES. This is particularly notable at low and average SES, where no ethnic minority groups have a significantly lower score than White British students, and indeed in 23 of the 32 comparisons the mean score for ethnic minority students is substantially higher than for comparable White British students.

(Strand, 2021, p. 5)

In summary, then, performance data have consistently confirmed the close link between social disadvantage and educational outcomes. Indeed, Andrews et al. (2016) make the point that, in general, 'a disadvantaged pupil falls two months behind their peers for each year of their time at secondary school and, by the end of school, that disadvantaged pupil is almost two years behind' (p. 40). While this relationship is replicated internationally, the effect of disadvantage appears to be stronger in England than elsewhere. Hansen and Vignoles (2005) found that England has one of the strongest correlations in the OECD between social class and educational outcomes; a finding replicated in Knowles and Evans' study, which found that 'the impact of pupils' socio-economic background is significantly higher than the OECD average' (Knowles and Evans, 2012, p. 1). Analyses such as these led Cassen and Kingdon (2007, p. 1) to conclude that 'England ranks internationally among the countries with relatively high average educational achievement but also high inequality in achievement'. Worryingly, there are recent signs that the gap between disadvantaged and more advantaged students has stopped narrowing and in some cases is widening (Hutchinson et al., 2020, p. 9). The COVID pandemic appears to have intensified this increasing gap: although, overall, grade levels at GCSE and A level in 2021 are significantly higher than in previous years, the increase is principally in the already-advantaged groups. At GCSE, 'independent schools had the biggest increase in top grades – 61.2% of results at grade 7/A, compared with 26.1% in comprehensives, 28.1% in academies' (Long et al., 2021, n.p.). At the same time, students with FSM slipped further behind. A similar pattern is true at A level, with independent school students achieving 70% of their results at A* or A, compared with 39% in comprehensive schools (Coughlan, 2021a).

It is evident from school examination and assessment data that there is a very real problem with educational inequalities in England. But there is also a potential problem in how we respond to these data. It can lead to deterministic attitudes or unconscious bias towards students from different groups, borne of an underlying belief that their social disadvantage means their educational outcomes are inevitable. It is important that this viewpoint is challenged. The data analyses draw on large-scale collated data, which are good at highlighting general differences between groups; however, these patterns may not be replicated within your school or even within your class. While the data can reveal 'big picture' *between-group* variation, they are not good at detecting *within-group* variation. Like Gillborn and Mirza (2000), Andrews et al. (2016) emphasise that national patterns of lower educational outcomes can be different in regional contexts. They cite the example of Newham, where socially disadvantaged five-year-olds achieve the same standards as five-year-olds without FSM nationally and conclude that this 'indicates the potential scope for dramatic improvements in narrowing the gaps across the rest of England' (Andrews et al., 2016, p. 6). Within-group variation, however, is not simply about regional variation – students are unique individuals, shaped by a unique constellation of experiences, and it is important 'to challenge the assumption that the white working class is one homogeneous cultural group' (Elliot Major, 2020, p. 1). Moreover, most of the studies using large datasets are *correlational*: that is, they identify a link between social disadvantage and educational outcomes. However, they are not *causal* and cannot tell us that social disadvantage causes poor educational outcomes. Nonetheless, national analyses of educational outcomes are important because they reveal hidden inequalities – but in your own settings, the data should be used to raise critical questions, provoke discussion and stimulate close analysis of the outcomes of students you teach. The data should not be the trigger for deficit discourses about social disadvantage nor a predictor of how students will attain.

Of course, knowing there is a problem is only the first step in achieving a solution to these inequalities in educational outcomes. In order to address these educational inequalities in your own professional practice, it is important to also understand the possible causes which create or exacerbate inequality. The next sections in this chapter look more closely at this, particularly at how the out-of-school home environment and the in-school practices might be contributory factors.

THE RELATIONSHIP BETWEEN HOME BACKGROUND AND EDUCATIONAL OUTCOMES

Understanding how home background might influence or shape a child's learning experiences in school is crucial if we hope to make interventions which support learning. Crenna-Jennings (2018) conducted a systematic literature review to establish the key drivers of the 'disadvantage gap' and synthesised the research into four main categories, each with sub-categories, as represented in Table 1.1.

Table 1.1   Key drivers of educational disadvantage: summarised from Crenna-Jennings (2018)

Main thematic category	Sub-categories
Inequalities in child development	Perinatal factors (affected by health inequalities)
	The physical and social home environment
	• The impact of material deprivation
	• Family stress and functioning
	• The home learning environment
	• Child-rearing strategies
	The role of community disadvantage

Table 1.1   (Continued)

Main thematic category	Sub-categories
Inequalities in school preparedness	Access to high-quality Early Years' education
Stressors experienced by disadvantaged children in school	Mobility (moving schools) Social psychological factors
Differential school practices	Teaching Unconscious bias Attainment grouping Curriculum

The table is helpful in foregrounding the complexity of the issue and the multiple ways in which inequality in educational outcomes might be shaped. Of her four key drivers, only one is directly related to home background (child development) and one indirectly, because access to high-quality Early Years' provision is strongly linked to where you live, with the most socially disadvantaged frequently having lesser access.

As noted earlier in this chapter, a dominant way of thinking about disadvantage is in terms of economic disadvantage, and it is very easy to understand how poverty might hamper progress in school. The increasing number of children living at or below the poverty line has risen since 2012, and about a third of all children in England are living in poverty (Social Mobility Commission [SMC], 2021, p. xvi). Living in poor housing, with limited resources, with insufficient food to eat and often also experiencing health inequalities may have a direct effect on a young learner's capacity to benefit from school (Connelly et al., 2014). To an extent, these are structural inequalities which are harder for schools to address, and yet many schools do attempt to do just that. Running breakfast clubs, organising uniform swap shops, hosting food banks and providing showering facilities are some examples of how schools try to help their students, making school a safe space to be. But poverty also directly affects learning in terms of access to books and other educational resources, digital access and additional support through extra tuition. More advantaged children come from homes better resourced to support learning, 'meaning pupils from poorer socio-economic backgrounds are less equipped for the school learning environment' (Early et al., 2020, p. 124).

The extent to which young children are equipped for the school learning environment is not only about financial resources, but crucially it is also about how the home environment and parenting prepare children for school. This includes both parenting practices in the home and the level of education of the parents, leading Field (2010, p. 38) to conclude that 'factors in the home environment, positive parenting, the home learning environment and parents' level of education' are most influential for later educational outcomes. However, Sylva et al.'s (2004) earlier research, involving more than 3,000 children, is important in cautioning against over-simplistic associations between home environment and school. They found that 'the quality of the home learning environment is more important for intellectual and social development than parental occupation, education or income. What parents do is more important than who parents are' (p. 5). In particular, this issue of the home learning environment relates to language and literacy development and how this is fostered at home. From a synthesis of research, Hannon et al. (2020) identify four strands of literacy which are particularly important in the pre-school experience: the exposure to print in the everyday social environment; experiences with books; oral language opportunities such as storytelling or rhymes, which develop phonological awareness; and talk about written language (p. 311). Siraj and Mayo (2014, p. 31) identify that practices, well aligned with Hannon's four strands, such as access to printed material, shared storybook reading, storytelling, mealtime talk and library visits, were more frequent and higher quality in higher SES families. The consequence of this is that young children arrive at pre-school or school settings differently prepared for the literacy demands of school.

What this highlights is that the relationship between the home environment and educational success is partly driven by economic disadvantage, but also by the nature of parenting and family life. This is important because many researchers emphasise that cultural and social differences between home and school explain why socially disadvantaged children have different educational outcomes from their more advantaged peers. Typically, this body of research refers to Bourdieu (1986) and his theory of social and cultural capital. Across society, different social groups have different forms of social and cultural capital, but those who have high SES and occupy positions of power, wealth and status have social and cultural capital which serves to reproduce and sustain that power and privilege. In other words, Bourdieu argued that an individual's social and cultural capital reproduces social inequalities, enabling those with powerful social and cultural capital to stay powerful and those without to remain less powerful. Precise definitions of social and cultural capital vary, but Table 1.2 offers a definition and some real educational examples of how some forms of capital might create educational advantage.

Table 1.2 Social and cultural capital

Term	Definition	Example
Social capital	This refers to the assets that an individual possesses, in terms of the social networks they can access to open doors and get things done; and the shared norms and values they share within a community.	• Having a friend who teaches Maths who can help your child's problems with Maths; • Knowing a lecturer at Oxford or Cambridge University who interviews students for entry, and can give your child a mock interview.
Cultural capital	This refers to the skills, knowledge, experiences and behaviours an individual possesses which enable them to access or belong to a particular group.	• Taking your children to the theatre; • Insisting on table manners; • Taking holidays which broaden cultural understanding; • Being able to help your child with their homework.

There is plenty of evidence of how the social and cultural capital of the privileged plays out into advantage for their children. Lareau's ethnographic study (2011) in the United States revealed how middle-class parents assertively intervened in their children's education, organising their children's time in activities of perceived educational value and being willing to challenge authority figures in school. In contrast, parents from lower SES backgrounds were much less interventionist and more likely to show dependency on the school. Parents understand how to play the system to get their children to their school of choice; they pay for extra tuition for their children to ensure examination success; they actively help with homework and are confident advising on university choices (Montacute and Cullinane, 2018). With the teacher assessment of GCSE and A level in 2021, 23% of parents with students in independent schools and 17% of parents in more affluent areas contacted schools about examination grades, compared with 11% in more disadvantaged areas (Coughlan, 2021b), with some concern that in some cases this constituted lobbying. This is not a uniquely British problem: Jæger and Møllegaard (2017) found that the effect of cultural capital on educational outcomes was stronger for students from high SES backgrounds, and they suggest this is because they are more likely to be in schools where they can convert their cultural capital into educational success. The capacity of middle-class parents to exercise cultural capital in their interactions with school is not mono-directional: Barg's study (2013) showed how teachers' decision-making and guidance to students is influenced by parental pressure. Indeed, Elliot Major and Machin (2018) argue that 'education has been commandeered by the middle classes to retain their advantage from one generation to the next' (p. 11), and it may be that social and cultural capital is one of the most powerful mechanisms explaining why more advantaged children achieve higher educational outcomes than others.

Sometimes, people talk about social and cultural capital as though it is something some students have and others do not, but everyone has their own social and cultural capital. Working-class learners, for example, do not *lack* capital, but they have *different* capital from other groups: the point is, however, that education is shaped by the interests and values of the more privileged groups in society and draws on their social and cultural capital, while at the same time, those with different social and cultural capital are marginalised. Reay (2017) suggests that classificatory indices such as social class, occupation and educational qualifications are only part of the story. What is most significant is understanding learners' experiences in school in terms of:

> *Confidence and entitlement in relation to education, the amount of knowledge and information about the school system that families have, the social networks that families have access to, wealth or lack of it; but also whether you come to school with a family history of educational success and recognition, or with a sense that education is not something you and your family are good at.*

> (Reay, 2017, p. 180)

THE IMPORTANCE OF THE SCHOOL

Throughout this chapter so far, one reverberating message has been that although social disadvantage has its sources *outside* the school, what happens *inside* the school is critical in addressing inequalities in educational outcomes. This section of the chapter explores in more detail how schools make a difference. Gillborn and Mirza (2000) and Andrews et al. (2016), among others, draw attention to local variation where the achievements of socially disadvantaged groups exceed national results; and research on social and cultural capital explains how some parents play the school system to their advantage. In other words, coming from a socially disadvantaged background should not determine future educational success. Macleod et al. (2015) found that up to two-thirds of the variance between schools in terms of attainment of socially disadvantaged students is attributable to school-level characteristics, not home background. They conclude that although 'schools' intake and circumstance are influential … they do not totally determine pupils' outcomes. It therefore implies that schools have meaningful scope to make a difference'

(p. 6). From their data, they synthesised seven principles which embody successful professional practice for raising educational outcomes (Table 1.3):

Table 1.3   Macleod et al.'s principles of successful practice (2015, p. 4)

1. Promote an ethos of attainment for all pupils, rather than stereotyping disadvantaged pupils as a group with less potential to succeed.
2. Have an individualised approach to addressing barriers to learning and emotional support, at an early stage, rather than providing access to generic support and focusing on pupils nearing their end-of-key-stage assessments.
3. Focus on high-quality teaching first rather than on bolt-on strategies and activities outside school hours.
4. Focus on outcomes for individual pupils rather than on providing strategies.
5. Deploy the best staff to support disadvantaged pupils; develop skills and roles of teachers and teaching assistants rather than using additional staff who do not know the pupils well.
6. Make decisions based on data and respond to evidence, using frequent, rather than one-off assessment and decision points.
7. Have clear, responsive leadership: setting ever higher aspirations and devolving responsibility for raising attainment to all staff, rather than accepting low aspirations and variable performance.

One aspect of difference relates to school quality: it has long been observed that children from socially disadvantaged backgrounds are more likely to attend schools judged to be lower quality (Lupton, 2005; Cassen and Kingdon, 2007; Jerrim and Sims, 2019). It is important not to accept this uncritically, however, as judgements of school quality are principally based on Ofsted inspection or school results, which may be insufficiently sensitive to the very real challenges for teachers and schools serving economically poor communities. At the same time, it may be all too easy to use a community environment of disadvantage as an excuse for what happens in school. The London Challenge was a government-funded initiative in the 2000s to raise educational outcomes through strengthening school leadership, making better use of data and focusing on teaching and learning through collaborative between-school support, and it was a significant success, raising educational outcomes for students of all backgrounds above the national average. The London Challenge is a pertinent reminder that background should not determine outcomes, and that schools can be significant in breaking the link between social disadvantage and poor educational outcomes. In an analysis of the characteristics of schools who were most effective in breaking this link, Ofsted found that these schools had 'a much wider definition of disadvantage' (2016, p. 10), aware not only of economic disadvantage but the broader issues which served to create disadvantage. This underlines the points made earlier in this chapter, noting that 'disadvantage' is not simply about financial poverty but includes social and cultural factors too.

Furthermore, a characteristic of our education system is that it is particularly segregated: Jenkins et al. (2006) point that we have 'a relatively high degree of social segregation in schools compared to other countries'. This plays out not only in terms of private and state schools but also in terms of local variations, such as the presence of grammar schools or the way one school in an area attracts the more privileged families. Grammar schools are often thought to enhance social mobility, but in fact they are often strongly populated by more socio-economically advantaged students. Jerrim and Sims (2019) found that disadvantaged students had more limited access to grammar schools, and that family income, parental school preferences and private tuition were key factors in securing a grammar school place. While the issues of school quality and school segregation are complex, nonetheless, there is little doubt that schools can make a real difference, which buck national trends of attainment and enable socially disadvantaged students to achieve highly (Hutchings et al., 2014).

To an extent, however, the questions of school quality and school segregation are between-school differences. But there are important within-school segregation choices which can exacerbate the effects of disadvantage, the most salient of which is the use of 'ability' grouping, the setting of students in classes by attainment. This has always been a contested subject but, perhaps surprisingly given the prevalence of 'ability' grouping in practice, there has never been any clear evidence that setting provides any educational benefit: indeed 'the evidence suggests that overall these practices are not of significant benefit to attainment, with a negative impact for lower sets and streams – those wherein pupils from lower socio-economic groups are over-represented' (Francis et al., 2017, p. 3). From their systematic review of research on setting, Francis et al. identify seven reasons why the practice of setting leads to a negative impact on students designated to lower sets:

- misallocation to groups;

- lack of fluidity of groups;

- quality of teaching for different groups;

- teacher expectations of pupils;

- pedagogy, curriculum and assessment applied to different groups;

- pupil perception and experiences of 'ability' grouping, and impact on their learner identities;

- these different factors working together to cause a self-fulfilling prophecy.

Francis et al. (2017, p. 4).

It is important not to underestimate the relationship between setting, social disadvantage and educational outcomes. A doctoral study by Travers (2016) adopted a qualitative approach to explore the experiences and perceptions of a group of white working-class males who had 'succeeded against the odds' and were studying at elite universities. This group repeatedly referred to the negative impact of being placed in a low set, believing that their teachers did not expect them to succeed academically, and that white working-class boys were positioned as subordinate to more advantaged students. In a more recent study, Francis et al. (2020) examining the effects of setting on learner confidence found that the gap in self-confidence widened between students in the top and bottom sets for maths after being placed in attainment groups, and in English, self-confidence in the top set increased significantly. In summary, as Elliot Major and Higgins (2019) point out, socially disadvantaged students are more likely to be placed into lower sets, frequently missing out on the most effective teaching; and the more rigid the setting, the more divisive it is.

The issue of teacher expectations, mentioned by both Francis and Travers, has itself been a focus for research. The views of the men in Travers' study concerning low expectations in lower sets are confirmed more widely. For example, teachers demonstrate high expectations of top sets by giving them challenging, fast-paced work (Boaler et al., 2000) and more homework (Ireson and Hallam, 2001): in contrast, students in lower sets covered less of the curriculum and at a slower pace. The everyday argument in favour of setting is that teachers are better able to differentiate their teaching to meet learners' needs, yet Boaler et al. (2000) found teachers were more likely to differentiate effectively when teaching mixed-ability groups than when teaching setted groups. More generally, Barbarin and Aikens (2015) highlight that, in their study, teachers were more likely to have low expectations of low-SES children than others. There is also evidence of teacher unconscious bias in assessing students from different social groups. Burgess and Greaves (2013) found that teachers systematically under-graded some ethnic groups, while over-grading others, and suggest this is attributable to stereotyping of particular groups. Similarly, Malouff and Thorsteinsson (2016) revealed grading bias when teachers were given information about the students' backgrounds or prior attainment. As a consequence of these low expectations and biases, Barbarin and Aikens argue that schools 'may replicate the effects of economic disadvantage in the family' (2015, p. 103) rather than challenging it.

What this tells us is that what happens in our classrooms is important. Successive studies have shown that within-school variation in student outcomes is greater than between-school variation (Reynolds, 2007; Husbands and Pearce, 2012), and that although this is an international phenomenon (McGaw, 2008), England has greater variation than most countries. In other words, the differences between teachers in a school are greater than the differences between schools. There is some evidence that teaching quality is poorer in schools in disadvantaged areas (Malouff et al., 2016; Allen and Sims, 2018), but if this observation is at school level this may be less about teacher competence than the challenging circumstances those teachers face (Gore et al., 2021). However, within-school variation is harder to argue away on these grounds: if teachers working with the same students in the same school are achieving different educational outcomes, then as Hattie argues 'what teachers do matters' (Hattie, 2009, p. 23). And teachers may matter even more for socially disadvantaged students. The Sutton Trust (2011) observe that 'the effects of high-quality teaching are especially significant for pupils from disadvantaged backgrounds' (p. 2) – their data reveal that these learners can gain 1.5 years' worth of learning with an effective teacher compared with 0.5 with a less effective teacher, and they conclude 'for poor pupils the difference between a good teacher and a bad teacher is a whole year's learning' (p. 2). Of course, data like these need to be taken with a pinch of salt as they described generalised patterns, not the individual outcomes of students in your classroom. They may also be over-reliant on test data to determine teacher effectiveness.

So if the quality of teaching is crucial, and teachers can really make a difference to the inequality of educational outcomes for learners from socially disadvantaged backgrounds, the sixty-four-dollar question is – what makes some teachers more effective than others? Teacher effectiveness is a substantial research area and has been for some time, though not surprisingly given its inevitable complexity, there has been no definitive answer to this mega-question. In Table 1.4, the findings from three studies seeking to identify the characteristics of high-quality teaching have been summarised. All three drew principally on statistical data collated from across multiple studies, frequently linked to test results, but the Sharples et al. (2011) study also looked at the findings of some qualitative data and was focused explicitly on raising educational outcomes for socially disadvantaged students.

Table 1.4   *Characteristics of effective teaching (summarised)*

Effective pedagogies:
- give serious consideration to pupil voice.
- depend on behaviour (what teachers do), knowledge and understanding (what teachers know) and beliefs (why teachers act as they do).
- involve clear thinking about longer term learning outcomes as well as short-term goals.
- build on pupils' prior learning and experience.
- involve scaffolding pupil learning.
- involve a range of techniques, including whole-class and structured group work, guided learning and individual activity.
- focus on developing higher order thinking and metacognition, and make good use of dialogue and questioning in order to do so.
- embed assessment for learning.
- are inclusive and take the diverse needs of a range of learners, as well as matters of student equity, into account.

(Husbands and Pearce, 2012, p. 3)

- the adoption of proven classroom management strategies (e.g. rapid pace of instruction, using all-pupil responses, developing a common language around discipline).
- the use of teaching strategies such as co-operative learning (structured group work), frequent assessment and meta-cognitive ('learning to learn') strategies.
- the use of interactive whiteboards and embedded multimedia with whole classes.
- the use of well-specified, well-supported and well-implemented programmes, incorporating extensive professional development.

(Sharples et al., 2011, p. 14)

- the importance of clear learning intentions
- a classroom environment that welcomes errors
- the challenge of the task
- effective feedback
- encouraging a sense of satisfaction, engagement and perseverance to succeed

(Hattie, 2009, p. 199)

Conclusions from Qualitative Research:
- rigorous monitoring and use of data
- raising pupil aspirations using engagement/aspiration programmes
- engaging parents (particularly hard-to-reach parents) and raising parental aspirations
- developing social and emotional competencies
- supporting school transitions

(Sharples et al., 2011, p. 14)

One thing that is missing from these syntheses of research findings on high-quality teaching is any reference to building constructive teacher–student relationships: this may be because they draw mainly on statistical datasets which may not naturally flag up relationships. Yet my own experience of teaching in an urban school with a high number of FSM students, principally white working-class, was that building a relationship with each student as an individual was a critical factor in creating a classroom climate where learning could flourish. There is a substantial body of research which confirms my own experience, signalling a link between positive teacher–student relationships and academic outcomes (e.g. Roorda et al., 2011; Lewis et al., 2012; Hughes and Cao, 2017; Scales et al., 2020). The positive relationships in these studies revolve around caring attitudes with clear boundaries, warmth, avoidance of conflict, fostering 'can do' attitudes and knowing the student as an individual. Some of the research links the constructive teacher–student relationships with culturally responsive pedagogies which recognise and understand students' cultures and experiences outside of school and which bridge ethnic and cultural differences (Ladson-Billings, 2009; Phillippo, 2012). There is a consensus in this research that positive teacher–student relationships can build students' motivation and engagement, leading to better outcomes. Curiously, almost all these studies are from the United States, suggesting a need to explore this area in more depth in England.

REFLECTION POINT

Look closely at Table 1.4 and reflect on these questions:

- Are there any common characteristics being flagged in all three reports?

- What are the differences in the findings from the qualitative studies, and why might they be so different from the statistical studies?

- Reflect on yourself as a teacher – are there aspects of effective teaching which you feel are already part of your professional practice; and are there aspects which you might need to develop further?

CONCLUSION

In summary, then, the research demonstrates an unquestionable link between social disadvantage and educational outcomes: this link is evident in most countries around the world but is particularly strong in England. The COVID-19 pandemic has thrown a particular spotlight on social and health inequalities and how they affect students' educational outcomes and on educational inequalities. COVID has not caused these – they were already firmly rooted pre-pandemic, but COVID has brought them into sharp relief. The research also explains unequal educational outcomes in terms of the home environment, particularly economic poverty and social and cultural misalignments; and in terms of the school environment, how schools can replicate and sustain the inequalities or challenge them to change educational trajectories. It underlines the risks of treating different social groups as homogeneous, be they ethnic groups, gender or class, thus failing to recognise the multi-dimensional nature of advantage and disadvantage and the uniqueness of individuals. Sociological research, in particular, also emphasises that the solution to this long-standing problem is not about making all students like 'successful' middle-class students, but to recognise and draw on the broader range of experiences, attitudes and perspectives of all students (Gewirtz, 2001; Elliot Major and Machin, 2018).

Following the success of the London Challenge initiative, Ofsted (2013) observed that 'material poverty is not in itself an insurmountable barrier to educational success. The significant improvements to London's schools and the outcomes for its pupils are evidence that disadvantaged pupils can achieve consistently well' (p. 16). If we, as teachers, are to tackle the pernicious connection between social disadvantage and poorer educational outcomes, we cannot simply locate the problem as outside the school, adopting 'deficit models where perceived shortcomings of the poor, rather than structural inequalities, are used to explain why children who live in economic disadvantage more often than not have poor educational outcomes. Negative stereotypes about impoverished children based on deficit assumptions can perpetuate inequality' (Ivinson et al., 2017, p. 9). At the same time, we cannot create a discourse which 'blames' teachers and gives them all the responsibility for challenging these structural inequalities. There are no quick fixes to this problem, or they would have been implemented years ago; there are no research studies which can tell you what steps to take to solve the problem; there are no super-teachers who have the problem cracked. But there are many individual teachers whose work building relationships supports learning and whose understanding of the learning and emotional needs of their students is indeed helping students to succeed against the odds. This is founded, not on a sense of teacher inadequacy, but on a sense of what is possible and why it matters, or as Dylan Wiliam put it: 'if we create a culture where every teacher believes they need to improve, not because they are not good enough but because they can be even better, there is no limit to what we can achieve' (2019).

2
BUILDING FOUNDATIONS FOR LITERACY IN THE EARLY YEARS

In my view, the most important thing a school can do for its pupils – and for society – is to teach them to read and write well. But to achieve this, we have to get in early and make sure that all young children get a good grounding in literacy before school starts.

Sir Kevan Collins, Chief Executive, Education Endowment Fund (2018, p. 4)

INTRODUCTION

This chapter will concentrate on the pre-school literacy education of children aged 3–5 years, with a focus on how the foundations for successful literacy learning can be laid, especially for socially disadvantaged young children. Children of this age in England are likely to spend some time within funded pre-school and Reception settings but will also be learning in their homes and communities. The chapter therefore considers the role of families, friends and caregivers, as well as professional educators, all of whom support children's early childhood literacy development.

UNDERSTANDING THE RESEARCH

DEFINING EARLY CHILDHOOD LITERACY

Early childhood literacy is widely regarded as a distinct phase of literacy, with its own body of interdisciplinary research that draws on a range of theoretical underpinnings (Larson and Marsh, 2012; Teale et al., 2020). From a research perspective, it is a relatively recent concept, involving young children's relationships with the full range of written language that they encounter in their social worlds (Gillen and Hall, 2012). As such, and for the purpose of this chapter, it can be distinguished from more wide-ranging ideas about language acquisition and interaction that involve acculturation into various ways of using the spoken word and non-verbal communication (e.g. gesturing) to make and convey meaning (Lancaster, 2013, p. 314). However, it must be acknowledged that all forms of language and its acquisition underpin and impact young children's literacy learning and cannot be separated from it – regardless of whether young learners are becoming literate in one language, or in many; and regardless of the nature of the social, economic and cultural worlds that children and their families occupy.

Specifically, views of early childhood literacy acknowledge that literacy and engagement with the written word begin before formal schooling starts. They also subscribe to the notion that from the earliest age, young children are strategic literacy learners who engage in a broad range of social and cultural experiences involving the written word, and that inform and extend beyond the print-based reading and writing activities we might associate with formal schooling and a primary phase classroom (Gillen and Hall, 2012, p. 7).

The term 'emergent literacy' has come to be widely understood to describe the genesis of this relationship with print and can be associated with scholars who have described children's early reading and writing behaviours and learning, for example, Clay (1966), Teale and Sulzby (1986) and Hall (1987). As Riley (2006) describes, emergent literacy can be regarded as the slow initiation into text and print, replacing the notion that there is a separate pre-reading stage with the idea that children engage in purposeful reading and writing behaviours that 'precede and develop into conventional literacy' (p. 50). The significant point here is that emergent literacy presumes that the young child is an active and purposeful learner who is seeking meaning in textual form (Wyse et al., 2018, p. 201). In the emergent literacy stage, young children use their fundamental abilities to make sense of the world around them in supportive contexts that allow them to engage in 'real literacy acts' (Hall, 1987, p. 9). These acts can include any 'strategic' meaning-making activity, where children pay attention to print (Gillen and Hall, 2012, p. 4). They will vary tremendously from child to child, depending on their access to resources and the activities that may promote them.

In a funded pre-school setting, these acts can be regarded as fairly standardised for each child, due to the statutory requirements for early literacy (DfE, 2021). They may include mandated activities, conducted with a practitioner, that are evidence-informed and widely regarded as being current 'best practice' by the policy-making and accountability-measuring organisations. In England, currently, this list would include activities such as storytelling and shared reading, the development of phonological awareness and phonics skills, and support for mark-making, as well as directed and undirected play-based activities that include the written word – for example, 'reading' and mark-making as part of role play (DfE, 2021; Education Endowment Fund, 2018, 2021).

Beyond the educational setting, these literacy acts will vary considerably from family to family. They may involve very different approaches and resources and may be conducted in a range of modes, including print and screen, and in more than one language. Parents and caregivers have long been regarded as instrumental in their children's early literacy learning (Clark, 2007; Hannon and Nutbrown, 1997). In the home, for example, children's literacy acts may involve directed and undirected learning and play, as children engage with the available family resources (human and non-human). This engagement may involve strategic sharing episodes introduced by caregivers to 'formally' help children become readers and writers, using educational resources akin to those of the school, for example, magnetic letters and early reading-scheme books designed to promote phonological awareness and grapheme-phoneme correspondence. Or it may involve undirected and unsupervised activities involving written words, for example, as children search for a favourite YouTube video on a tablet or write 'pretend' birthday messages and shopping lists as part of their work and play.

Beyond the home, these acts of emergent literacy may also occur in children's wider cultures and communities. Children may notice shop signs and logos on a trip to the shops. There may be literacy acts as a part of a visit to a local playgroup, library, event or an activity that relates to a family's wider social and cultural interests, perhaps linked to their beliefs and pastimes. The contexts for the development of emergent literacy are therefore multifarious and intertwined. As Flewitt (2013, p. 1) has argued:

> *... supporting children's early literacy learning is considered a task for the whole society, with responsibility no longer passed fully to families and education professionals, but extending into wider communities providing dynamic and stimulating literate environments.*

The variation in children's experiences in these contexts for emergent literacy development affects notions of the 'quality' of their preparation for more formal literacy learning and – as extensive research shows – can affect children's subsequent literacy outcomes, with particular implications for families with a label of disadvantage, as will be discussed in the next sections.

DEFINING EARLY CHILDHOOD LITERACY IN THE DIGITAL AGE

Recent research has expanded understandings of early childhood literacy practices to incorporate screen-based technologies, such as smartphones and tablets, and their multimodal affordances (Sefton-Green et al., 2016; Scott and Marsh, 2018; Erstad et al., 2020). Research also shows that children in England aged 3–4 increasingly access these technologies – both alone and with family members – to play and communicate, with 48% owning their own tablet and 4% owning their own smartphone (Ofcom, 2021, p. 47). These data clearly have implications for understandings of emergent literacy, as defining 'the written word' in the digital age is confounded by the communication affordances of the screen. In their review of young children's writing on screen, Kucirkova et al. (2019, p. 217) conceptualise writing as 'an active practice of producing signs and symbols on paper or any other solid medium' to accommodate these affordances. An example could include a young child's production of a piece of multimodal 'writing' composed using an app with digital images that interplay with written narration to convey meaning (see Dowdall, 2020). Equally, it could involve reading an electronic version of a well-known story on a tablet or e-reader with a teacher or caregiver (see Kucirkova et al., 2016). In the home, it could involve a child making meaning from an emoji as part of 'reading' a text message from a grandparent. Any consideration of contemporary early childhood literacy must therefore extend beyond print and paper-based resources to include making and constructing meaning in different media using multimodal symbolic resources (Lancaster, 2013, p. 318).

These examples demonstrate that while early childhood literacy could once be defined in relation to experiences with the written word alone (namely book sharing and mark making on paper), nowadays these experiences are more varied in materiality and in quality. This has implications for children who are more or less advantaged in social, cultural and economic terms, as access to the experiences that are currently most culturally valued in relation to formal literacy education is not equally distributed among all children. To understand this claim further, we will consider how the foundations of literacy are built at home, in the community and at school.

BUILDING THE FOUNDATIONS OF LITERACY AT HOME, IN THE COMMUNITY AND AT SCHOOL

Early childhood education, once seen as preparation for primary schooling, is currently understood by educators and researchers as an important educational phase in its own right (Taggart et al., 2015a). As noted already in this chapter, during this 'educational phase', the foundations of literacy are built at home and in the community, as well as in more formal educational settings. In the late 1990s, the Effective Provision of Pre-School Education (EPPE) research project (latterly known as the EPPSE research project) tracked 3,000 young children's development, initially between the ages of 3 and 7 years, in an attempt to understand the effectiveness of their early years' education on their subsequent learning outcomes (Siraj and Mayo, 2014). This influential study showed conclusively that all children's chances of success at 16+

are affected by their early learning experiences, with the findings going on to impact national and international education policy (Taggart et al., 2015; Education Endowment Fund, 2018; UNICEF, 2019).

More specifically, the EPPE project explored the impact of the home and childcare history, as well as any pre-school education, on children's development, for different groups of learners (Sylva et al., 2004, p. 1). Despite the fact that this longitudinal study began nearly 20 years ago, the results are still applicable when considering the educational attainment of children labelled as disadvantaged in relation to literacy. Findings for this group indicated that *good quality pre-school education*, and the quality of the *home learning environment*, can significantly impact children's attainment by the end of Key Stage 1 (Sylva et al., 2004, p. 1) and at a range of subsequent points during their education (Taggart et al., 2015). They argue that the provision of specialised support for language and pre-reading skills *and* the positive involvement of parents in their children's learning are central to a good-quality pre-school education for children who are disadvantaged.

The study is important for these key findings but also because it is overwhelmingly optimistic. It helps to challenge the deficit perspectives sometimes brought to bear on families with low socio-economic status (SES) and the potential for the children in these families to attain good literacy outcomes. The study does this by making the fundamental observation that regardless of economic advantage or disadvantage, the attuned actions of a caregiver can nevertheless support progress with early learning:

> … *what parents do with their children is more important than who parents are. Poor mothers with few qualifications can improve their children's progress and give them a better start at school by engaging in activities at home that engage and stretch the child's mind.*

> (Sylva et al., 2004, p. 5)

What is of significance here is the idea that early education in the pre-school and the home can help to reduce learning disadvantage for those with economic disadvantage. However, this will be contingent on the understandings that educators and caregivers have about the best strategies for helping children, in ways that are sensitive and responsive to the needs of each child and family. In the report, the following activities are noted as having a positive effect:

- Reading with a child
- Teaching songs and nursery rhymes
- Painting and drawing
- Playing with letters and numbers
- Visiting the library
- Teaching the alphabet and numbers
- Taking children on visits and
- Creating regular opportunities for them to play with their friends at home

> (Sylva et al., 2004, pp. 4–5).

This list can be regarded as a set of activities that will promote early literacy learning as well as general development. The challenge for caregivers and educators is to know about this set of activities, and to be supported to enact the recommendations, while also managing the range of factors that might impact on opportunities to do so. These will be different for educators and caregivers and will include personal and social factors, such as wealth, availability, time, access to resources, and in the case of educators, policy, accountability frameworks and statutory requirements – that may or may not seem sympathetic to the child and family in question.

To account for this complex context for literacy learning theoretically, Siraj and Mayo (2014) turn to the bioecological model of human development, proposed by Bronfenbrenner and colleagues in the 1990s. This model recognises that four interrelated defining properties weave together to account for human development: 'process, person, context and time'. Of these four properties, 'process' sits at the core of the model. As Siraj and Mayo explain: 'Proximal processes are particular forms of interaction between the child and environment that provide the child with culturally regulated experiences through which children's genetic potential for effective psychological functioning are actualized' (Bronfenbrenner and Ceci, 1994 as cited in Siraj and Mayo, 2014, p. 18).

An example of a proximal process might include any of the activities listed above, e.g. the sharing of songs and nursery rhymes between caregiver and child; between children as they play together; or in a formal pre-school setting with a teacher and classmates. However, the sharing may present very differently in different contexts. It might involve learning and reciting a 'traditional' nursery rhyme in a pre-school. It might involve joining in with a popular vernacular playground chant (Marsh and Richards, 2013). Or it may involve sharing nursery rhymes and songs located on the internet using a tablet or phone, as part of a generational 'handing down' of loved rhymes (Marsh et al., 2021, p. 292). These processes therefore happen between people, in specific places and at certain times. They are impacted by the culture of the family, community and setting, by the experiences and expectations of the individuals within these cultures, by the access to wealth and resources, and by the available forms of capital (social, economic and cultural) and agency that result.

As clearly exemplified by Brooker (2002) in her ethnographic study of children starting school, there are powerful consequences for the idiosyncratic experiences of young children and their home learning. In her study, Brooker describes the variably successful transition of culturally diverse four-year-old children from inner-city London into their Reception class, in relation to the social, economic and cultural capitals of their families. In this study, she demonstrates how variations in the family's practices and status in terms of agency and habitus support the children to make a more or less successful start to their educational journey, due to their match to the habitus of the classroom (Brooker, 2002). While some families hold high status in their communities, the lack of 'match' to school practices and expectations is shown to disadvantage the children from these families from the outset of their formal schooling.

A more recent review of research in this field upholds Brooker's findings, specifically for literacy. In their review of literature from English-speaking countries, Buckingham et al. (2013) observe that SES is positively related to literacy achievement in a complex interweaving of factors that are articulated at the level of the individual as well as at the level of teaching. Echoing Brooker's earlier study, they argue that low income alone is a minor contribution to literacy outcomes, but that it impacts literacy learning, by its association with other factors that amass to construct experiences that are more or less likely to support success; with the result being that children from lower SES backgrounds are unduly adversely affected and are less likely to become literate than their advantaged peers. This finding, while being relatively recent, is not new. The impact of the home environment on young children's learning, language and literacy has been the subject of extensive and much-cited research for over 50 years. Two key bodies of work are especially worthy of inclusion in this chapter, for their synergy with the work already presented.

As Bearne and Reedy describe in their recent overview (2018), the sociologist Basil Bernstein's ideas about the language of 'working class' and 'middle class' families, while being controversial, have formed the basis of many explanations for why middle-class children find more success educationally than their socially less advantaged peers (p. 24). In his work, Bernstein explored the role of what he called 'primary socialisers' (caregivers and peers) and 'socialising contexts' for their impact on children's language and learning. Working with theorists and researchers in the fields of sociology, psychology and linguistics, he argued that middle-class families have access to an 'elaborated' and universalistic form of language that can be aligned with the language of the school. Families with lower SES, on the other hand, are more likely to use language that involves 'restricted' and context-dependent forms of meaning. As an example, a restricted language form might involve a short context-dependent statement that presumes the listener understands the topic being discussed. By contrast, elaborated language forms are 'context-independent' and communicate ideas without recourse to shared contextual understanding. They 'give rise to universalistic orders of meaning, where principles are made verbally explicit' (Bernstein, 1971, p. 11).

An example of this context-independent language might involve an early year educator's careful explanation of how a caterpillar metamorphoses into a butterfly, as part of reading *The Very Hungry Caterpillar* to a group of pre-school children. While the context here is clearly central, and most likely supported by video material or even observation of the process, the language used could easily transfer from one early years' setting to another, to achieve the aim. It is a universal type of language, with recognisable features that belong to the educational context. In different family settings, however, the approach to talking about how a caterpillar changes into to butterfly may well vary, as caregivers draw on their own language and material resources.

The take-away from Bernstein's work is the view that the patterns of language (as used by teachers and early years educators when they talk, model ideas and provide explanations) are more likely to reflect the home language used sometimes (but not exclusively) by families with access to more material and social resources. This familiarity advantages these economically 'advantaged' children further, as they make their earliest steps into formal literacy education. In the meantime, children labelled as disadvantaged may be excluded from learning, as the register used is less familiar and less reassuring. As Bearne and Reedy explain, these ideas have been challenged, and Bernstein himself was clear that these statements are generalisations, recognising that patterns of speech are evoked by specific social contexts that vary under certain institutional and local conditions (1973, p. 9).

The work of Tizard and Hughes (2002) moved beyond Bernstein's account and is less deterministic. They explored four-year-old girls' and their mothers' language use in the nursery class and at home, to offer nuance to the starting point offered by Bernstein. Their study did not frame working-class children's and mothers' language use in deficit terms: rather it highlighted the aspects of home life that might contribute to educational success and the child's active involvement in their learning process. These aspects involve five elements:

- the extent of the range of activities experienced by children in the home;

- the shared history between caregiver and child used to make sense of the world;

- the conversation opportunities in the home between the caregiver and the child;

- the meaningful nature of home-based activities; and

- the close intense relationship between the individuals in the home.

(Dunn, as cited in Tizard and Hughes, 2002: Foreword)

These elements were observed in all children's homes in their study, regardless of their SES. Of significance, however, is Tizard and Hughes' observation that the use of language in children from working-class families varied markedly from their home setting to their nursery setting – presenting as more subdued and passive in the nursery class. As Tizard and Hughes explain, it is not hard to see how myths about working-class verbal deprivation arise – as educators may incorrectly presume that the quiet, passive working-class child is just the same at home (2002, Preface xv). Tizard and Hughes' well-regarded study illustrates that the factors that may influence a child's success before they come to school are complex and interwoven; they may be affected by SES, but cannot be accounted for in these terms alone.

This diversity of experience among the youngest children can lead to a sense of some children being better prepared for formal literacy learning than others, which in turn can lead to deficit framings of families from a lower SES, where access to book reading and the use of print-based resources may enjoy less prominence. This notion of deficit can be problematic, as it closes down opportunities to build from the communities of practice and literacy assets that these young children and their families possess. Instead, remedial intervention programmes to tackle this perceived deficit are often prescribed (Anderson et al., 2010, p. 49), resulting in the development of curriculum and pedagogies that seek to fill perceived gaps, rather than build bridges from home to the educational setting that will promote learning, rather than exclude (Dyson, 2018).

If we accept that a combination of good-quality pre-school education and the involvement of caregivers can positively impact children's early literacy, the question is how to facilitate these elements, so that all children can benefit. Family and community cultures vary, and caregivers will support children's early literacy in different ways. This in turn will impact the match between the foundations for literacy built in the home and community, and the expectations for literacy imposed by the formal curriculum of the educational setting. This means that educators need to be especially sensitive to this issue, in order that all types of literacy foundations can be used to launch children's formal literacy development, not just those reflected in the curriculum.

Hannon et al. (2020) recognise this and argue for schools and settings to enable all children to find success in early literacy by valuing the cultural attributes of all families. In their account of a study of an intervention programme designed to raise disadvantaged children's literacy achievement at school entry, they argue that securing children's success in literacy rests more on the educator's understanding that some 'advantaged' children's preparation for formal learning matches what happens in the classroom far more closely than others, thus giving 'advantaged' children a head start in finding success with early and emergent print-based reading and writing practices.

In the next section, we consider the ways that educators can work with parents to understand children's varied experiences and support families to build on these to achieve secure foundations for later literacy learning.

PARENTING PROGRAMMES AND INTERVENTIONS WITH PARENTS

Given the repeated evidence, addressed above, that there is a strong correlation between what happens at home and how children are able to cope with the literacy demands of the Early Years' curriculum, it is not surprising that one solution has been to run parenting programmes or interventions with parents which increase parental engagement with their child and their education in some way. There are consistent claims in the research that parenting programmes can have a positive effect on both parents and children (Goodall and Vorhaus, 2010; Breitenstein and Gross, 2013; Lindsay and Strand, 2013; Joo et al., 2020; EEF, 2021a), although the EEF best-evidence report (2021a) also acknowledges that there can be variability in the effectiveness of different interventions. Joo et al. (2020) argue, from their synthesis of the research, that 'young children whose parents engage in more accepting, nurturing, and cognitively stimulating behaviours are more likely to exhibit greater growth in their academic skills and have higher self-esteem and academic achievement than children whose parents do not engage in such behaviours' (p. 3). This notion of parental engagement is generally broadly interpreted: including, for example, learning in the home, the communication between school and home, bringing parents into schools, and parental involvement, through roles such as being a parent governor. More recently, the EEF explained parental engagement as 'actively involving parents in supporting their children's learning and development' (2021a) and include strategies to help parents talk and read more with their children, direct interventions in particular aspects of parenting, and family initiatives within the community. It is important to underline here that the phrase 'parental engagement' is thus *both* about parents' engaging with school *and* schools engaging with parents.

Interventions to address parental engagement are not restricted to literacy interventions – they address health (Hingle et al., 2010), school readiness (Holmes, 2019), emotional and behavioural issues, and relationships and numeracy (Brooks and Hutchinson, 2002). Lindsay and Strand (2013), for example, evaluated the government's Parenting Early Intervention Programme (PEIP), a programme which specifically targeted parents whose children displayed or were at risk of behavioural and emotion difficulties. Such programmes are not irrelevant to literacy, as it is difficult for a child to thrive in an Early Years' setting if they are not ready for learning or struggle with relationships, emotion and behaviour. But our principal interest here is in interventions which do address literacy. In a nutshell, most of these are predicated on the idea that if we know how the home environment can nurture emergent literacy, then interventions or programmes might help parents to recreate that nurturing home environment. Perhaps not surprisingly, many parenting interventions target socially disadvantaged families or communities, and the parents of early years children so are particularly relevant for our interests in this chapter.

Literacy interventions have predominantly focused on either supporting parents in developing their children's oral language or on reading. In general, these show modest positive results in relation to changing family practices and behaviours, although these are not always accompanied by evidence of improved literacy outcomes for children. For example, Canfield et al. (2018) found that an intervention which helped low-income parents to access the public library increased the amount of parent–child book sharing and reading together, while Leung et al. (2018), reporting on a programme designed to foster a rich home language environment, found that it increased parental understanding about language development and increased the amount of turn-taking conversations between parents and children. A meta-analysis synthesising the results of 25 different language interventions with low SES families found some positive benefit on expressive vocabulary and language, but not a strong effect (Heidlage et al., 2020). There is also recurrent evidence that parental engagement interventions are *less* effective for disadvantaged groups (Mol et al., 2008; Manz et al., 2010; Carpentieri et al., 2011; van Steensel et al., 2011; EEF, 2021a) – in other words, they may be least effective for the very groups they intend to support. More promising outcomes derived from an intervention with parents of 5- to 6-year-olds in an inner-city disadvantaged community which focused both on supporting parents' management of their children's behaviour and on word reading and writing (Sylva et al., 2008). The literacy element of the intervention tutored parents on reading strategies using video recordings, drawing on the principles of the Reading Recovery Programme (see European Centre for Reading Recovery, 2012 for more detail) and emphasising the importance of making meaning, connecting written texts with children's own experiences and context. This intervention had a significant positive effect, both on how parents read with their children and on the children's word reading and writing skills.

The study of Hannon et al. (2020) is particularly worth noting for its approach. It was designed to be mindful of the evidence that family interventions in literacy often have lower results for disadvantaged families, thus achieving the perverse effect of *increasing* the achievement gap. They were also mindful of the problematic nature of the term 'disadvantaged' as we discussed in Chapter 1 and resisted the simplistic causal link between disadvantage and educational outcomes, arguing that 'disadvantage does not inhere in individuals; it is about the relationship between individuals, society and, particularly in the context of this paper, the institution of schooling' (p. 311). They also distinguish between *facilitative* interventions, which help parents capitalise on everyday opportunities to develop emergent literacy and *instructional* interventions which try to help parents reproduce what teachers do in school. In light of this thinking, their intervention was designed for teachers to work with parents 'from a value position of mutual respect and partnership with families. Their starting points were the individual circumstances of each family with the aim of building respectful, collaborative partnerships on this foundation, where each partner could contribute their own distinct knowledge and skills to their joint work' (p. 318). The intervention itself addressed four strands of emergent literacy – environmental print; book sharing; writing and oral language – and was implemented through a combination of home visits, centre-based activities, special events and postal communications between the child and the teacher. Access to literacy resources was also provided. There was a high take-up of the programme by parents, perhaps because of the relationships and respect that were built, and a significant impact on emergent literacy, which was stronger for socially disadvantaged children.

What is evident from this overview of research into parenting programmes and interventions for socially disadvantaged children is that the evidence of effectiveness is rather mixed. This may be because it is more challenging to change academic outcomes of children than it is to change parents' behaviour and practices. Gao et al. (2020) suggest that these programmes do support parenting but do not necessarily lead to children's development. Similarly, Joo et al. (2020) found that parenting interventions seem to have benefits for health, behaviour and socio-emotional outcomes but not for pre-academic cognitive skills. The EEF (2021a) concludes that 'though it is clear that parental engagement is valuable, much less is known about how to increase it, particularly in low-income communities'. There have also been critiques of the research itself: the poor quality of the interventions (Gorard and Huat See, 2013); limited information about whether and how parents implemented the programme (Hannon et al., 2020); limited measures related to parent training procedures and parent outcomes (Heidlage et al., 2019) and too much reliance on correlational studies, rather than those which look at causal relationships (EEF, 2021a). Nonetheless, the Hannon et al. study (2020) is important in pointing to possible ways forward. One criticism of underpinning beliefs implicit in many interventions is that they see the solution as trying to make all parents more like middle-class parents (Gewirtz, 2001; van Steensel et al., 2011), and that these programmes 'could be a poor fit with families' wishes or circumstances' (Hannon et al., 2020, p. 315). In contrast, the Hannon et al. study was built on an ethical stance which resisted deficit views of socially disadvantaged parents and was founded instead on respect for the parents they worked with and on principles of collaboration and trust.

CRITICAL QUESTIONS

- The research points to the critical importance of the home environment in building the foun-dations for literacy, but there is also a tendency to describe this as a deficit evident in some families. Re-read this chapter so far and marshal different points which confirm or challenge this idea. What is your own view?

- Why do you think so many interventions are less successful in homes with disadvantage?

IN PRACTICE IN THE EARLY YEARS SETTING

BUILDING LITERACY RICH ENVIRONMENTS

So given the variable findings from research into the efficacy of parenting programmes for promoting early literacy, how might you ensure that you support children's early literacy from within the pre-school setting. As stated earlier in this chapter a *good-quality pre-school education*, along with the quality of the *home learning environment*, can significantly impact children's attainment by the end of Key Stage 1 (Sylva et al., 2004, p. 1). The provision of a good-quality literacy education involves the construction of a literacy environment that is both familiar and enriching. When building literacy-rich environments in pre-school settings, you might consider the environment that the setting offers for literacy, as well as the range of textual experiences that are provided for their learners and their families. These choices and insights should then be informed by careful consideration of how to build from understandings of families' assets and needs; as well as by exploring ways to actively engage caregivers in their children's literacy learning.

The EEF advocate the use of 'early literacy approaches' to 'improve children's skills, knowledge or understanding related to reading and writing' (2021b). They describe a range of activities, based on a meta-analysis of 15 studies, mainly from the United States and exploring reading, that include the use of storytelling and group reading; the explicit teaching of letter knowledge, sounds and phonics; and exposure to different kinds of writing, to benefit all children's literacy learning. They also note that these activities may involve parents and caregivers (EEF, 2021b). Some of the listed strategies, including targeted small group interaction, are recognised as potentially having particularly positive effects on children from disadvantaged backgrounds. However, it is also noted that benefits may not be long-lived and single interventions may not be sufficient to support those with disadvantage. The Nuffield Early Language Intervention (NELI) (Nuffield Foundation Education Limited, 2021) is an example of an early literacy approach. As the NELI website states, the programme is designed for children in Reception (aged 4–5 years) and involves regular small group sessions and individual sessions each week for 20 weeks, targeting small groups of learners. The intervention aims to first develop vocabulary, listening and storytelling (narrative) skills, followed by a focus on activities to build phonological awareness and early sound-letter knowledge as a basis for reading success (Nuffield Foundation Education Limited, 2021). Its evaluation in 2016 showed a greater positive impact on language skills, than on word-level skills (Sibieta et al., 2016), but it has nevertheless been developed as an intervention programme, subsequently, reaching two-fifths of primary schools and involving 62,000 children in English schools in 2020–2021.

In their guidance report *Preparing for Literacy*, the EEF proposed seven practical evidence-based recommendations for improving children's communication, language and literacy in the early years. Listed here are the recommendations that seem most apposite when considering children with disadvantage (EEF, 2018):

1. Prioritise the development of communication and language

    - use high-quality adult–child interactions, where talking with and talking to children is involved

    - model effective language

    - use a range of approaches including shared story reading and telling, to build vocabulary.

2. Develop children's early reading using a balanced approach

    - recognise the need for a broad range of capabilities (decoding as well as language comprehension)

    - focus on multiple aspects of early reading

    - include storytelling, letter and sound knowledge, and singing and rhyming activities for phonological awareness

    - build from phonological awareness and an interest in sounds, to systematic phonics.

3. Develop children's capability and motivation to write

    - prioritise expressive language use

    - provide a wide range of opportunities and develop motivation to write

    - develop the foundations of fast, accurate and efficient handwriting

    - monitor the progress of handwriting and support as needed.

4. Embed opportunities to develop self-regulation.

5. Support parents to understand how to help their children to learn

    - encourage parents to read to children before they can read

    - read with children

    - run workshops for parents to help them develop skills of reading with children and talking about reading.

6. Use high-quality assessment to ensure all children make good progress.

7. Use high-quality targeted support to help struggling children.

DEVELOPING CONSTRUCTIVE RELATIONSHIPS WITH PARENTS

The research on parenting programmes and interventions with parents shows that it is not always easy to achieve positive results when addressing literacy with parents in socially disadvantaged contexts. However, the research also offers some clear pointers which might maximise the likelihood of success.

A good place to start is to think critically about your own attitudes and assumptions and ensure that you do not adopt a deficit position towards socially disadvantaged parents or view them as poor parents. Poor parenting exists across the whole social spectrum, regardless of social status! And much of the research on differential educational outcomes for children from different social groups highlights that the problem is principally about a misalignment of school expectations and practices with those in the home. It is also helpful to understand the wider community within which your EY setting is located – its challenges and its possibilities, and the spaces, resources and people who might help.

From this base, you can work actively to develop positive relationships with parents, founded on mutual respect and a shared desire to work together. Sometimes parents who live in areas of social disadvantage may be hard to reach or reluctant to engage, so identify these parents and explicitly try to draw them in. These parents may have very negative memories of schools themselves or feel intimidated by other parents: just make sure you don't sound like a teacher scolding them and that you don't only speak to parents when there is a 'problem' with their child. Keep remembering that constructive relationships are more likely to grow when parents do not feel you are telling them what to do, but are supporting them and engaging with their needs and concerns. These relationships can also flourish where there are plenty of informal opportunities to meet together. You might think about how you invite parents into your teaching space and how they can interact with literacy activities in that environment. You might also arrange events which parents and children attend together: such as an oral games afternoon; a community storytelling session; an author visit or a 'special memories' shared writing session.

REFLECTION POINT

In their Early Years Toolkit, the EEF (2021a) suggests you ask yourself and reflect upon the following key questions:

- Have you provided simple guidance to parents about how they can support their child?

- Home visits can help parental engagement, but aren't always essential. How can you make your setting welcoming to encourage regular attendance from parents?

- How will you monitor the impact of your parental engagement approach?

- Have you considered the specific needs of the families of your school's pupils?

One particularly positive step you might consider is to develop a programme designed to build parents' confidence and knowledge in how to support their children's emergent literacy. At the heart of this should be collaboration with parents, understanding their concerns and needs in relation to their home environment, and building relationships founded on mutual respect. You might find it helpful to use the resources that Hannon et al. (2020) used in their research with parents, and created to help teachers generate constructive ways of working with parents. They begin by thinking about emergent literacy in terms of four complementary strands, elaborated with examples that are appropriate for attention in the home environment (see Figure 2.1).

Environmental Print	Books	Writing	Oral Language		

⇩   ⇩   ⇕   ⇩   ⇕   ⇩   ⇩

		Form:	**Content:**	**Phonological**	**Literacy**	**Storytelling:**
notices; comics; magazines; hand written texts; letters, notes; advertisements; leaflets, posters, signs; television print ...	commercial texts; fiction; non-fiction; home-made books; picture books; adult information texts...	scribbling; drawing; mark-making; handwriting	story writing; personal writing; labelling; lists; letters; cards...	**awareness:** alphabetic knowledge; nursery rhymes...	**talk:** literacy vocabulary; critical vocabulary...	listening, speaking and telling; creating spoken narrative...

Figure 2.1   The four strands of emergent literacy (Nutbrown and Hannon, 2011)

Before designing your programme, you might reflect on your current practice in your own EY setting and how your learning environment and activities map on to these four strands.

Hannon et al. (2020) call their overall framework the **ORIM** framework because, in addition to the four literacy strands above, they have four ways in which parents can build their children's literacy: providing **O**pportunities for literacy development; showing **R**ecognition of and valuing what their children achieve; sharing **I**nteraction with literacy through talk and activities; and acting as a **M**odel of being literate so their children can see their parents engaged in literacy practices in their everyday life. The ORIM framework is presented as a matrix (see Table 2.1) to support planning, and Nutbrown and Hannon (2011) suggest that EY professionals think about each cell in the matrix in terms of What can school do to support the parent's role here? and What can we do to help parents improve children's experiences here?

Table 2.1   The ORIM framework (Nutbrown and Hannon, 2011)

		Strands of literacy			
Parents can provide		Environmental print	Books	Writing	Oral language
	Opportunities				
	Recognition				
	Interaction				
	Model				

ACTION POINT

Use the ORIM matrix to develop the outline of a possible session with parents addressing just one of the four strands of literacy (or one of the sub-strands, such as phonological awareness). Think about:

- Your own professional knowledge of that aspect of emergent literacy;

- What activities you might use in a session with parents to address Opportunities, Recognition; Interaction and being a Model;

- How you will explain things to parents in clear, everyday language;

- How you will create space to listen to parents' voices.

CONCLUSION

As stated by Hannon et al. (2020), in England, Early Years educators are confronted with a significant challenge when trying to promote access to mandated school literacy for children whose families are labelled as disadvantaged. The challenge is two-fold. It requires the teacher (educator) to recognise that they may need to build a bridge from their pre-school children's diverse everyday family literacy experiences that extends to the print-centric story and skills-based context of many early years' literacy classrooms; and second with the need to value the informal teaching of emergent literacy practices by the families themselves. Hannon et al. are clear that while children labelled from their earliest years as 'disadvantaged' typically achieve less well in school than their 'advantaged' peers, this is not necessarily as a result of their background. Rather, they argue that securing children's success in literacy rests more on the educator's understanding that some 'advantaged' children's preparation for formal learning matches what happens in the classroom far more closely than others, thus giving 'advantaged' children a head start in finding success with early and emergent print-based reading and writing practices.

VIGNETTE

In the United Kingdom, as in other countries, the COVID pandemic has disrupted education on an unprecedented scale and over a prolonged period of time. Pupils in primary schools have faced periods of total lockdown, when schools were only open to children of key workers or vulnerable children, and everyone else was asked to stay at home. Many have also experienced ongoing low-level disruption as the disease has continued to circulate among staff and pupils in schools, causing those with COVID or in close contact with someone else with the disease to self-isolate at home.

All of this has meant that many children have been confined to home for a considerable period of time, with home schooling substituting for learning in school. Parents and teachers have had to negotiate with each other and with their children to enable this to work. Nobody yet knows quite how significant this break in normal patterns of school attendance will prove to be, and indeed, quite which groups of children will be affected the most, or in what ways.

What restricting children to their homes has highlighted, however, is just how important a role schools play in a society which tolerates, and indeed seems to do so little to address, the very real and material effects of poverty on many children's lives. What made learning at home during lockdowns so difficult for many children was inadequate food and heating, overcrowded housing that didn't afford the space for more than one child to be online at any particular time, where only a single mobile phone might be available, shared with several siblings, with no access to outside space and with parents worrying about paying the bills or even knowing who to turn to at such a time. Primary schools serving these kinds of communities were quick to act. They recognised at the start of the pandemic that some families would be struggling to put food on the table and went to considerable lengths to ensure no children went hungry. They checked in regularly with families where they thought children might be at risk from mental health issues, domestic violence, compounded by sub-standard, temporary housing. They did everything they could to find other sources of support in their communities that families could turn to.

In so many ways they refused a policy logic that prioritises maintaining curriculum delivery at all costs, regardless of what else is going on in children's lives. In the aftermath of COVID, it is worth taking stock of the relentless drive to hold schools to account for test performance with 'no excuses' accepted for poverty's material effects on children's capacity to learn. In reality, this vastly underestimates the harms poverty causes. It remains to be seen how resilient children can be under pandemic conditions and how quickly they can recover, given access to the kind of holistic support schools really do routinely provide. Greater recognition for the work schools do in holding communities together and finding ways to motivate and empower children to learn, whatever the circumstances in which they are growing up, is key to redressing the harms that high levels of inequality within our society create.

Gemma Moss

Professor of Literacy and Director of the International Literacy Centre, UCL Institute of Education

To see more about Gemma's research on COVID: https://iris.ucl.ac.uk/iris/browse/profile?upi=PJGMO52

3
TALK FOR LEARNING AND DEMOCRATIC PARTICIPATION

INTRODUCTION

Communication is a fundamental human right, expressed in Article 19 of the Universal Declaration of Human Rights: 'Everyone has the right to freedom of opinion and expression; this right includes freedom to hold opinions without interference and to seek, receive and impart information and ideas through any media and regardless of frontiers' (United Nations [UN], 1948). Crucially, literacy learning enables the enactment of this right, empowering humans with the language necessary for communication and expression, while supporting personal, social and economic well-being. This chapter focuses particularly on spoken language – also referred to here as 'talk' – as an object of study its own right, as a crucial foundation for literacy learning and as an enabler of democratic participation in society.

As explained in the previous chapter, the early development of children's spoken language is crucial for literacy learning and for managing the challenges of school and later life. It is well documented that children with underdeveloped language and communication skills may face more academic, social and emotional challenges (Department for Children, Schools and Families, 2008; The Children's Communication Charity [I CAN] and Royal College of Speech and Language Therapists [RCSLT], 2018). In fact, Speech, Language and Communication Needs (SLCN) often underlie behavioural difficulties and are common among children excluded from school (Stiles, 2013; Owen, 2015) or in the justice system (I CAN, n.d.; I CAN and RCSLT, 2018). It is significant then that a considerable proportion of children entering school have an (often unidentified) SLCN, and, as stated in the 2008 Bercow Report, that 50% of children and young people in some socioeconomically disadvantaged populations have speech and language skills significantly lower than those of other children of the same age (Department for Children, Schools and Families [DCFS], 2008, p. 13). Indicative of persisting inequalities and insufficient resourcing, I CAN and RCSLT in 2018 and Public Health England in 2020 report that while approximately 10% of all children have long-term SLCN, in some deprived areas, 50% of children start school with an SLCN. The COVID-19 pandemic has further exacerbated concerns about the numbers of children starting school with poor language and communication skills (Bowyer-Crane et al., 2021). It is important to note of course the distinction between SLCN which is the result of, for example, lifelong disabilities, and SLCN which may be the result of social and environmental factors and which may improve with teaching and intervention.

Sensitivity to children's language needs and experience is also important given school success is often predicated on implicit expectations around language use which is not familiar to all children. For many children, the language of school and the curriculum – the Standard English variety – is not the language of the home, and many children will not have experienced the spoken language forms stipulated in curricula (e.g. debate). Moreover, many children will not have experienced ways of talking which support learning in school: as Mercer and Littleton assert, 'social experience does not provide all children with the same language experiences, so we cannot assume that all children naturally have access to the same opportunities for developing their use of language as a tool for learning, reasoning and solving problems' (2007, p. 2).

Although teachers cannot correct for inequalities in children's early language experiences, teachers can harness talk in the classroom as a powerful pedagogical tool; teachers can celebrate linguistic diversity by drawing on pupils' knowledge and experience to foster confident use of spoken language repertoires, including Standard English. As Alexander argues, 'The educational consequences of social disadvantage are compounded by children's difficulties in oral development and communication; and that talk can be an effective means of re-engaging the disengaged and closing the overlapping gaps of equity and attainment' (Alexander, 2020, p. 19). As far as possible, children should leave school empowered to enact their fundamental human right to communication and expression, equipped for democratic participation in an ever changing and unpredictable world.

UNDERSTANDING THE RESEARCH
SOCIOECONOMIC STATUS (SES) AND LANGUAGE EXPERIENCE

Children benefit linguistically, cognitively and academically from early exposure to and experience of diverse and complex spoken language (Tamis-Le Monda et al., 2017; Romeo et al., 2018). However, research indicates the disparities in language experience associated with socioeconomic status (SES) (Neuman et al., 2018; Romeo et al., 2018; Rowe, 2018; Kalil and Ryan, 2020). Reviewing evidence linking parenting practices and socioeconomic gaps in childhood outcomes, Kalil and Ryan (2020) posit that SES parents – characterised as those with more education and income – tend to use greater spoken language stimulation when interacting with their young children than do their lower SES counterparts, arguing that 'SES-based differences in linguistic environments could plausibly contribute to SES-based gaps in children's early language skills' (p. 32). Research evidence also indicates that school-level SES, in some cases more than student-level SES, may influence the quality of the spoken interactions children experience in school. Examining language processes and interactions during kindergarten year, Neuman et al. (2018, p. 102) found that children living in more concentrated poverty were more likely to experience more limited language complexity and diversity in both home *and* school contexts, resulting in a 'double dose of disadvantage' in their first year of school. This finding also serves as a reminder of the effects of living in concentrated poverty, that 'neighbourhoods... clustered in social settings, may exercise affordances or constraints and create "social milieus" that foster educational advantages or disadvantages' (Neuman et al., 2018, p. 113).

However, as discussed in Chapter 1, it is important to interpret cautiously claims which arise from comparisons of socioeconomic groups and to recognise that these studies report *average* differences (Rowe, 2018) which can mask variation within groups and lead to unhelpful generalisations. The debates and research arising from the oft-cited Hart and Risley (1995) study highlight the importance of early language experiences but also serve as an illustration of why it is important to be attentive to the way that findings are reported and to the way that different research methods can yield different results: Hart and Risley's (1995) observations of words spoken to young children in the homes of families from different socioeconomic backgrounds led to the hugely influential finding that 30 million more words are spoken directly to young children in higher SES families than lower SES families. More recently, using less intrusive and more sophisticated data collection methods, Gilkerson et al. (2017) place this figure at a more modest, yet still significant, 4 million. Unlike Hart and Risley (1995), Sperry et al. (2019) established the quantity of speech *overheard* as well as *directed* at the child and found that differences in home language environments were equally distributed across different socioeconomic groups. Golinkoff et al. (2019), however, drawing attention to the risky implications of denying the existence of the word gap, argue that talk *directed* to a child – talk which is conversational and responsive, and may account for the differences between SES groups (Romeo et al., 2018) – is developmentally more valuable than talk overheard. In taking different methodological approaches, these studies, when considered together, illuminate important issues, but they also highlight the need to avoid over-generalisations about SES groups and the way they communicate.

It is also important to recognise that research evidence reveals mainly *correlational* relationships between SES and language experience. SES itself is not a direct, *causal* factor in children's language development: it is the *contextual* factors *associated* with parent and school SES which may influence interactional practices which affect language development in young children (Rowe, 2018; Kalil and Ryan, 2020). SES affects quality of life, including access to resources and quality of services, all of which contribute to SES-related differences (Neuman et al., 2018, pp. 102–103): parents' communication with their children is shaped by a variety of environmental and economic factors, as well as beliefs and values. Understanding the factors that shape parents' communication with their children is essential for identifying ways to reduce disparities in children's language development (Rowe, 2018).

Research evidence suggests that children who have more limited experience of language are disadvantaged by fewer opportunities to engage in the cognitively challenging exchanges valued in school (Neuman et al., 2018, p. 104; Romeo et al., 2018). However, a key message, here, and throughout the book, is that lower SES families should not be viewed as a homogeneous group: different components of SES relate to families in different ways (Rowe, 2018), and parenting and linguistic practices should not be assumed deficit. Children in lower SES families may well be exposed to rich and varied language practices (Heath, 1983; Avineri et al., 2015) or have linguistic strengths which serve them well in their immediate settings (Hoff, 2013), but may find that the language and expectations these foster do not fit with the expectations of school. Finally, it is also important to challenge discourses around SES and aspirations: most parents, regardless of income and education, believe in the importance of developing life skills which will prepare their children for success in school and later life (Kalil and Ryan, 2020).

LANGUAGE FOR LEARNING

In the classroom, talk is an essential pedagogic tool: 'Of all the tools for educational intervention in students' development, talk is perhaps the most pervasive in its use and powerful in its possibilities' (Alexander, 2020, p. 15). A considerable body of research on classroom talk conducted since the 1960s demonstrates the clear benefits of talk for learning and cognitive development (Resnick et al., 2015). Much of this research is underpinned by Vygotsky's (1978) theories about language and the socially constructed nature of learning. According to Vygotsky (1978), the acquisition of language itself is a cultural process, supported in early childhood by the agreement between adult and child on referents which provide an 'entry point' to social interactions. Children gradually begin to master words and recognise their potential for meaning: at first, speech is external, then egocentric, and as it converts to inner speech, comes to organise thought; inner speech retains the functions of social interactions, with discussion and argument becoming the basis for reasoning. Individual thinking, therefore, is the internalisation of cognitive processes experienced first through social interactions and mediated through the mechanism of language; for Vygotsky, 'Thought development is determined by language, i.e. by the linguistic tools of thought and by the sociocultural experience of the child' (1986, p. 94). This theoretical perspective, therefore, brings into sharp relief the importance of children's early language experiences: as Halliday said, 'when children learn language, they are not simply engaging in one kind of learning among many; rather, they are learning the foundation of learning itself' (1993, p. 93).

In framing learning as an active and social process, these theoretical perspectives draw attention to the crucial role of dialogue between learner and 'other': for awakening 'a variety of internal developmental processes that are able to operate only when the child is interacting with people in his environment and in cooperation with his peers' (Vygotsky, 1978, p. 90). Describing the space between what a learner can do alone, and what they can achieve with support and guidance, the Zone of Proximal Development (ZPD) – a concept central to Vygotsky's theory of learning – is allied closely with the concept of 'scaffolding'. A term first coined by Bruner (1975), scaffolding describes the process through which an adult uses inter-actional strategies to support a child in carrying out a task beyond the child's capability (Stone, 1998). Vygotsky did not specify the particular form of interactions within the ZPD (Stone, 1998), but interactions characterised as 'dialogic' are considered particularly productive for learning (Mercer, 1995; Nystrand et al., 1997; Alexander, 2020). Dialogic talk is searching and reciprocal, opening a 'space' (Wegerif, 2007) for the exploration of ideas; in dialogic teacher–student interactions, querying and elaboration have been highlighted as particularly productive for learning (Hennessy et al., 2021; Howe et al., 2019).

Dialogic *teaching*, an approach, which, promoting egalitarian participation and pupil voice, places talk firmly at the heart of students' learning and teachers' practice (Alexander, 2020, p. 1), has been shown to positively impact pupil attainment (Jay et al., 2017; Alexander, 2018) and is a powerful tool for teacher assessment:

> *Dialogic teaching is good for students. It harnesses the power of talk to engage students' interest, stimulate their thinking, advance their understanding, expand their ideas and build and evaluate argument, empowering them for lifelong learning...Dialogic teaching helps teachers. By encouraging students to share their thinking, it enables teachers to diagnose needs, devise learning tasks, enhance understanding, assess progress and assist students through the challenges they encounter.*

> (Alexander, 2020, p. 1)

Alexander outlines six principles to guide the planning of classroom talk, and as criteria for 'dialogic' classrooms (see Alexander, 2020, for more extensive frameworks):

Collective	*The classroom is a site of joint learning and enquiry, and, whether in groups or as a class, students and teachers are willing and able to address learning tasks together.*
Supportive	*Students feel able to express ideas freely, without risk of embarrassment over contributions that are hesitant or tentative, or that might be judged 'wrong', and they help each other to reach common understandings.*
Reciprocal	*Participants listen to each other, share ideas, ask questions and consider alternative viewpoints; and teachers ensure that they have ample opportunities to do so.*

Deliberative	Participants discuss and seek to resolve different points of view, they present and evaluate arguments and they work towards reasoned positions and outcomes.
Cumulative	Participants build on their own and each other's contributions and chain them into coherent lines of thinking and understanding.
Purposeful	Classroom talk, though sometimes open-ended, is nevertheless structured with specific learning goals in mind.

(Alexander, 2020, p. 131)

Central to Alexander's principles for dialogic teaching is the notion of *repertoire* – teaching which involves a 'broad array of interactive skills, strategies and moves' (2020, p. 2) – and through which pupils listen to and engage in different ways of talking which support different kinds of thinking and understanding (Alexander, 2018). Repertoires of talk include 'broad forms and functions of talk that extend across exchanges and transactions, for example, discussion and argumentation; enabling patterns of group work; norms for talk which are as much about the student's attitude and relationship to others as talk itself; and specific moves such as questioning and extending' (Alexander, 2020, p. 136). Crucially, in the dialogic classroom, teachers utilise and orchestrate a *range* of interactional strategies according to learning purpose and context.

The teacher's role, therefore, is crucial in dialogic teaching because 'it is through the teacher's talk that the student's talk is mainly prompted, accelerated and enriched – or not, as the case may be' (Alexander, 2020, p. 3). Dialogic teaching is, though, more than the talk, but enacts 'a dialogic stance on knowledge, learning, social relations and education itself' (Alexander, 2020, p. 1). Snell and Lefstein (2018) draw attention to the way that teacher ideology, and specifically perceptions of pupil ability, may clash with the principles of dialogic teaching, compounding the potentially threatening expectations of the dialogic classroom for some pupils; they argue that: 'dialogic pedagogy's potential as a lever for equity and social justice can only be realized if it is enacted within an ideology that views ability as dynamic, context-dependent and socially constructed' (pp. 47–48). Teachers who believe in cognitively challenging participation for *all* pupils, regardless of perceived ability or background, and who foster an atmosphere of mutual respect in the classroom, create conditions for classroom dialogue and support pupils' identities as 'competent and accountable members of the classroom community' (Snell and Lefstein, 2018, p. 45).

TALK, READING AND WRITING

Spoken language lays a foundation for literacy learning – as Britton famously said, 'reading and writing float on a sea of talk' (Britton, 1970, p. 29). Yet, despite the symbiotic relationship between talk, reading and writing, spoken language has historically been attributed less prominence than the teaching of reading and writing in England; and in the classroom, talk often fails to be harnessed in a way which exploits the potential complementarity of reading, writing and spoken language. Spoken language is fundamental in the process of becoming a reader – in both learning to decode and comprehend (Department for Education and Skills [DfES], 2006) – and in developing the metalinguistic knowledge which underlies writing competency (Myhill and Newman, 2016). Spoken language is also fundamental to the way learners' *experience* English – to the meanings derived from stories told or read aloud, plays performed and poems heard.

In the teaching of reading, spoken language lays a crucial foundation for phonics instruction, in which the relationship between the written and spoken – or phoneme and grapheme – is fundamental (Department for Education and Skills [DfES], 2006). Furthermore, the verbal interactions that can surround reading, for example, between parent and child as they read a picture book, support the development of pre-reading skills such as auditory and visual discrimination. Reading aloud to children and talking about what has been read, through the early to teen years, is a valuable way of making 'bridges, from the written to the oral and back again' (Rosen, 2019). In the classroom, talking about what has been read is also a crucial means of constructing meaning from and responding to text. In fact, dialogue-intense approaches have been shown to be specifically beneficial for literal and inferential comprehension (Wilkinson et al., 2019). Comprehension may be supported through questioning and discussion which supports the cognitive and metacognitive strategies – *making connections, predicting, questioning, monitoring, visualising and summarising* (New South Wales [NSW] Department of Education and Training, 2010) – that enable readers to make sense of text. Talking about text – treating text as 'multi-voiced' (Bakhtin, 1986) and reading as social – is also a crucial part of fostering a love of reading. The role of talk about texts, and in the teaching of comprehension strategies, is discussed in more depth in Chapter 4.

Like reading, writing, often viewed as silent and solitary, is also a social activity. While we draw on cognitive processes as we write, what and how we write is shaped by our social experiences. In the classroom, talking about writing not only supports the cognitive processes involved in writing, it enables the creation of writing communities who generate their own norms and values (Cremin and Myhill, 2013). Talk can be used in a range of ways to support young writers: for example, talk can help pupils generate ideas for writing (Fisher et al., 2010); oral rehearsal can ease the cognitive demand of writing and may support the transfer of spoken words to written text – an 'interface' which is hard to bridge (Cremin and Myhill, 2013); metacognitive modelling (Quigley and Coleman, 2019) – when a teacher (or perhaps pupil) talks about how they re-read, revise or overcome obstacles when writing – is also a useful scaffolding strategy which helps writers develop metacognitive control of the writing process.

An accumulating body of research also sheds light on how talk about writing – what Myhill and Newman (2016, 2019) call 'metatalk' – can support the development of learners' metalinguistic understanding. In the context of writing, 'metalinguistic understanding' involves *recognising* how written text is crafted for meaning and effect and being able to control one's own writing choices. Metatalk opens up discussion about writers' linguistic choices, developing knowledge about language and supporting metalinguistic thinking. Metatalk may be agentic and 'consciousness-raising' (Schleppegrell, 2013) in its capacity to enable learners' deliberate control *of* language. Instructional approaches, such as these, which recognise the generative relationship between talk and writing may well be key in the effective teaching of writing (Department for Children, Schools and Families [DCSF], 2008; Ofsted, 2009).

TEACHING TALK AND STANDARD ENGLISH

Before turning to practical strategies for teaching talk, this section will consider how spoken language, and particularly Standard English, is positioned in the curriculum in England. In the United Kingdom, spoken language is variously weighted, in terms of value, content and assessment, across different curricula and examination syllabi (see Jones, 2017). The status of spoken language has shifted over time – for example, the current version of the National Curriculum in England (Department for Education [DfE] 2014) places less emphasis on spoken language than previous iterations, and the term 'spoken language' in the current version replaces the previously used term 'speaking and listening'. In contrast, the Welsh curriculum, for example, refers to 'oracy', a term coined by Wilkinson (1965) and which encapsulates more spoken language as a fundamental part of literacy. These terms and the talk types stipulated in curricula are indicative of how (and which) spoken language is valued by their associated governments (as Alexander notes, language is an intensely political matter). The curriculum in England places emphasis on particular presentational types of talk – talk which is adjusted to the needs of an audience (e.g. debate is specified in the spoken language curriculum for Key Stages 1–4). Whatever talk 'types' are the focus of teaching, it is important to consider the form and expectations associated with these different ways with words, and to make these explicit to students.

The remainder of this section will consider the teaching of Standard English and some of the associated issues and debates, bearing in mind that those most likely to speak non-Standard English are socially disadvantaged learners. The National Curriculum in England states that 'Pupils should be taught to speak clearly and convey ideas confidently using Standard English' (Department for Education [DfE], 2014). This statement is mirrored in the Teaching Standards, a document outlining a set of minimum requirements for teachers' practice and conduct, and which specifies that teachers must use and promote Standard English (DfE, 2013). Standard English is a dialect spoken by a small proportion of the population and is associated with social status and power; there are very many other varieties of English, all of which are important and embody identity and heritage (Myhill et al., 2016). Standard English enables speakers and writers from varying backgrounds to communicate, and it is the language of choice in settings where power is exercised or decisions made, including in education (Alexander, 2020, p. 88). Children who can use Standard English are, therefore, advantaged (Myhill et al., 2016).

As Cushing (2021a) argues, however, a consequence of Standard English as a form which is both con-structed by and associated with powerful social groups, and which is a gatekeeping mechanism to employment and education opportunities, is that non-Standard forms are often considered subordinate, or even deviant. The equation of non-Standard versions of language with poor standards and crime is evident in Norman Tebbit's comments in 1985 – that 'if you allow standards to slip to the stage where good English is no better than bad English, where people turn up filthy to school…all those things cause people to have no standards at all, and once you lose standards there's no imperative to stay out of crime' – and more recently when the actions of London rioters were linked to the 'wilful distortions' of 'inchoate street slang' (Johns, 2011). Cushing (2021a) argues that the 2014 National Curriculum also foregrounds an elitist stance which associates Standard English with notions of citizenship and societal expectations. Examining how this Standard Language ideology surfaces in primary school language policy documents, Cushing found schools that *position teachers as* "standard language role models" who have the authority to police, regulate and suppress students' language' (2021a, p. 321). Cushing (2021b) posits that strict language policies and approaches advocated by 'toolkits' such as *Teach Like A Champion* (Lemov, 2015, in Cushing, 2021b) can, in 'correcting' non-Standard forms, for example, deny speakers the opportunity to draw on their own linguistic resources, while embarrassing individuals and detracting from the learning focus of the lesson. Cushing warns that by reinforcing the Standard English ideology and a deficit view of non-Standard varieties, curriculum policy and how this surfaces in schools can lead to the 'entrenchment' (2021a, 2021b) of linguistic and social inequality.

Denying access to Standard English risks social and economic marginalisation: being able to use Standard English is empowering, and being able to 'code-switch' – moving between standard and non-Standard, formal and informal language, etc. – is an important skill. But given the issues raised by Cushing, and the close connection between language and identity, it is important for teachers to think carefully and critically about how to approach the teaching of Standard English in a way that doesn't mean stamping out non-Standard dialects. It is important too to be alert to a tendency to align discourses of language with discourses of behaviour and standards and to avoid promoting a view of non-Standard language as deficit. Cushing argues the importance of critical literacies, as a way of teaching *about* standardised English, including its association with status, race, class and power and which problematise the historical realities by which a dialect becomes the 'Standard' (2021a, p. 333).

CRITICAL QUESTIONS

Teachers might find that some of the principles for teaching Standard English advocated here are at odds with what they encounter in school and policy. However, while teachers are inevitably constrained by policy (and other factors), they do 'retain a creative licence in how they appropriate and re-contextualise policies for their own needs' (Cushing, 2021a, p. 333). Think critically about the following:

- What is your response to the arguments presented above?

- How does your school approach the teaching of Standard English and manage linguistic diversity?

- What knowledge and experience do you have of using different dialects and how might you draw on this in the classroom?

- In light of the arguments above, what strategies might you use to promote understanding of Standard English and other varieties of English?

IN THE CLASSROOM

TALK FOR LEARNING IN ACTION

To illustrate how teachers can harness talk to support reading and writing, and to exemplify teacher–pupil interactions, three transcribed episodes – two from a secondary English classroom and one from a primary classroom – are presented below.

The first two episodes below, taken from two consecutive year 9 lessons (age 13–14), focus on the novella *Of Mice and Men* by John Steinbeck: the first lesson explores the author's choice of character names; the second lesson, using the text as a springboard for writing, focuses pupils on developing noun phrases to alter the impression of the characters discussed. In an interview with the observing researcher, the class teacher explained her rationale for these lessons: 'being able to play around with [language]...to create these multi-faceted characters, giving them that freedom to experiment meant that they would be able to develop their own understanding'. The teacher's intention was that pupils' reading and analysis of the text would support subsequent linguistic decision-making, and that the process of writing would help pupils to think more deeply about Steinbeck's linguistic choices. These episodes illustrate the potential complementarity of reading and writing instruction and how it is the talk that mediates the learning.

Teacher: *We've talked a lot about Curley's wife being a possession...We haven't talked about that in relation to Candy's dog, did anybody think about the significance of this?...Poppy?*

Poppy: *I think it shows that they're both_they're not given the individuality, like they aren't important enough to be given names.*

Teacher: *Nice. Not important enough to be given their own title, so definite connections with status there and them being unequal_ Leo?*

Leo: *I think like Flora was saying about Candy_it also says something about Candy's character, about him being quite kind and caring_he cares about the dog.*

Teacher: *And what's in his name which suggests that he's caring?*

Leo: *Candy, it's almost_ it's also like the American word for sweet.*

Immediately prior to this short episode, pupils discussed character names in pairs; here, the teacher elicits feedback. Poppy recognises the similarity between Curley's wife and Candy's dog, noting that they are not important enough to be given names. The teacher reformulates and expands Poppy's response, using the words 'status' and 'unequal'. Leo, building on Flora's earlier response (not featured here), adds that the name 'Candy' suggests something kind about his character; the teacher poses a follow-up question, prompting Leo to make a more specific connection between the name 'Candy' and the word 'sweet'. This brief exchange illustrates how teachers can expand pupil responses and ask probing questions to encourage elaboration; it also illustrates how pupils can build on and develop peer responses, and how talk makes pupils' thinking 'visible'. In this first episode, the teacher uses questions and reformulation to steer pupils towards a particular response; in the second episode, we see an example of more exploratory questioning as the teacher supports a pupil to recognise the significance of her word choice.

Teacher: *Lucia, share one of yours [noun phrase] that you either liked or was your favourite or didn't work as well.*

Lucia: *I think one that didn't work as well was '**Crook, a useless being of the world**'.*

Teacher: *A '**useless being**' of the world?*

Lucia: *Yeah.*

Teacher: *Okay, why?*

Lucia: *Because I don't know, it just... I don't think it was as imaginative as the other one, as saying you're a '**useless being**' doesn't really show anything else except for the fact that no one really likes you.*

Teacher: *You've... you've played around with the noun choice again though, haven't you? So we've thought about '**man**', yesterday you thought about '**failure**', we thought about '**creature**', you've put in '**being**', why '**being**'?*

Lucia: *It's kind of like... I don't know, it's kind of like a human but like lower down than a human, it's like...*

Teacher: *Yeah, it's interesting, knocking off the... the '**human**' being, the '**human**' part before that. There's also a sense of absence...*

Lucia: *A bit empty.*

Teacher: *Yeah, that... that human part is perhaps missing. I'm just thinking through my ideas here, it's not something I'd considered before, so if you're a '**being**' does that suggest then that the human part of you is missing and you're perhaps... what would you be?*

Lucia: *It can be, yeah, kind of means that you're... you're not like everyone else, you're different...*

Teacher: *Yeah.*

Lucia: *And your soul isn't connected up.*

In this episode, Lucia shares her least favourite noun phrase, explaining that the choice 'useless being' doesn't reveal much about the character. However, the teacher's response, recalling prior discussion of alternatives, draws attention to and questions the specific word choice 'being', prompting Lucia to consider its significance in more depth. The teacher builds on Lucia's response to highlight the absence of the pre-modifying 'human'; the reciprocal exchange of ideas which follows explores the significance of this linguistic choice. The teacher here opens a space for dialogue and supports Lucia to verbalise the significance of her linguistic choice. This episode exemplifies how *why* (and *how!*) questions can prompt elaboration and develop thinking, but also the importance of the 'third turn' – where the teacher makes interactional moves which *function* to develop pupils' responses, and which keep the pupils' voices in the dialogue (Boyd and Markarian, 2015). For Alexander (2020), the third turn move which functions to develop thinking might be an indicator of genuine dialogic talk. This episode also illustrates the meta-linguistic learning, discussed above, that can arise from embedding opportunities for talk and reflection throughout the writing process.

In the third transcript below, taken from a year 2 (age 6–7) primary classroom, the teacher is working with children to create a description of what it feels like to ride a bike. Before this, the class read a story about a child learning to ride a bike; the teacher also asked the children to close their eyes and imagine what it feels like to be riding fast on a bike. After the children have written descriptive sentences, the teacher invites them to share their best sentence, and to choose their favourite word.

Teacher: *When you've thought of some really good words you can sit up. I'll write a few of them up here for ideas and then you can go away and do your own.*

Child 1:   *I can hear the wind whistling.*

Teacher: *I can hear the wind whistling – good girl. I can hear the wind whistling. Good description. Any other ideas?*

Child 2:   *I can see the blurry trees.*

Teacher: *Good, excellent. Why are they blurry, who can tell me – it's a really good word but why are the blurry?*

Child 3:   *They are going so fast.*

Teacher: *They are going so fast. They are rushing past.*

Child 4:   *I can see the bushes go past.*

Teacher: *I can see the bushes go past – but that's not quite so expressive. We've got a 'hear' and a 'see' has anyone got a 'feel' they can give me?*

Child 5:   *I can feel the air brushing against my face.*

Teacher: *Ooh lovely I can feel the air brushing, good word, against my face. Super ideas.*

Source: Taken from Fisher et al. (2010, p. 164).

REFLECTION POINT

In the episode above, the teacher elicits ideas from several children and uses questioning to emphasise and explore the meaning of words and children's own linguistic choices. Reflect upon this using the following prompts:

- In this episode, which questions posed by the teacher prompt elaboration and develop thinking about word choice?

- Is there evidence here of a 'third-turn move' which functions to develop children's responses?

- What aspects of the interactional exchanges observed in the secondary and primary episodes above might be usefully incorporated into your own practice?

As noted, talk comes in many forms: it is shaped according to learning purpose, and it is responsive to pupils' needs and understandings. These brief episodes provide only a snippet of dialogue that extends far back and beyond the lessons from which they are taken; but the episodes point to the powerful potential of talk and to its imperfect nature, while revealing the complexity of orchestrating talk that supports learning. This is why reflecting on and developing the quality and breadth of classroom talk repertoires is a valuable and ongoing part of being a dialogic teacher.

DEVELOPING INTERPERSONAL SKILLS FOR LEARNING DIALOGUES

Dialogue – between teachers and pupils, and between pupils in pairs or groups – which involves sharing and challenging perspectives, negotiating and resolving differences, is productive for learning. Yet, pupils are not always aware of the implicit interpersonal norms of such talk: making these explicit can support pupils' productive participation. Mercer uses the concept of *ground rules* – 'the normative principles, usually implicit, which govern social behaviour…to examine how talk is actually used by teachers and their students' (Mercer and Dawes, 2008, p. 55) – to promote pupils' participation in exploratory talk. Generating ground rules for exploratory talk with a class, such as those listed below, is a way of promoting a shared understanding of how to engage in productive exploratory talk which supports learning.

Ground Rules for Exploratory Talk:

- *Partners engage critically but constructively with each other's ideas*

- *Everyone participates*

- *Tentative ideas are treated with respect*

- *Ideas offered for joint consideration may be challenged*

- *Challenges are justified and alternative ideas or understandings are offered*

- *Opinions are sought and considered before decisions are jointly made*

- *Knowledge is made publically accountable (and so reasoning is visible in the talk)*

(Mercer and Dawes, 2008, p. 66).

Also drawing on the principles of dialogic teaching, Newman's (2016) framework (Table 3.1), which describes collaborative talk as a process of *participating, understanding and managing,* is a pedagogical tool intended to support pupils in reflecting on and analysing talk. The framework is not a checklist for collaborative talk but is a tool that supports metatalk – in this context, 'talk about talk' – which fosters pupils' dialogic talk about the interpersonal dimension of discussion. Developing awareness of this interpersonal dimension and evaluating how its features surface in collaborative talk may develop and encourage pupils' application of interpersonal skills in their own talk.

Table 3.1   A Framework for Collaborative Talk (Newman, 2016, p. 109)

	During collaborative talk, speakers:
Participating	Speak clearly and concisely
	Share experiences and challenge ideas without conflict
	Show respect for other people's ideas
	Build on other people's ideas
Understanding	Listen carefully in order to understand what's being said
	Listen with an open mind
	Use questions to explore ideas and ensure understanding
	Make sure that they and everyone in the group understands
Managing	Manage the talk to make sure that goals are met
	Keep the talk focused on the goal
	Manage challenges and objections with sensitivity
	Encourage others to contribute

REFLECTION POINT

Reflect on your own management of talk in the classroom:

- What strategies do you use to develop pupils' talk for learning?
- How do you encourage all pupils to speak?
- How aware are you of the contributions made by your socially disadvantaged pupils?
- How do you ensure that what they say is treated respectfully?

TEACHING AND EXPANDING SPOKEN LANGUAGE REPERTOIRES

Developing pupils' knowledge about spoken language, and of the linguistic forms associated with different forms, also broadens awareness of and participation in repertoires of talk. Examining the differences between spoken and written forms is a good place to start, helping pupils to develop a meta-language for talking about talk, while supporting recognition that written and spoken forms are not dichotomous but 'overlapping continua with structures and functions that are both distinct and shared' (Heath, in Alexander, 2020, p. 86). Carter's work (see QCA, 2004) is useful for this purpose: Carter's 'grammar of talk' describes (not prescribes!) how talk works, with the aim of 'making talk visible'. Carter's grammar includes three key characteristics which can be used to support analysis of spoken language:

1. ***Signalling the shape and structure of talk****: In spoken communication, speakers and listeners constantly signal how they want things to be taken and interpreted. This spoken punctuation reflects the need for speakers to give structure and shape to their talk.*

2. ***Communicating in real time and space****: Spoken language is a process of real-time communication. It takes place in real time and space.*

3. ***Communicating face to face****: Spoken language is normally a process of face-to-face communication. We are alert to feedback and constantly adjust what we say in the light of an ongoing situation.*

(QCA, 2004, pp. 9–11)

Developing pupils' linguistic and interpersonal awareness of spoken language enables teachers to broaden pupils' talk repertoires, introducing them to the various forms and functions of different talk types, such as those stipulated in curricula.

In the following sequence, we exemplify an approach to teaching oral storytelling which incorporates attention to the difference between spoken and written forms, and which develops confidence, fluency and coherence. In the interest of expanding talk *repertoires* and literacy experience, we have chosen storytelling deliberately because of the power and relevance of story and storytelling to children at all stages of schooling, and because of the way that stories and storytelling can celebrate and promote diversity – in all its forms; part of democratic participation, storytelling is fundamental to how we understand ourselves and our world. The strategies outlined here can, however, be adapted to the teaching of other spoken language forms and for different age groups.

▬ A LEARNING SEQUENCE TO TEACH STORYTELLING ▬

Elicit Prior knowledge: What do pupils already know about storytelling? What stories have they been told? What do they think makes a good or bad story telling?

Explore non-verbal communication: Watch a storyteller telling a story (or record yourself telling a story!) on mute and ask pupils to consider how the non-verbal – for example, body language, gesture, eye contact - creates meaning. This approach is important too when exploring, for example, speeches and presentations because of how the non-verbal conditions how what is said is received, as Carter indicates in his third characteristic – important if we want pupils to engage critically with, for example, political messaging (Alexander, 2020; QCA, 2004).

Develop confidence with performance: Discuss how the storyteller develops the story and engages the listener by varying pause, pace and tone. Build in activities to develop pupils' confidence with these skills: for example, pupils could mimic a few lines from the story, then try to alter the effect of delivery and meaning through pause, pace and tone. Working at first with just a line or two eases the cognitive challenge involved in storytelling, freeing up pupils to focus on a specific performance skill.

Focus on form and structure: Listen to the story - using audio only. There is an opportunity here to focus on the differences between the written and spoken form by inviting pupils to compare the oral re-telling of the story to a written version. Attention could be drawn to, for example, how the written form uses full sentences where the spoken form uses chains of clauses and discourse markers to signpost transitions in the story (resonant with Carter's first characteristic). Pupils could then plot key moments or transitions in the storytelling, perhaps as a story mountain, noting any particular words or phrases which they might later use to structure the telling of their own story.

Playing with story: There are a variety of drama games which can support pupils in devising and performing their own story. For example, 'Super-Size Stories' starts with one pupil recounting something mundane about, for example, their weekend; another pupil then 'super-sizes' the story – re-telling it with more drama and detail – and so on and so on; the basic structure of the first story shouldn't change, but it should become more elaborate and dramatic with each telling! 'Story in a Bag' invites pupils to take an object from a bag and improvise part of a story: with each new object the story should change direction. In 'Story in a Bag', the objective should be for the whole class to devise a whole story; as in 'Super-Size Stories', pupils need to listen carefully to their peers but this time think about narrative coherence.

Devising a story: The focus should be on the *telling* of the story so there is no need for pupils to devise lengthy or complicated stories. You could provide pupils with a short written story to adapt; a series of images which they could sequence into a narrative; or, pupils could recount a personal experience or anecdote. It's helpful to plot key moments or transitions in the story, perhaps using key words or phrases identified earlier; memorising just a sequence of prompt words or phrases discourages reliance on scripts, retains the spontaneous and improvised nature of storytelling and supports pupils in thinking about narrative coherence. It's also good to talk with pupils about what to do should they forget what they were going to say - *e.g. pause, take a breath, repeat or summarise what has just been said to prompt memory.*

Delivery and reflection: Pupils can tell their stories to each other in small groups, or to the whole class, if appropriate. Pupils should always be reminded of what to expect from an audience: close and respectful engagement with the performance. After the stories have been told, pupils should engage in individual and group reflection, inviting pupils to talk *about* the talk, identifying what made a good story telling, and how their observations match with their expectations of this oral tradition.

ACTION POINT

Using the sequence above as a guide, sketch a teaching sequence for a class of your choice, focusing on a different spoken language form (e.g. debate or presentation). In doing so, think carefully about:

- how the lesson builds on pupils' existing knowledge and experience of language

- what additional strategies you might need to scaffold learning and develop confidence

Note too how the sequence above makes use of whole class/peer exploratory discussion: when planning for the teaching of talk - and other topics - it is also helpful to plan for the kinds of talk that will support pupils in their learning (Reedy and Bearne, 2021).

TEACHING ABOUT STANDARD ENGLISH

Language diversity can be an asset in the classroom, providing scope for discussion about Standard and non-Standard constructions. 'Language Detective' tasks (see Myhill et al., 2016), which involve pupils in language investigation can broaden pupils' awareness of linguistic variation and dialect. Asking pupils to listen to someone speaking in a local dialect and comparing this to Standard English, or inviting pupils to investigate their own dialects and those of the people in their community, are approaches which draw on and value pupils' linguistic experience and knowledge. Comparing Standard and non-Standard varieties, and how language shifts between contexts, also highlights how speakers tend in verbal reality to mix language varieties – that the line between Standard and non-Standard language is quite blurred. Because the spoken form is different from the written, comparing spoken and written Standard English also provides an opportunity to explore misconceptions: for example, the erroneous conflation of written and spoken forms often seen in language policy and underpinning 'rules' such as 'speak in full sentences' (Cushing, 2021a). Exploring how non-Standard dialects are used to create character voice is another engaging way of developing knowledge about language: consider the dialect of *The BFG* – 'Just because I is a giant, you think I is a man-gobbling cannybull!' – and imagine how his character would be diminished by speaking instead in Standard English (see Myhill et al., 2016). It is worth noting, as apparent in the BFG's exclamation, a common difference between Standard and non-Standard dialect is verb use – in this case subject-verb agreement – and a common error in written Standard English. Look out for these common issues and teach these explicitly.

This latter section of the chapter has focused specifically on strategies for teaching spoken language: to develop learning dialogues, to teach spoken language forms and to teach about Standard English. To reiterate, however, the quality of pupils' talk hinges on the quality of teachers' talk. As a teacher, reflecting critically on your own use of talk, and talk in your classroom, is a valuable and ongoing process.

Analysing and developing the quality and management of classroom talk is greatly assisted by video recording and group discussion of your own practice (Lefstein and Snell, 2013). Organising a small 'video club' (ibid, p. 176), comprised of colleagues with similar problems or interests, who record and discuss snippets of their own lessons is a valuable, and dialogic approach, to teacher development. If recording your own lessons feels too threatening, at least at first, there are materials available elsewhere to prompt critical discussion about classroom talk (see e.g. Lefstein and Snell, 2013).

CONCLUSION

As Alexander notes, some pupils will find the norms of pedagogical, curricular and wider cultural discourses more or less in harmony; yet, some will experience dissonances of class, race and gender and will find that academic and everyday registers diverge (2020, p. 7). Alexander warns that this confrontation of discourses may be even more strident in light of recent political events, the rise of populist leaders, social media and fake news, but points to *dialogue*, not as a panacea, but as a response – as 'purposive social action, as well as a vital ingredient of effective teaching and a worthy educational end in itself, and hence a manifesto for hope' (Alexander, 2019, p. 14).

This chapter emphasises the potential of talk as a powerful pedagogical tool for learning and literacy and advocates the teaching of talk in its own right: so that pupils are equipped with spoken language repertoires that enable their participation in and movement between different social, academic and employment contexts. This chapter has emphasised the importance of dialogic teaching because of the way that it can address social inequality, by promoting egalitarian, democratic participation, giving individual and collective voice: 'Among the promises of dialogic teaching is that it distributes classroom talk more equitably, first between teacher and students collectively, then among students themselves; and that this redistribution will contribute to the larger cause of reducing social inequality' (Alexander, 2019, pp. 9–10). It is the teacher who has the potential to harness the power of talk and to realise the promise of dialogic teaching: as Wood et al. remark 'what distinguishes man as a species is not only his capacity for learning, but for teaching as well' (1976, p. 89).

VIGNETTE

As a young person growing up in the 1960s and 1970s I was not very politically or socially aware and was certainly not explicitly conscious of issues of social disadvantage or privilege, other than rather vague notions of rich and poor. I definitely did not see myself as disadvantaged! I was clothed, fed and looked after within a caring home. But neither of my parents had any academic qualifications or any great leanings towards learning and education – they were doers: capable, pragmatic, industrious, with a strong work ethic. And, to be honest, they harboured a slight suspicion about 'clever people'. At the same time, somewhat paradoxically, they were keen that I and my siblings succeeded at school. But this was more of a desire than a practical endeavour. I was not read to at home (though my parents did teach me nursery rhymes and songs) and as a young child, there were virtually no books in the house. The only book I remember was a gardening book my father, a keen gardener, kept in the airing cupboard (no idea why it was stored there!) which I read again and again, and believe now accounts for my own love of gardening. They were supportive of school but had no experience or knowledge of how a home environment can allow literacy to thrive.

It was school that changed my life chances, particularly secondary school. I bumbled my way through primary school without any particular problems, and with no sense of my level of achievement or how I compared with others – the joys of a time before national testing and accountability! But at secondary school, for the first time, I discovered a joy in learning – especially debating, critical thinking and reasoning. It awakened a curiosity about the world, a thirst for ideas and issues, and 'rights and wrongs'. Two teachers, in particular, my geography and English teachers, surfaced a love of words, images, ideas and places which remains with me. More than this, though, the school recognised me as an individual and had time for me. They gave me roles of responsibility, they pushed me to volunteer for things, they invited me to join school societies – just at a time when I was becoming aware that it was not girls like me who did these things. And academically, they challenged me, not accepting work that I could have done better. Significantly, they encouraged me to stay on into the Sixth Form, and when I decided I wanted a career as a teacher, they raised the possibility of doing a degree at university, rather than a professional qualification at a Teacher Training college.

In the end, I was the first person in my family, and the only one of my siblings, to stay on into the Sixth Form and to go to university. My parents were somehow simultaneously proud of my achievements and disappointed that I had not got a job at age 16, as my siblings had. Later, as a secondary English teacher, I found myself repeatedly irritated in staff meetings, where assumptions about family backgrounds were capping what teachers felt was possible for certain children. Schools do make a difference!

Mary Hunt

Retired Secondary English Teacher

4
READING THE WORLD

INTRODUCTION

It is always very easy to make an argument for the importance of reading, as this is one of the few topics where politicians, parents and teachers would all agree. Being able to read is a foundational skill for accessing education, and for being able to cope with the demands of life: it is 'not only seen as a necessary foundation for performance in other subject areas within an educational context, but it is also a pre-requisite for successful participation in most areas of adult life' (Organisation for Economic Development [OECD], 2002, p. 103). It is no surprise, therefore, that one of the United Nations sustainability devel-opment goals is to ensure quality education for all people around the globe, and being able to read is core to this goal. The United Nations note that 'more than half of all children and adolescents worldwide are not meeting minimum proficiency standards in reading and mathematics' (United Nations, n.d.). The 2019 OECD report on the international PISA results, which draws on the reading test results, observes that home and family background 'exerts a powerful influence on student performance across countries' (OECD, 2010, p. 45) in reading, and our own national assessment data indicate that in 2019, 38% of children identified as 'disadvantaged' did not achieve the 'expected' standard in the key stage 2 Reading test, compared with 22% of their peers (DfE, 2019, Table N4a). These statistics underline both the global and national challenge of ensuring that social background does not exclude children from accessing the written word. Indeed, the effect of the rapid expansion of the internet and social media have only intensified the significance of being a competent reader, as more and more of our everyday communi-cation and access to information and services is conducted through online affordances. At the same time, reading is a source of personal pleasure for many people, allowing us to enter imaginary worlds, to read about people like ourselves and people who are very different, and to engage with new ideas and new perspectives.

In choosing the title for this chapter, we have deliberately drawn on a phrase used repeatedly by Brazilian educator, Paolo Freire – reading the world (Freire, 1985; Freire and Macedo, 1987). Freire himself grew up in considerable poverty and initially struggled at school, not because he was not interested but because 'my social condition didn't allow me to have an education', an experience which reinforced for him 'the relationship between social class and knowledge' (Gadotti, 1994, p. 5). As a consequence, he saw literacy as the route to empowerment, a way out of disadvantage, and argued that the process of making sense of written text involves both reading the word and reading the world. In other words, when we read, we are not simply reading words on the page, but we are connecting this with our previous experiences and creating a new 're-reading of the world' (Freire, 1985, p. 19). Being able to read opens up the possibilities of critical engagement with texts, developing the capacity to think about who is and who is not represented in a text, where are the silences and the gaps, and whose voices are privileged. In this chapter, we start from the premise that reading is powerful and consider how to support developing readers, not only in reading words, but in making sense of texts, print and digital, in the context of their own lives and imagined futures.

UNDERSTANDING THE RESEARCH

THE RELATIONSHIP BETWEEN READING AND SOCIAL DISADVANTAGE

Perhaps because of the primacy of reading in accessing education and social engagement, there is a substantial and long-standing body of research on the relationship between reading and social disadvantage (for example: Shannon, 1985; Clark and Akerman, 2006; Buckingham et al., 2013). The OECD reported that, for every country represented in the PISA tests, 'the occupational status of the parents, books in the home, home educational resources and cultural communication are correlated with achievement in reading literacy' (OECD, 2002, p. 124). Dolean et al. (2019) established a direct link between poverty and the development of reading comprehension in Roma children, a finding echoed by Vinopal and Morrisey (2020) who identified an effect of poverty on reading in pre-kindergarten children in the United States. Many studies indicate that young children from socially disadvantaged backgrounds are more likely to begin school with more limited skills in phonological awareness (Raz and Bryant, 1990; Locke et al., 2002; McDowell et al., 2007; Lundberg et al., 2012; Dodur et al., 2021) and in oral language skills (Hay and Fielding-Barnsley, 2009; Hirsh-Pasek et al., 2015; Rowe et al., 2005). And we have already noted that children eligible for Free School Meals (FSMs) do not achieve so highly in national reading tests as their peers.

A common trend in the research is to explain this link between social disadvantage and poorer reading in terms of the home environment (for example, Melhuish, 2008; Bhattacharya, 2010; Siraj and Mayo, 2014; Hannon et al., 2020). An Australian literature review synthesis on the link between socio-economic status and reading achievement (Buckingham et al., 2013) argues that significant factors in the home environment include the time spent reading, the number of books in the home, as well as parents' academic aspirations for their children. Drawing on a substantial sample of 3,172 pre-school children and families, Crampton and Hall (2017) investigated how the home environment was associated with reading development. They defined 'home environment' drawing on characteristics of interactions which support reading development, namely whether children were read to; visited a library; were taught letters and numbers; painted and drew; played with numbers; and were sung songs and rhymes. They found a direct relationship between social disadvantage and home environments which then affected later reading development. They also found an indirect effect on children's self-concept as readers (their own judgement of their reading competence). Similarly, Aikens and Barbarin (2008) and Bergen et al. (2016) identified correlations between early reading competency and the home environment for literacy, including the number of books in the home. These findings echo findings discussed in Chapter 1: that exposure to print, shared experiences with books and storytelling, rhymes and language play which develop phonological awareness, and library visits are important foundations for learning to read, and are more evident in socially advantaged homes (Siraj and Mayo, 2014; Hannon et al., 2020).

Studies also highlight some very real issues of access to reading for socially disadvantaged children. Children experiencing economic poverty have more limited access not only to books but also to computers, and toys and games which support reading (Bradley et al., 2001). Clark and Akerman's survey (2006) found that access to books in the home correlated with self-confidence as readers, and that disadvantaged children were less likely to have books of their own. The same children reported that they would read more if 'books had more pictures; someone read aloud to them; libraries were closer; they found reading easier; their family encouraged them more; and they had better eyesight' (Clark and

Akerman, 2006, p. 7). This echoes Fisher and Frey's argument (2018) that access to reading material is a key factor for all readers, but perhaps especially those whose home situation renders them more vulnerable. Wood et al. (2020) found a significant relationship for students eligible for FSM who used their school libraries and their reading: they were more likely to read for pleasure and to read more diverse range of texts. In Clark and Akerman's survey, children receiving FSM were significantly more likely to report that they enjoyed going to the library (2006, p. 5), yet access to libraries is known to be problematic for this group of children (Neuman and Moland, 2019; Mackey, 2021). Of course, school and public library closures during the pandemic have intensified this (Clark and Picton, 2020), and teachers believe that poor access to books was a major barrier to reading for pleasure (CLPE, 2021). The issue of access to reading material is not only about young children, but is also important in the secondary school. The OECD (2002) analysis of reading habits and engagement with reading in 15-year-olds found only a weak link to socio-economic background per se, but a much stronger link between access to books at home and reading habits:

> Fifteen-year-olds who have access to a limited number of books at home will, on average, be poorly diversified in reading. They mainly read magazines and newspapers. Students who have access to a larger number of books at home are more diversified in their reading and are more interested in reading other material, such as books (fiction and non-fiction) or comics.

> (OECD, 2002, p. 106)

These studies on the relationship between home environment and access to reading resources emphasise two important factors. Firstly, the link between social disadvantage and reading is sometimes linked to material poverty, a lack of financial resource to support reading in the home and access to books. But equally crucially, it is strongly linked to the nature of the social interactions around reading experienced in the home, and how adults engage young learners in the pre-reading and reading activities which lay the foundations for later reading competence and enjoyment.

It is important, of course, to recognise that many studies making this connection between social disadvantage and reading attainment rely on statistical data for their results. There are alternative perspectives, which draw more on the voices of the students themselves which are strong reminders that students from different backgrounds are not homogeneous groups, but unique individuals. Scholes's study (2019), looking at working-class boys in Australia, challenges research which offers 'simplistic accounts of how working-class masculinities are at odds with feminine pursuits such as reading' (p. 344). Instead, her in-depth qualitative study interviewing working-class boys highlights many differences within this group: some boys love reading while others are less positive. She argues that 'classroom pedagogies that take into account the boys' histories and life-worlds as assets and productive resources can be used in the design of powerful curriculum and critical pedagogy, producing productive relationships between literacy learning and place-conscious pedagogy for schools located in high poverty locales' (p. 359).

However, the link between social disadvantage and reading proficiency is not simply about home environment and access to books, but is sustained into the school system. Buckingham et al. (2013) distinguish between individual and school level factors, noting the quality of early teaching of reading is important in relation to developing phonemic awareness, phonics, fluency, vocabulary and comprehension. And yet, as noted in Chapter 1, schools with a high proportion of learners from socially disadvantaged communities are less likely to have the best teachers and less likely to achieve well academically. Such schools are also less likely to have access to in-school library resources, including library staffing, than more advantaged schools (Pribesh et al., 2011). In the context of reading, this underlines the significance of teachers who understand best practice in the teaching of reading and are well supported by the school leadership and broader local networks.

Data from Feinstein and Bynner's analysis (2004) show that if socially disadvantaged children begin school as poor readers, they are highly likely to remain poor readers throughout primary school. As Buckingham et al. (2013) point out, the 'adverse effects of the risk factors for poor literacy are not just cumulative but amplified among socioeconomically disadvantaged students' (p. 192). On the other hand, their analysis indicates that about one-third of these poor readers *do* improve their reading capacity in school, and thus that schools can make a substantial difference. The risk in discourses which present socio-economic background as a determinant of educational success is that it becomes a self-fulfilling prophecy, with the consequence that instead of breaking the link between social disadvantage and reading outcomes 'schooling often appears to reinforce its effects' (OECD, 2019, p. 13). Looking at reading results in the international PISA tests, this report shows that the strength of the link between socio-economic background and reading competence is uneven, with some countries having a weaker association than others. Typically, countries which have a more equitable distribution of resources across schools, and which are less socially segregated have a less strong effect of social background. The report is a powerful reminder that 'disadvantage is not destiny' (OECD, 2019, p. 15).

READING FOR PLEASURE

Reading for pleasure and personal enjoyment is an important way to broaden and extend both reading proficiency and the broader benefits of reading to understand ourselves and our world. Leisure reading is linked with improved comprehension (Torppa et al., 2020), higher academic performance (Twist et al., 2007; Schiefele et al., 2012) and with supporting general cognitive development (Sullivan and Brown, 2015). It is important not to assume that reading by choice *causes* better reading performance – indeed it is easy to see how being a capable reader might motivate reading for pleasure. Some research suggests the relationship is bidirectional (Morgan and Fuchs, 2007), while other research notes that the evidence is not yet clear (Sullivan and Brown, 2015). Yet, students receiving FSM, particularly boys, are less likely to enjoy reading, and they are 'significantly more likely to agree that reading is more for girls than for boys, that reading is boring and hard, and that they cannot find books that interest them' (Clark and Akerman, 2006, p. 5). This disengagement from reading is across both primary and secondary, but may be particularly pronounced in secondary as in general, interest in reading declines during ages 11–16 (Best et al., 2020). Perhaps not surprisingly, this lower interest in reading is paralleled by a lower likelihood of reading outside school – although as these conclusions are drawn from surveys, it is possible that students do not count digital reading as reading. Clark and Picton's 2020 survey of children's reading habits suggests that enjoyment of reading has increased during lockdown and school closures. However, the survey does not reveal which children are reading more in terms of their social background, and it does show that 20% of those who didn't generally enjoy reading before the pandemic are now enjoying reading even less (Clark and Picton, 2020, p. 4). It seems reasonable to infer from this that those who did not enjoy reading pre-pandemic are in the group eligible for FSM, and that the pandemic has intensified the difference between social groups. The OECD (2002) reports that despite the strong link between social background and reading results in the PISA tests, this relationship is not deterministic: 'the correlation between engagement in reading and socio-economic background is only about one-third of the correlation with achievement' (p. 124). Instead, the report indicates that engagement is more strongly linked to books in the home, rather than social background per se. They argue for the importance of cultivating an engagement in reading, in terms of attitude, motivation and reading practices because this 'has the potential to reduce the gaps between the reading proficiency scores of students from differing back- grounds' (OECD, 2002, p. 132). Sullivan and Brown's study found that reading for pleasure correlates more strongly with cognitive progress than parental education and they conclude that 'supporting reading for pleasure among disadvantaged children could potentially provide a powerful tool in closing educational gaps' (2015, p. 987).

Given the importance of engagement in reading in supporting reading development, schools have a key role to play in ensuring all children have the opportunity to read for pleasure. The Centre for Literacy in Primary Education (CLPE) reports the extraordinary efforts that primary teachers made during the pandemic to get books to children with limited access to books in the home (2021). At the same time, there is some evidence that in the classroom, socially disadvantaged children who are not keen readers receive a narrowed experience of reading for pleasure. Westbrook et al. (2019) note that readers in low-attaining sets in secondary schools, in whom socially disadvantaged children are disproportionally represented, are more likely to experience reading in terms of exercises with text extracts and simplified readers. Hempel-Jorgensen et al. (2018) undertook an in-depth ethnographic study in schools with a high number of children eligible for FSM, and which espoused the Reading for Pleasure principles (Cremin et al., 2014). They found, however, that the teaching of reading focused more on 'technical proficiency' (Hempel-Jorgensen et al., 2018, p. 89) than reading for pleasure, and observed 'the restrictive and restricting nature of pedagogy in relation to children's volition and social interaction as readers' (Hempel-Jorgensen et al., 2018, p. 93).

The choice and variety of reading material available to learners is intrinsically linked to engagement and enjoyment of reading. Studies also show that when given a choice about what they read, there are benefits in terms of motivation to read (Allington and Gabriel, 2012; Pruzinsky, 2014) and gains in reading comprehension (Guthrie and Humenick, 2004), including children from low-income backgrounds (Fraumeni-McBride, 2017). And what children read matters. Research over time has persistently recorded that many learners do not have access to books which reflect their own experiences, with particular reference to gender, ethnicity and disability (Golos and Moses, 2011; Mantei and Kervin, 2014; McGeown, 2015; Gritter et al., 2017; CLPE, 2018; Elliott et al., 2021). These studies emphasise the importance of access to reading which provides young readers with representations of their own lives and social expe- riences. Jones (2008) and Dutro (2010) both consider this through the lens of social class. Jones' analysis of children's literature suggests a need 'to question the invisibility of working-class and poor lives in mainstream children's literature' (2008, abstract). Dutro's study in the United States examined the responses of children living in poverty when reading a mandated fictional text about the Great Depres- sion. She found that the curriculum promoted class-privileged perspectives on the text, giving no space for readers to bring their own understandings into dialogue with the text, and yet students' responses were rich and powerful. She argues for both texts and teaching to acknowledge and create space for the experiences of children living in poverty. From a slightly different perspective, Jerrim and Moss's (2019) analysis of PISA data found a strong correlation between reading fiction and reading skills, and they suggest that interventions which encourage boys from socially disadvantaged background to choose to read fiction may be particularly helpful.

WHAT READING INTERVENTIONS ARE EFFECTIVE IN SUPPORTING SOCIALLY DISADVANTAGED READERS?

Given the considerable research which establishes the connections between social disadvantage and reading proficiency, there are surprisingly few studies which investigate effective classroom practices for supporting progress in reading specifically for this group of learners. Table 4.1 summarises some of the most recent studies and includes studies which targeted less proficient readers, as these are likely to include a high proportion of socially disadvantaged students.

Table 4.1   Summary of reading interventions

Author/s	Description of intervention and findings	Age group and country
Henning et al. (2010)	Intervention involving an oral language and phonological awareness programme. While the study found short-term positive benefits, the programme did not enhance socially disadvantaged students' reading in the long term.	6- to 7-year-olds Australia
Allington et al. (2010)	Intervention providing books for students from low-income families to choose and take home for summer reading. The intervention had a positive effect on reading attainment.	Primary United States
Machin et al. (2018)	*Synthetic Phonics* intervention: using data from national pilot and subsequent roll-out of synthetic phonics teaching. The intervention provided a positive benefit on reading outcomes at KS2 for socially disadvantaged students.	Primary United Kingdom
Kennedy (2018)	*Write to Read* intervention: providing access to rich and meaningful literature developing creative, emotional, aesthetic and cognitive responses. Included high-quality books, giving students choice and time to read. The intervention increased students' motivation and engagement in reading.	Lower primary Ireland
O'Hare et al. (2019)	*Reciprocal Reading* intervention: providing direct teaching of four metacognitive comprehension strategies (predicting; clarifying; questioning; summarising) in a collaborative group context. Targeted poor comprehenders. The intervention had a positive effect on reading comprehension outcomes, including for children eligible for FSM.	Upper Primary United Kingdom
Thurston et al. (2020)	*Reciprocal Reading* intervention: as above. Targeted poor comprehenders. The intervention had a positive effect on reading comprehension outcomes.	11- to 13-year-olds United Kingdom
Westbrook et al. (2019)	Intervention involving reading complex texts at a fast pace: reading of two challenging novels at a faster pace than usual in 12 weeks. The intervention had a positive effect on all readers, but a particularly strong effect on poorer readers, repositioning them as 'good readers' with a more engaged reading experience.	12- to 13-year-olds United Kingdom

---

CRITICAL QUESTIONS

- The majority of studies reported here draw their conclusions from statistical data. Chapter 1 has highlighted how statistical data can help to identify broad patterns and relationships but also how it cannot always be generalised to the level of a particular class or particular learner. Reflect on the key findings from this 'Understanding the Research' section and consider how they might or might not be relevant to the learners that you teach.

- There is little or no reference in most of this research to digital reading practices – what do you think about this?

IN THE CLASSROOM

In terms of teaching reading, one important element to draw out of the research review above is, that to ensure all students become confident, engaged readers, effective teaching involves rich reading experiences, not narrowed 'basic skills' teaching. The Machin et al. study (2018) highlights the importance of phonics teaching in initial reading, but on its own this is insufficient. Learners who have shared books with parents or other adults and who understand how stories work bring an understanding of being a reader to the decoding of texts, and phonics teaching is amplified when it takes place alongside opportunities to share and engage with high-quality texts. Indeed, Camilli et al. (2003) found through a meta-analysis that phonics teaching was most effective when it was combined with meaning-making language tasks and appropriate individual support. It is important to be aware that as children grow older they may have successfully mastered how to decode written text, but may still be poor comprehenders, and there is little point in reading if you cannot understand it. Scarborough's Reading Rope (2001) is a helpful way to think about the complexity of becoming a reader and how different skills are inter-related (Search the internet for 'Scarborough's Reading Rope' to see the visual representation). Using the visual metaphor of a rope, she shows that the decoding element of reading becomes increasingly automatic, whereas elements of comprehension should be used in an increasingly strategic way to develop skilled reading.

The recommendations for effective practice presented in the rest of this chapter draw principally on these ideas, emphasising the importance of developing comprehension within the context of an environment where reading is engaging, shared and enjoyed.

MAKING SENSE OF TEXT

Understanding text begins way before school starts through interactions with text in the world around us – in the supermarket choosing favourite foods, recognising brand names and of course recognising what your own name looks like in print. When books are shared with babies and toddlers, they learn how books work and how they represent the world they live in, and when adults engage with young children in talk which explores the ideas in the books, they are sharing in making sense of text. This is why the research repeatedly confirms the importance of parental engagement in reading with their children. In school, we can think about how to sustain these practices, relative to the age and learning needs of the students. Core to this are opportunities for active discussion – about students' responses to the ideas in texts, how they connect with their own lives and experiences, what emotions the texts convey or evoke and increasingly, as readers mature, how the author has written the text. These discursive opportunities are building blocks for developing comprehension in tandem with enjoying the experience of reading and are also drawing on the importance of talk for learning as discussed in Chapter 3. Maine's research in primary school (2015) used dialogic talk strategies to facilitate peer-to-peer discussion and showed how the talk enabled the students to make meaning from text and to think critically and creatively. Table 4.1 highlighted the effectiveness of 'Reciprocal Reading' interventions in both primary and secondary contexts, and a key aspect of this is creating opportunities for rich, collaborative talk about reading. You might consider to what extent your normal classroom practice when teaching reading is dominated by teacher talk or whether you open up space for student discussion and response to what they are reading.

In addition to establishing a classroom environment where talking about texts is standard practice, there are also real benefits in explicitly teaching students about comprehension strategies. These are cognitive and metacognitive strategies which help readers to make sense of text: they are not 'teaching strategies', but strategies that readers (of every age – they are equally useful for academic reading!) can be taught to use to support comprehension. Proficient readers use cognitive strategies as they read: for example, you will probably have re-read a section of text because you felt you had missed something. This is the 'monitoring' strategy. You may not have been aware that you were using this strategy because it has become automatic, but struggling readers need to learn these strategies. One very real benefit of teaching comprehension strategies is that you are equipping learners to manage any comprehension problems they face, thus helping them to become more independent. This is because, at their best, they are meta-cognitive – learners are conscious of using a strategy and become increasingly adept at self-regulating what strategy is needed. Multiple EEF reports flag the effectiveness of comprehension strategies in closing the gap between proficient and struggling readers – at KS2 (EEFa, n.d.); in Secondary Schools (EEFb, n.d.); and the Teaching and Learning Toolkit (EEFc, n.d.) judges teaching comprehension strategies to be 'very high impact for very low cost based on extensive evidence'.

So what are these comprehension strategies? A quick search on the internet will throw up numerous websites and posters of comprehension strategies, but there is no single definitive list. Table 4.2 illustrates three different sites and their respective lists of strategies. You can see that three of them are common across these websites: *monitoring, questioning* and *summarising*; and similarly, *making connections* and *visualising* are common to two, so you may find it helpful to use these initially.

A further important factor in using comprehension strategies is that most of the intervention studies emphasise the role of collaborative talk while using any comprehension strategy, a factor which links back to the point made earlier about the learning significance of rich talk about texts. Below are two teaching examples, each focussing on a different comprehensive strategy and incorporating opportunities for discussion. You might like to look at each one and observe, not only how the strategy is integrated into the teaching and where there are opportunities for talk but also how the teacher is explicit about the particular strategy, raising the learners' metacognitive awareness, and how the text is always shared and enjoyed, before working on the comprehension strategy.

Table 4.2   Reading comprehension strategies

Highland literacy	Choice literacy	Reading rockets
Monitoring: being alert to when something you've read doesn't make sense	*Repairing understanding when meaning breaks down.*	Monitoring comprehension
Questioning: readers (not teachers) asking questions of the text	*Questioning the text.*	Answering questions Generating questions
Summarising: in your own words	*Synthesising information.*	Summarising
Making connections: comparing ideas within a text, across other texts you've read and with life experiences you have had	*Activating background knowledge to make connections between new and known information.*	
Visualising: creating mental representations of people, places, activities in the text	Creating mental images	
Predicting: anticipating what will happen next	*Drawing inferences.* Determining importance	Metacognition Recognising story structure Graphic and semantic organisers

Source: https://highlandliteracy.com/reading-2/strategies-2/super-six/; https://choiceliteracy.com/article/what-are-the-seven-reading-comprehension-strategies/; https://www.readingrockets.org/article/seven-strategies-teach-students-text-comprehension

---

PRIMARY EXAMPLE

Using **Visualisation** with the description of Kensuke in Morpurgo's *Kensuke's Kingdom.*

He was diminutive, no taller than me, and as old a man as I had ever seen. He wore nothing but a pair of tattered breeches bunched at the waist, and there was a large knife in his belt. He was thin, too. In places – under his arms, round his neck and his midriff – his copper brown skin lay in folds about him, almost as if he'd shrunk inside it. What little hair he had on his head and his chin was long and wispy and white. I could see at once that he was very agitated, his chin trembling, his heavily hooded eyes accusing and angry.

- This description is the first time that the reader, and the lead character, Michael, see Kensuke. After reading Chapter 5 together and sharing thoughts and responses about what has happened, return to this description, displayed on a whiteboard or screen.

- First of all, ask students individually to try to picture this character and what he would look like; if you had to paint a picture of him, what would you want to include? Explain that being able to

(Continued)

visualise information from a text is an important part of reading, and that this is a strategy we can use as readers to help us understand the text better.

- Then invite them to share their ideas in groups, explaining what parts of the text made them visualise Kensuke in this way.

- Finally, discussing as a whole class, share responses, drawing out the clues in the text itself, but also additional visualisations of Kensuke which the description has prompted in their mind's eye. Note how we often create unique visualisations prompted by the text (which is why we are sometimes disappointed by film versions of books!)

SECONDARY EXAMPLE

Using **Prediction** with the opening paragraph of Dickens' *A Christmas Carol*.

Marley was dead: to begin with. There is no doubt whatever about that. The register of his burial was signed by the clergyman, the clerk, the undertaker, and the chief mourner. Scrooge signed it: and Scrooge's name was good upon 'change, for anything he chose to put his hand to. Old Marley was as dead as a door-nail.

- After reading the first chapter of the story together, and sharing initial responses to the text, return to the opening paragraph and ask students in pairs to consider:

    a. whether this opening paragraph makes them predict or anticipate what the story might be about;

    b. what is it in the text which makes them think this.

- Take feedback, inviting students to elaborate and justify their answers, and to question each other's responses. Draw out the use of the colon, which interrupts the flow of ideas, and the clause 'to begin with' which undermines the certainty of the first clause and the rest of the paragraph. If appropriate, draw out how authors sometimes use our readerly inclination to predict to create a narrative hook.

- End by noting that *predicting* what is going to happen in a text is a good strategy to use when trying to make sense of text because we have to use the information in the text, and our background knowledge to anticipate what might happen.

Explicit metacognitive awareness of how to use different comprehension strategies is useful for all readers – consider, for example, how summarising your reading about Vygotsky's Zone of Proximal Development in your own words might help you become aware of what you don't yet fully understand. But in most of the research studies with struggling learners, there is an emphasis on targeting particular groups of learners with strategy which matches their particular needs, and this may be a particularly important consideration for socially disadvantaged readers.

> **ACTION POINT**
>
> Develop a teaching sequence, along the lines of those above, but for a different comprehension strategy, trying to address the following points:
>
> • Integrating the comprehension strategy into your usual teaching of a text;
>
> • Matching the strategy to particular learners' needs;
>
> • Being specific about the strategy being used;
>
> • Creating opportunities for collaborative talk;
>
> • Developing students' metacognitive awareness of the strategy for future use.

CREATING A SUPPORTIVE CULTURE FOR READING

As the review of research above highlights, it is critical to ensure that students experience a rich and engaging reading culture in school, and yet there is also evidence that struggling readers are more likely to experience a narrow and impoverished diet of reading, focused more on 'basic skills' than fostering reading enjoyment. Simply having catch-up reading sessions, where no thought is given to the learner's experience is likely to cement negative attitudes to reading and foster feelings of low self-efficacy. It seems axiomatic that building a classroom environment where reading is a pleasurable experience is more likely to create a secure foundation for more explicit teaching about reading and being a reader. And this is not just an issue for primary schools – the heavy emphasis on literature in GCSE makes it equally important to establish a rich and engaging reading culture, which makes tackling challenging texts more possible.

The work of Cremin's team on *Reading for Pleasure* (2014) and the CLPE work on the *Power of Reading* (2015) are evidence-based and offer many supporting resources for teachers. Cremin's pedagogy for reading for pleasure foregrounds the importance of the social environment for reading, thinking about the classroom organisation and how it might offer spaces for relaxing and enjoying reading as a shared activity or independently. The social environment also includes what happens in those spaces, particularly purposeful opportunities to talk about books, both formally and informally. Significantly, Cremin emphasises how reading aloud 'enabled children to access rich and challenging texts, offered a model for silent independent reading, prompted the children's affective engagement and created a class repertoire of "texts in common" to discuss' (Open University, n.d.) something which might be particularly supportive for socially disadvantaged students.

The CLPE principles have a strong overlap with the *Reading for Pleasure* pedagogy:

• Developing an ethos and an environment that excites, enthuses, inspires and values;

• High-quality texts with depth and interest in story, character, illustration, vocabulary, structure and subject matter;

- A read-aloud programme;

- Teachers who are knowledgeable about children's literature;

- Creating a community of readers with opportunities to share responses and opinions;

- Planning for talking about books and stories, providing structures within which to do this;

- Working with authors and author/illustrators to understand the process of creating books.

(CLPE, 2021, p. 2)

Both Cremin and the CLPE promote reading aloud as a powerful mechanism for generating engagement. You might also consider making more use of audio-books or digitised texts, both for use that engagement with audiobooks can impact positively on reading skills and enjoyment (Best et al., 2020). Listening to a text being read aloud bypasses decoding, thus allowing access to books that a student might find difficult to read in print form. Audio-books have grown considerably in popularity, even with keen readers, because of their portability and because of the sheer pleasure of being read to. Being able to access more challenging texts in this way builds readerly knowledge of texts, for example of story structures, and builds comprehension, because a listening reader still has to make sense of the text. They can be significant in generating engagement with texts and could be a useful resource in the secondary classroom for addressing GCSE English Literature texts. One positive outcome of the pandemic has been the way schools have been incredibly creative in finding ways for socially disadvantaged students to access reading material, and this has often involved listening to text. Some teachers, for example, have created videos or podcasts of themselves reading stories aloud, or parents and grandparents have made audio texts.

Another element of establishing a vibrant social environment for reading is providing more time to read (Clark and Picton, 2020) and engaging 'children in the planning and delivery of reading and library activities, offering them the opportunity to select and purchase reading materials for their use' (Clark and Akerman, 2006, p. 8). The possibilities for this may be different in primary and secondary contexts, and depending on school size. Not only do classrooms vary in size and shape, but in some secondary settings, a teacher may not have their own dedicated teaching room for English, making it harder to alter the physical environment (although it is still very possible to ensure the interpersonal social environment is engaging). Remember that time for reading and opportunities for choosing texts and requesting reading materials can be positively achieved through a school library. Indeed, Wood et al. (2020) argue that 'effective school libraries can be a significant resource in supporting engagement with self-motivated literacy practices in children from low-income families'. School librarians are often keen to work with literacy/English teachers and make the library a place that students love to visit – a hub for reading for pleasure. Many libraries also provide access to ebooks, and you might consider making more use of these in the classroom too. One study found a significant positive impact on both reading enjoyment and reading progress when students were given the opportunity to take part in an ebook intervention (Picton and Clark, 2015). Specifically, they found that students who read more ebooks made greater progress than those who read less, and the percentage of boys who felt reading was 'cool' doubled over the period of the intervention from 34.4% to 66.5%.

One helpful way to think about the reading environment is proved by Mackey (2021) who maps the different conditions which enable positive reading experiences (see Figure 4.1). She places the reader at the heart of this mapping and traces what constitutes positive personal dispositions towards reading. You might think about reluctant readers in your own classes and how you might foster these positive

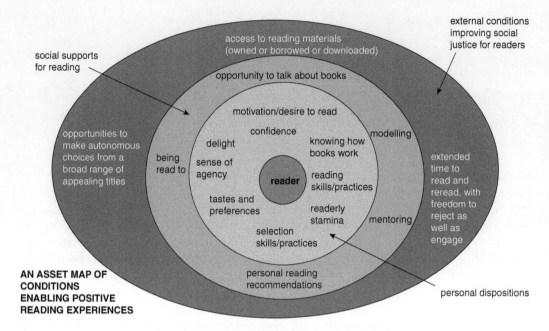

Figure 4.1   Asset map of conditions enabling positive reading experiences (Mackey, 2021)

dispositions. The map also flags the broader territory of social supports for reading, which you could ensure are part of your routine teaching of reading and the external context which facilitates all of these positive experiences.

What was the last children's book you read? Creating a supporting reading environment, as both Cremin and the CLPE stress, requires teachers who are knowledgeable about the books written for children and young people, and keep themselves up-to-date with the latest publications. Book talk is only truly possible if you can engage directly and meaningfully with students as readers. This makes it easier to recommend texts which match a reader's capability and interest, so it is important to ensure breadth and diversity in what you read, including books from a wide range of cultures and backgrounds, and different genres. We are fortunate to have such strong publishing in children's literature, all the way from pre-school picture books through to Young Adult fiction. Book awards such as the United Kingdom Literacy Association (UKLA) annual book awards or the Carnegie Award are excellent opportunities to build your own knowledge of the latest publications and to share the reading experience with students, finding out their perspectives as readers.

REFLECTION POINT

Think about and reflect on the reading environment that you establish in your classroom:

• Write down three things which you feel align with the ideas in this section;

• Write down three things which you might change to create a stronger reading environment;

(Continued)

- How do you make active use of the school library and the librarian's expertise?
- Consider asking the students you teach what they think about their experiences of reading in school, and any changes they feel would motivate them more.

CONCLUSION

This chapter has outlined the strong correlation that exists between social disadvantage and reading proficiency, including how economic poverty can limit access to both books and reading resources, and how the nature of home experiences and interactions about books can support or limit reading interest and development. Moreover, because in general the more you read, the better you become at reading, the critical risk for students is what is called the Matthew effect (the rich get richer and the poor get poorer), where the effect of disadvantage, or advantage, is accumulative (Cunningham and Stanovich, 1997). Young learners who are slow to pick up reading can fall into a vicious cycle where struggling to read means they read less, thus developing reading competence more slowly than those who have made a quicker start. And, as they get older, this is compounded by a sense of failure and subsequent reluctance to read. However, the research described in this chapter has also emphasised that this relationship is not deterministic: in other words, appropriate support and intervention can mitigate the effect of social background, and readers who make a slow start can become proficient and confident readers.

One recurrent theme which runs through this chapter is the importance of engagement with reading, not simply in terms of how parents engage with their children in the early years, but how teachers and schools can establish a reading environment in which learners can thrive. The OECD report on reading found that 15-year-olds from socially disadvantaged backgrounds who are highly engaged in reading achieve higher results than students from more advantaged backgrounds who do not enjoy reading, and they conclude that 'finding ways to engage students in reading may be one of the most effective ways to leverage social change' (OECD, 2002, p. 3). This conclusion is strengthened by studies which show that narrowing the reading curriculum for struggling readers to focus only on phonics or simplified texts is an ineffective strategy (Camilli et al., 2003; Hempel-Jorgensen et al., 2018; Westbrook et al., 2019). A clear implication for practice is to ensure that, whether at primary or secondary phases, the classroom and the school offer high-quality environments for reading, both print and digital texts, create opportunities for students' choice of reading material and employ teaching strategies which foster collaborative and challenging talk about texts.

VIGNETTE

In the bitter battleground of marital breakdown there isn't much time for quiet reading and reflection with your children. For so much of my upbringing my mum and dad were engaged in a desperate fight for survival. I wasn't neglected. I didn't go hungry. I suffered only occasional beatings at the hands of my angry father.

For my mum and dad, learning was what happened at school. Communal family activity was sitting in front of a flickering TV screen. That, and the annual summer trip to Cornwall to a caravan park under large electricity pylons by the golden sands of Hayle. My life lacked what Pierre Bourdieu called cultural capital – the middle-class assets needed to succeed in middle-class society. In our home there was no nurturing of words, numbers or ideas.

That all changed at the age of 13 when I met an English teacher called Mr Francis, affectionately known as 'BJF' (Brian John Francis). BJF resembled a post-war fictional character: an impeccably dressed, pot-bellied, rosy-cheeked, moustachioed gentleman. He had once served in the Navy. He had been a teacher at the former grammar school and had agreed to stay on to teach at our newly formed all boys comprehensive. We were the last class he ever taught.

In BJF's loving hands, dry printed words were transported into magical flights of imagination revealing the universal stuff of life. I still relate to Prince Hal's struggles in Shakespeare's *King Henry IV, Part 1* and remember the eerily accurate dystopian future depicted in EM Forster's 'The Machine Stops'. I fell in love with the young poets of Ypres and Verdun.

One day BJF brought me into his office to give me some encouraging feedback on one of my essays. That two-minute conversation meant the world to me – one of the first times someone had bothered to consider my work and help improve what I was trying to say. Over the months my grades went from D's to B's and even to A's. We took our English literature O-level a year early. A year later, after our English language O-level, Mr Francis retired.

I would say BJF's spark ignited a burning fire. But my passion was more sponge-like. I scoured second-hand book shops in search of literary classics, devouring whatever I could find, from Homer to Solzhenitsyn to Fitzgerald, and of course the Romantics, Keats, Byron and Shelley. What an odd book collector I must have seemed: all bleached blond spikey hair, hooped earrings and 1980s eyeliner.

Those were precarious times. By the start of A-levels, I was living on my own and had stopped attending lessons. These were the days of my first loves, and drugs and clubs in London. I lost most of my possessions moving from one place to another. Yet somehow my books stayed with me. I can see them now as I write, staring back at me from my shelves in my family home.

How I wish BJF could also see me now. I became the first person in my family to enter university. I have published four books, and I'm a university Professor. I've even advised the Government on improving literacy. I still feel an awkward shame about coming from a broken home. For good and ill, your history stays with you. But my love of words transformed my life.

Lee Elliot Major

Professor of Social Mobility, University of Exeter

Former Chief Executive of the Sutton Trust

5

WORDS AND WORLDS: THE CHALLENGE OF VOCABULARY

INTRODUCTION

This chapter considers the particular role of vocabulary in literacy development, something which has received a lot of attention recently in both research and wider educational discourse (Quigley, 2018). Words are fundamental to thought, as Vygotsky famously claimed:

> *Real concepts are impossible without words, and thinking in concepts does not exist beyond verbal thinking. That is why the central moment in concept formation … is a specific use of words as functional tools.*

> (1986, p. 107)

While there is debate about the extent to which abstract thought can occur without verbal language (e.g. Blackburn, n.d.), Vygotsky's view that words are *tools* for thinking is widely accepted. Each word we know represents a concept in our minds, and having a *word* for a concept allows us to combine it with other concepts, helping us to make connections and generate ideas. This chapter will explore how these tools particularly enable us to decode and comprehend texts, and to express ideas and communicate with others. It will also consider how we can address vocabulary development in a way which is inclusive and avoids a 'deficit discourse' (Kuchirko, 2019; Johnson, 2015). We start, however, by specifically examining the relationship between vocabulary and disadvantage.

UNDERSTANDING THE RESEARCH

THE RELATIONSHIP BETWEEN VOCABULARY AND DISADVANTAGE

The concept of a 'word gap' – that is, a difference in the number of words known by children from relatively advantaged or disadvantaged backgrounds – has been popular since the 1990s, when Hart and Risley published the results of a longitudinal study comparing the words spoken at home to young children in families from different socio-economic backgrounds in the United States (1992, 1995). Their phenomenally influential work presented a number of interesting results, but the one which most caught hold in educational discourse became the '30 million Word Gap' – the suggestion that extrapolating from their data revealed that 30 million more individual words were spoken to children in families of high socio-economic status compared to those from families in receipt of welfare, between the ages of 7–9 months and 3 years old.

This finding precipitated a wave of further study into the 'language environments' experienced by children in their early years at home. To understand or be able to use a word, a child has to have encountered it, so many studies have measured the amount of parental talk in households with infants – both talk directly to the child, and talk more generally in the home environment – and related this to children's own vocabulary development, language processing and educational attainment. While the '30 million' estimate has been revised downwards to 4 million by the age of 4 (Gilkerson et al., 2017), some studies have found that children who experience less 'child-directed' talk have less developed vocabularies of their own (Weisleder and Fernald, 2013; see also Hoff, 2013). It has been posited that language experiences in infancy are particularly crucial for children's auditory discrimination, including their ability to hear the speech sounds of their native language (Kuhl et al., 2005) as well as 'language processing abilities', 'memory, reasoning, vocabulary and cognitive skills' (Kuchirko, 2019, p. 541).

However, these studies have also pointed to a range of complicating factors which are often obscured by the attention-grabbing '30 million' headline. Firstly, Weisleder and Fernald (2013) noted that their study, which looked only at low socio-economic status families, found almost as much difference among their participants as Hart and Risley found between the high and low socio-economic status families. This is an important reminder that we must not over-generalise, or expect all households of low socio-economic status to communicate in the same ways. Indeed, there has been a substantial amount of criticism relating to Hart and Risley's methods of collecting data from households (e.g. Johnson, 2015; Baugh, 2017), all of which suggests that their findings are likely to significantly over-estimate the differences between different socio-economic groups.

Secondly, recent research has suggested that it can be very difficult to separate language disadvantage from specific language impairments, noting that children from low socio-economic status families are more likely to experience language disorders (Norbury et al., 2021), and are less likely to have been referred for speech and language therapy if they need it (Roy et al., 2014). In addition, the majority of studies have examined correlation between speech in the home and a range of performance measures in the children, rather than interrogating causal relationships or factors which might explain or confound the relationship between social or economic disadvantage and language learning, such as 'variability in parents' own verbal abilities or conversational style' or the 'activities that parents tend to engage in with their children' or 'parental stress and emotional well-being' or 'parental beliefs' (Weisleder and Fernald, 2013, p. 9).

There is also an important argument that the focus on comparing low and high socio-economic status populations masks the impact of cultural differences among different communities, and that it is not a language 'deficit' but rather language 'difference' that occurs (Kuchirko, 2019, p. 543; see also Baugh, 2017). Seminal studies conducted by Brice-Heath in the 1980s (1982, 1983) found distinctly different social patterns of talk in different communities in the United States. In a detailed ethnographic study, she compared the home literacy practices of children in three communities: Maintown, predominantly representing middle-class culture; Roadville, a white working-class community; and Trackton, a black working-class community. She found equally rich and sophisticated but very *different* patterns of interaction within different communities, and crucially found that the Maintown children had experiences more closely aligned to constructions of literacy which are privileged in school. Differences in relation to storytelling, for example, included the emphasis placed on linearity and chronology, on individual storytelling vs co-constructed narratives, and the extent to which non-verbal communication is valued. The school-aligned, middle-class practices are not inherently *better* than those of the other communities, but the coherence between home and school literacies serves to advantage the middle-class children. If you would like to know more about some of the problematic assumptions which underpin both the procedure and the reporting of the Hart and Risley study, see Kuchirko (2019) and Baugh (2017). Shanahan also presents a useful concise overview in his blog (2018).

CRITICAL QUESTIONS

The section above alludes to the fact that there are differences in the ways in which families from different cultures and communities tend to interact and communicate in the home. It suggests that middle-class talk is closer to the types of talk that are valued in school. There is more on this later, but for now, can you identify 'types' of literacy which are privileged in school? You might think about:

- How far literacy in school is seen as something practiced by an individual speaker or author, compared to literacy as a social interaction, with multiple authors working together

- Specific forms – including vocabulary and grammar – which are taught as 'correct'

- The genres of speech and writing which are valued, and the conventions of these genres

- How far literacy is associated with knowledge of language only, rather than multimodal forms in which language is combined with gesture, sound or image.

WHY VOCABULARY MATTERS

When categorising vocabulary knowledge, we can separate out receptive and productive vocabulary. Receptive vocabulary refers to the words that a person will understand if they hear or read them, while productive vocabulary (sometimes called 'expressive vocabulary') refers to the words that a person can use in their own speech or writing. The relationship between reading and receptive vocabulary has been studied in some detail.

VOCABULARY AND READING

On a fundamental level, receptive vocabulary knowledge supports decoding, as children are quicker to decode well-known words than unfamiliar ones (Perfetti, 2010; Tunmer and Chapman, 2012). Fluent decoding supports comprehension by freeing up working memory, allowing readers to focus on meaning (Klauda and Guthrie, 2008). As well as supporting decoding fluency, receptive vocabulary also has direct relationship with reading comprehension: we need to understand words to make sense of text. This is, of course, a reciprocal relationship: familiarity with words helps us to read, and reading helps us to learn new words and to develop deeper knowledge of words with which we're already familiar (Cain and Oakhill, 2011).

The concepts of *lexical breadth* and *lexical depth* are useful when thinking about this. Lexical breadth refers to the number or range of individual words that we know, while lexical depth refers to how detailed our knowledge of a word is: how much we understand a word's range of meanings and associations. Both breadth and depth of lexical knowledge is strongly associated with reading comprehension (Oakhill and

Cain, 2012), and particularly with the ability to draw inferences from texts. As we read a text, we don't remember it word for word, but rather construct a mental model of it, one which becomes richer and more detailed as we read. We integrate information from different parts of a text, and read between the lines to fill in missing details, inferring meaning (Cain and Oakhill, 2014). Lexical depth appears to be particularly important in helping readers to draw inferences and make links between different parts of a text. As Cain and Oakhill explain, 'having rich, detailed and precise semantic representations of words makes it more likely that thematically-related inferences will be made to establish coherence' (2014, p. 651). To make this more concrete, they give the example of a story where the setting is not given explicitly, but can be inferred by making links between 'concepts such as "building sandcastles", "paddling in the water" and the presence of a "pier"' to suggest that the story takes place at the seaside (ibid, p. x). As an aside, it's interesting to consider which words in their example might be unfamiliar to children from different regional or cultural backgrounds. To what extent might 'sandcastles' or a 'pier' be familiar everyday concepts to children who live in different urban, rural or coastal communities, or children who are recent immigrants?

Receptive vocabulary, therefore, plays an important role in supporting a range of different interrelated processes involved in reading: fluency of decoding, general comprehension and inference. Vocabulary knowledge itself can be developed through reading, so a virtuous circle can be created where 'gains in vocabulary knowledge through reading practice may enhance reading comprehension performance' (Cain and Oakhill, 2011). Alternatively, a cycle of failure can persist, where children who struggle to read at the expected level in class experience poor self-efficacy and loss of intrinsic motivation, which leads to them reading less (Walker, 2003; Guthrie et al., 2007; Schiefele et al., 2012). Given the importance of literacy across all curriculum areas, this can have a significant impact on a student's academic attainment more widely.

VOCABULARY AND WRITING

Productive or expressive vocabulary and its relation to writing development has received much less attention in comparison to receptive vocabulary and reading. Nevertheless, attempts to correlate quality of writing with various measures of vocabulary use have yielded some interesting results. Research has typically measured diversity or sophistication of vocabulary – broadly defined as the range of different words used and how uncommon and task-appropriate they are. Olinghouse and Wilson (2013) highlighted that different genres of school writing place different demands on vocabulary: high scores in narrative writing were associated with diversity of vocabulary; in persuasive writing, register and content words (that is, technical words which are specific to the subject being discussed) were important; and in information texts, content words and maturity of vocabulary were important. There is also evidence that children develop more 'register-appropriate' vocabulary as they progress through school: while they tend to use words 'typical of fiction texts' from the outset, they accrue disciplinary vocabulary over time, and increasingly deploy this appropriately in non-fiction writing (Durrant and Brenchley, 2019, p. 1951). This points to the importance of disciplinary or genre-specific vocabularies for success in school writing: the idea that 'distinct parts of the curriculum pose distinctive communicative challenges' (Durrant and Durrant, 2022, p. 13), and the fact that students need to learn how to use vocabulary that is appropriate for a particular subject, genre or task.

This issue of 'disciplinary vocabularies' is incorporated into Beck et al.'s vocabulary tiers (2013), where a distinction is made between more general, cross-disciplinary academic language and the special technical terminology associated with different subjects. Their three vocabulary tiers separate words hierarchically: tier one comprising words common in everyday usage; tier two including words which are academic but commonly used *in school* across the curriculum; tier three comprising subject-specific academic vocabulary, or 'terminology'. Of course, words can move between the tiers depending on their usage, and indeed some tier three subject specific words cause problems because they also exist in everyday forms (for example, the term 'complex sentence' has a specific technical meaning which isn't the same as the more everyday notion of 'complicated sentence' – although it's typical for students to confuse the two). While most teachers readily identify and teach the technical tier 3 vocabulary, Quigley (2018) has highlighted the importance of addressing tier 2 as well. This is particularly important as tier 2 includes words which are often used as examination cues (e.g. explain, analyse and estimate), and words which students use to increase expressive sophistication and to structure and organise their writing (e.g. discourse markers such as *conversely, however, notably*).

ACTION POINT

Research tier 2 and tier 3 vocabulary lists for your phase and/or subject. Quigley (2018) lists a number of useful examples, but you will also find a wealth of ideas on the internet.

- Review words which you think might cause problems or misconceptions for your students. Are there any cases where 'everyday understandings' might interfere with the technical understanding of a word?

- If you're working in Primary or Early Years, consider which tier 2 words you might want to teach explicitly. Which words will provide useful concepts for understanding 'academic language' and help them to express their ideas as students' progress through their early formal education?

- If you're working in Secondary, are there any subject-specific meanings of tier 2 words that you might need to make sure that students understand – such as the difference between 'analyse' in a literary essay and 'analyse' in a scientific report?

AVOIDING THE DEFICIT DISCOURSE: VOCABULARY, LITERACY AND STANDARD ENGLISH IN SCHOOLS

We know, then, that there is a clear relationship between vocabulary knowledge and both reading and writing. We also know that there are patterns of difference in household communication which can have an impact on children's vocabulary knowledge. Before looking at the implications for teaching more closely, it's important to think through some of the critiques of how the relationship between language and socio-economic disadvantage has been framed. This is a sensitive and complex issue.

The 'deficit discourse' refers to a view which positions the talk and language of low socio-economic status families – and indeed their culture more broadly too – as inherently lesser than that of more advantaged communities. This view presents their language and communicative practices as less valuable, less rich, less sophisticated and less informed or knowledgeable. Arguments which take this position can also carry an implication that the inferior home language environment leads to inferior cognitive development. It's important to recognise that there is no evidence to support this idea (Johnson, 2015).

We can see this deficit discourse in the original Hart and Risley studies; as Johnson (2015, p. 44) explains, phrases such as 'poverty of experience' (in relation to low socio-economic status families), 'enriched language' (in relation to high socio-economic status) and measures of linguistic 'richness' which are based purely on word counts, are value-driven, theoretically questionable and clearly imply that the language of middle-class or professional households is innately superior to those in the socio-economically disadvantaged group. A similar implication is present in Basil Bernstein's theories of *elaborated* and *restricted* codes, another idea that has regained popularity recently (Quigley, 2018) and was also discussed in Chapter 2. Working in the 1960s and 1970s, Bernstein argued that the cause of poor academic performance among students from socio-economically disadvantaged backgrounds could be attributed to the ways in which language was used in the home. He suggested that it is possible to identify fundamentally different ways of using language within different communities – not entirely dissimilarly to Brice-Heath's findings which were noted above. A key difference in their work, however, is the value judgements implied in their analyses of language. While Brice-Heath aimed to represent the richness and complexity of all different talk and communication habits, the labels which Bernstein chose to distinguish between 'middle class' and 'lower working class' (1971, p. 46) leant themselves all too readily to the deficit discourse, with the language of the lower working class represented as 'restricted' in comparison to the implicit sophistication of the 'elaborated' middle-class code (p. 59). The terms which Bernstein chose are easy to misinterpret – the restricted code does not refer to limited vocabulary, but rather primarily to syntax, the way in which words are combined to convey meaning, with the restricted code relying more on shared understanding and the elaborated code being more explicit in explaining information. However, his work has been heavily criticised (Baugh even claims that it has been 'debunked' (2017, p. 41)) for implying that the language of low socio-economic status communities is inferior to that of the middle classes.

DEBUNKING DEFICIT

In counter to the deficit discourse, linguists argue that the language and communication of disadvantaged communities is just as rich and sophisticated as that of advantaged communities. It is important to remember, for example, that there is nothing inherently more sophisticated about Standard English than any other dialect form. Trudgill (2011) offers a range of examples of ways in which Standard English has fewer options than regional dialects, arguably rendering it less sophisticated. These include the fact that it doesn't distinguish between the pronoun for second person singular and plural ('You') unlike dialects which use 'Youse' for the plural form. Another example is the fact that there are only two singular demonstrative pronouns: 'this' for objects close to the speaker and 'that' for objects further away. In contrast, many regional dialects have three options – 'this' for objects close to the speaker, 'that' for objects close to the listener, and 'yon' for objects away from both speaker and listener. In the United States, the seminal work of Labov in the 1970s presented a compelling analysis of the language of 'Negro children' who had previously been thought to live in 'verbal deprivation', to 'hear very little well-formed language', and consequently to be 'impoverished in their means of verbal expression' (1973, p. 21). In contrast to this deficit view, Labov's analysis presented a picture of children who 'receive a great deal of verbal stimulation, hear more well-formed sentences than middle-class children, and participate fully in a highly verbal culture' (p. 21).

This argument, echoed by Brice-Heath (1983), and more recently by Baugh (2017), Au (2013) and Zentella (2005), and many others, emphasises the fact that it is the sociocultural assumptions and values of our education system that underpins the relationship between language and disadvantage. As well as issues of Standard English, they point particularly to the mismatch between the collaborative, multimodal talk patterns of some communities and the individualist, linguistically orientated talk which is valued in school. It is not the case that students from socio-economically disadvantaged communities experience an 'impoverished' language, and it is not even primarily an issue of diminished vocabulary that hinders their progress in school. Rather, it is a mismatch between the patterns of speech in the home and in formal education that creates a hurdle, and these differences in patterns of communication reach beyond vocabulary into syntax, the structuring of spoken language and multimodal communication.

One important comment to note in relation to research in this area is that much of it has taken place in the United States, where there is a much stronger history of research which considers ethnicity in relation to social and economic disadvantage. Many of the studies outlined above have included a focus on specific ethnic communities, as can be seen in relation to Labov. Studies of disadvantage in the United Kingdom are less likely to focus on specific ethnic demographic groups, and tend to focus more on class or economic categories (see Chapter 1).

IMPLICATIONS FOR TEACHERS

There are deeply important implications of this anti-deficit view for teachers. Crucially, we know that teacher expectations can have a major impact on student attainment (Kolb and Jussim, 1994), so it is vitally important that you are mindful of your own assumptions, and that you don't reduce or lower your expectations for students who might not readily demonstrate 'middle class' literacies. Equally important is the way in which you talk about home literacies in school. It is possible to teach students how to use standard forms of language while not insisting that these are 'correct' regardless of context, or 'superior' to the language spoken at home. As discussed in Chapter 3, linguists use the term 'code-switching' to refer to the ways in which we change register, referring to our ability to change the formality of speech or writing, or to how we use particular vocabulary and phrasing that is appropriate in different contexts. This concept is a useful way to explain to students what you're teaching them to do: you are not correcting their use of words when you amend their dialect to Standard English or teach them to use more formal vocabulary, but rather helping them to 'switch' to the appropriate 'code', or way of using words.

Of course, it would be naive to say that the literacy privileged in school – including Standard English and academic vocabulary – is not also valued more highly in wider society. The relationship between disadvantage and literacy is influenced by social and cultural values and attitudes across society, not just within the classroom. Many justifications for teaching 'Standard English' refer not only to the value of vocabulary for academic progress but also for subsequent careers and status. This puts schools and teachers in a very difficult position – one where it is easy for them to unintentionally reinforce values which are discriminatory. This is discussed in some detail in Chapter 3, drawing on Cushing's work which critically interrogates how positioning Standard English as inherently 'correct' can 'marginalise and stigmatise' students who come from non-standard speaking backgrounds (2021a, p. 332). It is worth reiterating here in relation to 'word gap' policies, as there is potential for a devastating impact on a student's sense of identity and belonging. If the message that they receive from their teachers – explicitly or implicitly – is that the language spoken in the home is inferior and incorrect, this can create shame, anger or defiance. We know that one of the most important factors in enabling students from socially disadvantaged backgrounds to succeed in education is the extent to which they feel that they belong in school (Siraj-Blatchford et al., 2011). Factors which support disadvantaged children include a 'positive perception of themselves as learners, their appreciation for what school and education can bring them, and their willingness and ability to build and sustain meaningful relationships with the people around them that actually serve to facilitate their learning' (p. 69), as well as a positive, cooperative relationship between home and school. For all of these reasons, it is important that students' use of vocabulary and wider interaction in the home is not presented in deficit terms when it is compared to Standard English, but rather recognised explicitly as having value and sophistication. Vocabulary teaching can be framed as positive development of academic and disciplinary language, rather than addressing a 'problem' in students' home language.

As well as the emotive impact on students, their perception of themselves and their attitude to school, it's also important to recognise that enforcing Standard English vocabulary in classroom talk can create further disadvantages. Standard English is primarily a written not spoken dialect (Trudgill, 1999) – nobody consistently speaks in full Standard English sentences. Policies which require students to speak in Standard English create an additional barrier to learners' ability to engage productively in classroom talk and express their ideas. If we consider the importance of dialogic talk (see Chapter 3), it's easy to identify how being asked to speak in an unfamiliar register might inhibit students' ability to express partial thoughts aloud, to reason, speculate and share opinions. In cognitive terms, the additional pressure on working memory is also substantial as students have to expend cognitive resources on remembering how to phrase their ideas in standard forms, rather than having the freedom to use their full range of linguistic resources (Cushing, 2021a, p. 331).

REFLECTION POINT

Now is a good time to consider your own unconscious biases. The first stage in overcoming these is to bring them to consciousness, to think explicitly and critically about them, and to try to challenge yourself to consider different viewpoints.

- To what extent does the way that someone speaks affect your attitudes towards them? How and why does your perception of someone change according to the language that they use?

- How can you ensure that your students are not disadvantaged by your unconscious bias?

- How can you talk about the difference between Standard and Non-Standard English without implying that Non-Standard forms are incorrect, less sophisticated or inferior to Standard forms?

IN THE CLASSROOM

VOCABULARY GROWTH THROUGH EXPOSURE TO WORDS

There is a long-standing assumption that reading widely will automatically develop vocabulary knowledge. That assumption is not wrong – Cain and Oakhill have found that 'both reading habits and reading comprehension appear to have specific and direct effects on vocabulary growth' (2011, p. 441). One implication here is the importance of developing reading for pleasure, as discussed in Chapter 4: indeed Cain and Oakhill note that 'an early enjoyment of books should be nurtured but can be further developed in the early years of schooling' (p. 441).

Exposure to words does not only occur through reading, of course, and classroom talk can be equally valuable for supporting students' ability to 'code-switch' effectively. Quigley discusses the value of 'Academic talk' (2018, p. 149) in which teachers deliberately model academic language and sophisticated vocabulary choices, and use questioning which prompts students to develop, explain and justify their ideas, asking 'why' questions' to 'get children to better trigger their prior knowledge and think harder' (p. 152). As noted in the section above, you should think about the extent to which you want to prioritise *students'* use of academic register and Standard English when they speak in class. There may be occasions where you want to focus on dialogic exploration of ideas and do not want to impose an additional hurdle or barrier for how students express their thoughts, and other occasions where you explicitly want students to focus on how they are expressing their ideas clearly in academic code.

VOCABULARY GROWTH THROUGH PLANNED TEACHING

Despite the benefits of general reading and talk outlined briefly above, just presenting opportunities for students to be 'exposed' to words is unlikely to be sufficient, particularly if you want to support students from non-advantaged backgrounds to be able to code-switch effectively. Two seminal meta-analyses have synthesised evidence on interventions to support vocabulary development, with a particular focus on examining the impact of the interventions on reading comprehension. Again, note that there is significantly more research on receptive vocabulary and reading in comparison to productive vocabulary and writing. Both of these analyses – the first by Elleman et al. (2009) and the more recent by Wright and Cervetti (2017) – suggest that it is very difficult to develop general comprehension ability through vocabulary training. As Elleman et al. summarise: 'vocabulary instruction does not transfer beyond the taught target words and texts in which it is learned' (2009, p. 33).

However, this does not mean that there is no point in teaching vocabulary explicitly. Both meta-analyses found that teaching *relevant* vocabulary supports comprehension of specific texts, and that vocabulary instruction can develop both depth and breadth of word knowledge. Elleman et al. specifically contrasted students with reading difficulties to a comparison group, and found that vocabulary instruction was particularly beneficial in supporting comprehension for students 'with reading problems' (2009, p. 34). This means that teaching selected vocabulary can help students to access and understand texts – so selecting useful vocabulary is an important first step in teaching.

— ACTION POINT —

Take any text that you ask your students to read. Make a list of vocabulary that you might want to teach explicitly in order to support students' comprehension.

- Which words might students find difficult?

- Are there any words which require cultural or historical knowledge to understand?

- Are there any words that trigger misconceptions?

- Are there any words which might require depth of knowledge to understand fully – an appreciation of different meanings or associations that the word has?

- Are there any words which might also be useful for understanding *other* texts?

- What else, other than vocabulary, might make the text hard to comprehend?

Wright and Cervetti's analysis focused more specifically on exploring the impact of different types of vocabulary teaching. Again, they discovered that teaching vocabulary supported comprehension of the 'target words', but that there was only 'very limited evidence that direct teaching of word meanings, even long-term, multifaceted interventions of large numbers of words, can improve generalized

Table 5.1 Summary of comprehensive vocabulary development

Type of knowledge taught	Goal of instruction	Methods taught
Procedural knowledge: knowing how…	Learning strategies to understand and clarify the meaning of a word	• Activities supporting memorisation of words and meanings • Structural analysis of words – using morphological and etymological knowledge • Using contextual clues • Exploring synonyms
Conditional knowledge: knowing when…	Learning metacognitive and self-regulation strategies to use during independent reading	• Self-monitoring of comprehension • Self-regulation of word-learning strategies
Declarative knowledge: knowing that…	Building word knowledge	• Interactive work with words • Use of a journal to record work with words • Repeated exposure to words • Graphic organisers

Source: Adapted from Lubliner and Smetana (2005).

comprehension' (2017, p. 219). However, they did note that there were some indications that teaching strategies for working out what words mean *alongside* metacognitive and self-regulation strategies might be more widely beneficial: specifically approaches which 'actively teach students to monitor their understanding of vocabulary and use multiple, flexible strategies for solving word meanings' (ibid). In relation to this, they pointed to a study by Lubliner and Smetana (2005) which took this multidimensional approach to vocabulary teaching and reported positive results. The different types of strategies are outlined in Table 5.1.

The table highlights three different strands of teaching: teaching strategies for working out the meaning of words; teaching metacognitive strategies for recognising when you don't fully comprehend the meaning of a word and for selecting strategies to use to work it out; and teaching words meanings directly. The last one of these is arguably the most straightforward, and Quigley presents a simple model for introducing words, which he labels the 'SEEC' method (2018, p. 139). This involves *selecting* the word to teach, *explaining* its meaning, including giving a student-friendly definition, plenty of examples, and talk to explore variety of meanings and clarify misconceptions, *exploring* the word by, for example, looking at synonyms, words which share etymological roots, different ways in which the word might be used, and *consolidating* knowledge of the word by revisiting it, asking students to use it in their own writing, asking students to research it, and so on.

Table 5.2   Teaching activities to support the development of strategies for learning vocabulary and deducing new word meanings, drawing on Lubliner and Smetana (2005) and Quigley (2018)

Methods	Pedagogical activities and approaches
Activities supporting memorisation of words and meanings	• Flashcards of key words and definitions • Visual organisers – e.g. of clusters of semantically or thematically related words • Spaced recall quizzes on key word definitions • Repeated exposure to a key word • Repeated opportunities to actively use of a word (in writing or talk) • Use of a journal, word bank or word list which a student compiles over time
Structural analysis of words – using morphological and etymological knowledge	• Explicit teaching of morphological elements – e.g. prefixes, suffixes, inflected endings, high frequency Latin and Greek root words • Investigation and play with etymological relationships between root words – finding the meaningful relationships between words which share roots. For example, exploring the meaning of 'tele' (Greek: far) and how it operates in words such as television, telephone, telegraph and telescope.

(Continued)

Table 5.2 (Continued)

Methods	Pedagogical activities and approaches

Using contextual clues	• Explicitly teaching students to look for clues as to the meaning of a word – e.g. by modelling:
	  • Careful reading of the sentence the unknown word is in
	  • Looking for words which might be thematically related to the target word elsewhere in the text.

Exploring synonyms	• Building 'word webs' or other graphic representations of synonymous or near-synonymous words, to develop depth of knowledge of meanings and associations.

If we combine the first and last set of methods outlined by Lubliner and Smetana (2005), we can develop a range of pedagogical activities which both teach key vocabulary explicitly, *and* teach students strategies for deducing the meaning of new words. Many of these are expanded on, with a wealth of specific examples, in Quigley (2018). Drawing on a range of research, Quigley has created a model of a 'Word Rich Classroom' which incorporates four key strands: reading with purpose and pleasure; making connections and categorising; academic talk; and word play (p. 145). These combine techniques which focus on exposure and immersion with explicit teaching of targeted words and deductive strategies. Table 5.2 presents an overview of pedagogical approaches which combines Lubliner and Smetana's theorised approach to vocabulary instruction with some of Quigley's useful pedagogical activities.

It's worth noting at this point that the meta-analyses also highlight the benefit of active and contextual vocabulary instruction. Active approaches are those in which students are asked to use the target words in their own speech and writing, and to engage more generally in collaborative talk about and investigation of words. This recalls Quigley's 'word play' dimension, which emphasises the potential of puns, idioms, proverbs, catchphrases, slogans, anagrams, palindromes (to lift but a few from his extensive list) for facilitating creative experimentation and fostering a love of words.

Contextual instruction refers to the learning of words which are relevant to a text or topic being studied, where they are seen in context in speech or written text, rather than as a separate list of words and definitions. A key point here, raised by Oliver (2016), is that this is not incidental or accidental teaching of words, but rather still planned, deliberate introduction of vocabulary. The work of Nash and Snowling (2006) has been important in highlighting the value of this approach. In a study which compared students who were taught definitions of words directly, with students who were taught strategies to work out what words mean from context, they found that there was significantly more benefit from the latter approach. Children who were taught how to use clues in the text to work out the meaning of a word and investigated words collaboratively retained a deeper understanding of the words they learned, and were able to express 'more meanings' (Nash and Snowling, 2006, p. 350). Nash and Snowling offer a range of suggestions as to why their contextual approach was beneficial, including the idea that it may have been a result of active engagement as much as seeing words in context. Nevertheless, they also raised a particularly important implication in relation to students with poor vocabulary: they suggested that these children may be less likely to 'automatically infer the meaning of new words from context', but crucially that they 'can be taught to do so' (p. 349).

The other important strand in Lubliner and Smetana's approach is the teaching of metacognitive and self-regulation strategies. Wright and Cervetti suggest that this might be the key to making vocabulary instruction transfer to more general improvement in comprehension. Lubliner and Smetana used approaches such as traffic lights to help children monitor their understanding of words, teaching them to think about whether they don't know a word at all (red), have heard of it but aren't confident that they can use it or explain what it means (yellow), or know the word confidently and can use it in a sentence (green). This sort of comprehension monitoring (Palincsar and Brown, 1984) is important if we want students to deliberately and consciously use strategies to deduce the meanings of unfamiliar words.

ACTION POINT

Taking the text that you analysed above, consider the opportunities it presents for teaching strategies for solving word meanings.

- Are there words which can be deduced from contextual clues? How could you help students to identify those cues?

- Are there words that could be deduced from morphological clues? What aspects of morphology could you teach to help students work out what those words means?

- What strategies could you use to help students to monitor their comprehension of words as they read?

Table 5.3   Examples of word banks for different genres of writing

Word bank for a persuasive speech	Word bank for descriptive writing
Linking Conjunctions: Furthermore; In addition; Moreover	Colours: azure, lilac, rose-red, bone-white and steel-grey
Contrasting Conjunctions: On the other hand; However; In Contrast	Touch: clammy, slippery, gritty, coarse, silken, prickly and frosty
Logical Conjunctions: Therefore; Consequently; In conclusion	Sound: rumbling, crackling, gurgling and hissing
Inclusive pronouns: We feel, You know	Smell: Musty, rotten, sharp and smoky
Intensifiers: Crucially, Vitally, Importantly and Exceptionally	

TEACHING VOCABULARY FOR WRITING

The fact that research on vocabulary focuses primarily on reading comprehension has become a recurrent theme in this chapter. There is very little research that investigates the impact of explicit vocabulary instruction on the writing of native speakers. However, there has been some consideration of the value of teaching vocabulary for the planning stage of the writing process, and particularly for generating ideas, with Duin and Graves (1987) finding that teaching relevant vocabulary improved the overall quality of students' expository essay writing. In practice, teachers commonly help students to compile banks of words and phrases before writing (see Table 5.3).

Given what we know about the value of focusing on words in context, it is worth noting that the most useful word banks will be compiled in response to a specific task, rather than as generic tools. They should also be compiled *with* students rather than simply presented *to* them, so that they comprise active discussion of and engagement with words, though you might also purposefully introduce some key vocabulary that you want to include. Consider how to use these to support depth not just breadth of vocabulary knowledge, and the different types of word that you might want to include too; Myhill et al. (forthcoming) note that much teaching of descriptive writing tends to over-emphasise adjectives and adverbs at the expense of recognising the descriptive power of well-chosen nouns and verbs, for example. Vocabulary banks can scaffold all stages of the writing process, triggering ideas, helping students to express themselves with sophisticated, register-appropriate vocabulary, and providing support when students evaluate and revise their writing.

BEYOND VOCABULARY

Many points in this chapter have signalled that it's not always possible or useful to focus on vocabulary in isolation. Vocabulary knowledge does play an important role in reading comprehension, but there are many more processes involved, as discussed in Chapter 4. Similarly, word difficulty is only one facet of text difficulty, which also includes 'sentence structure, length, elaboration, coherence, text structure, familiarity of context and background knowledge required, audience appropriateness, quality and verve of writing and interest' (Graves and Philippot, 2002, p. 180). Vocabulary is also only one facet of writing quality. While we want to foreground the power of words – not least to highlight the dangers of the deficit discourse – it's also important not to over-emphasise vocabulary as the explanation for achievement gaps between advantaged and disadvantaged students. Addressing vocabulary in an explicit, targeted, active, contextual way, teaching strategies and expanding students' repertoire of productive academic vocabulary will support reading and writing development. However, fixating on vocabulary as the single most important factor is likely to be unhelpful (Baugh, 2017).

VIGNETTE

The *Centre for Literacy in Primary Education* has a long tradition of creating resources and programmes, putting quality children's books at the heart of all learning, and making connections between being a reader and being a writer. In 2014, we became aware that there was something particularly transformative for children in using picture books and visual approaches to engage children as readers and writers, and so we developed the *Power of Pictures* programme in collaboration with award-winning author, Ed Vere. This programme is based on the principles that:

- Picture books are an important genre of children's literature and support the development of sophisticated reading skills.

- Children need time, space and planned opportunities to develop their ideas for truly creative and independent writing.

- When children are given opportunities to draw as part of the writing process, this helps them to formulate, develop and extend ideas for writing, making their independent, self-initiated writing richer.

The visual element of this programme attracted learners who traditionally have difficulties engaging in literacy activities and the experience of working alongside a published author was beneficial for improving pupils and teachers understanding of the writing process. (to read more about this, see https://educationendowmentfoundation.org.uk/projects-and-evaluation/projects/power-of-pictures.)

Vinny Dawson, Year 5 Class teacher at Harrow Gate Primary Academy in Stockton-on-Tees, reflects on the impact of the programme and approaches:

The project provided a range of excellent teaching ideas and suggestions – each supported by detailed planning that I could deliver in school. The first sequence was based around a picture book and analysed features of this text. Ultimately, this sequence wasn't just a revelation for me – but also for my children. The opportunity to explore this high-quality text in such detail led to focussed discussions and incredible writing outcomes. Using pictures to fuel our English processing helped all children engage with the learning – and the idea that "anyone can read a picture" removed previous barriers like reading and spelling ability.

As well as working with this incredible and engaging planning, my class were given a chance to Newcastle to take part in a workshop with a picture book author, Tim Hopgood, which will remain as one of my favourite days teaching for a very long time. The children were awe-struck that a real author wasn't just taking the time to work with them, but was also deeply interested in everything they were doing. Tim and the class shared their expertise – and the day gave a unique chance to truly live and breathe this incredible learning.

After the session, we used the planning to develop their new learning and understanding to put together personalised, individual stories – and their creativity really came to life when they were given the freedom to do something completely unique. The sequence allowed children of all abilities to thrive. More able writers could really flourish, and disengaged children were able to turn a new leaf, breaking through unspoken barriers that had previously confined their learning. Many of our parents and carers face severe and multiple disadvantage and our pupil premium figure is currently at 78%, so a programme like this has been a real leveller, enabling all children to shine and integral to closing disadvantage gaps.

Charlotte Hacking

Learning and Programmes Director, Centre for Literacy in Primary Education.

https://clpe.org.uk/

6

CREATING A COMMUNITY OF WRITERS

INTRODUCTION

Writing in the 21st century is more important and more ubiquitous than at any point in history, largely due to the possibilities created by digital technologies. Writing is no longer confined to personally handwritten texts, or professionally printed texts: we can create our own print versions, and even more significantly we can create digital texts which can reach millions of people. The repertoire of writing has expanded exponentially: we routinely text, message, tweet and email using the written word; we can develop our own blogs and websites and contribute to the websites of others. In some ways, we could argue that digital technologies have brought about a democratisation of writing and publishing. In the light of this, it is a curious fact that there is less research on writing and the teaching of writing, particularly beyond the Early Years, than on any other aspect of literacy (Slavin et al., 2019), and in parallel with this, there is less research explicitly addressing how social disadvantage may affect learning and development as a writer. Brandt (2019, p. 39) suggests that one reason for this is that historically becoming literate was synonymous with learning to *read*, not to write – when ordinary people could read the religious texts of their culture, they were empowered to access and interpret it for themselves.

And yet the national data for key stage 2 writing assessments in 2019 (DfE, 2019, Table N4a) show that 32% of children identified as 'disadvantaged' did not achieve the expected standard in writing, compared with 17% of their peers. The attainment gap of 15% is almost identical to the gap in the reading tests, but writing is rarely highlighted as the focus for attention. Apart from these key stage 2 data, there are very little data on writing attainment, as they are not disaggregated from the overall result, and the international PISA tests do not test writing (because it is too difficult to test fairly across different countries and languages as there is no internationally agreed understanding of what constitutes good writing).

Underpinning this more limited attention to writing may be a common assumption that reading underpins writing, and thus that learning to be a competent reader will also make you a better writer. However, research on cognitive processes which we use when reading suggests the relationship is bidirectional and interactive (Shanahan, 2006; Parodi, 2007): in other words, writing and reading are mutually supportive. This is also a finding of more pedagogical research: Barrs and Cork (2001) explored the idea of 'the reader in the writer', and the reciprocality of reading and writing is clearly articulated by Smith (1983) who maintained that a learner 'must read like a writer, in order to learn how to write like a writer. There is no other way in which the intricate complexity of a writer's knowledge can be acquired' (p. 562). It is important to recognise this reciprocality between reading and writing, and to avoid positioning writing development as dependent upon reading.

Given the relative sparsity of research on writing, it is an additional irony that researching writing and writing pedagogy is our own primary research focus, and thus we will draw substantially on our research to inform the explanations and recommendations in this chapter. Wherever possible, we will note studies which do consider the needs of students living with disadvantage, and we will highlight current understanding about the best practices in the teaching of writing.

UNDERSTANDING THE RESEARCH
WRITING AS A CRAFT: BECOMING A WRITER

Perhaps one reason that reading has been prioritised over writing for research may be because of the particular complexity of writing. It is a *physical* activity: young writers, in particular, have to develop the motor skills to use a pencil expertly and shape letters on the page in straight lines; and older writers need to learn fluent keyboard skills (Ferreiro and Teberosky, 1982; van Waes et al., 2021). It is a *cognitive* activity: all writers are using mental processes to generate ideas and language to verbalise those ideas, and to plan and revise their writing (Kellogg, 2008). It is a *linguistic* activity: writers need to know how best to express their ideas in ways that will be appropriate for the kind of text they are writing and for their intended audience (Perera, 1984; Myhill, 2009). And it is a *social* activity: texts are written within communities of writers who have different ways of working and different understandings of what constitutes 'good' writing (Prior, 2006; Dyson, 2009). Students learning to write have to learn to master all these demands: 'writing requires an integration of muscle, mind, knowledge, language or languages, tools, and social worlds. Writing is effortful and remains effortful at all ages' (Brandt, 2019, p. 46). Indeed, Kellogg (2008) maintains that writing is as cognitively demanding as playing chess. Perhaps it is not surprising that many learners struggle with writing and lose interest or motivation to write.

One way to address this is by thinking of writing as a craft which incorporates these different aspects of writing in a holistic way. The idea of writing as a craft has its origins principally in the work of professional creative writers and the verbal or written advice they offer about writing well. Novelists Stephen King and Ursula Le Guin both use the word 'craft' to talk about writing in the titles (*Steering the Craft*, Le Guin, 2015; *On Writing: A Memoir of the Craft*, King, 2012), and Le Guin advises writers that 'once we're keenly and clearly aware of these elements of our craft, we can use and practice them until – the point of all practice – we don't have to think about them consciously at all, because they have become skills' (p. xiii). There is no romanticism in what these writers say: they recognise the hard work involved in writing, that practice is important, and that writing can be learned. The founders of creative writing organisation, Arvon, argue that 'all art is achieved through the exercise of a craft, and every craft has its rudiments that must be taught. The craft of writing is no exception' (Fairfax and Moat, 1998, p. 1). From an educational perspective, Twiselton (2006), Moon (2012) and Brandt (2019), among others, have conceived of writing as a craft as a way of thinking about teaching writing. In our own research (Myhill et al., 2021), we have developed a framework to describe writing as a craft, drawing on data from interviews with creative writers and observations of writing workshops and tutorials they led with teachers. This framework has five components, as outlined below, and incorporates cognitive, linguistic and social demands of writing:

The writing process (cognitive):	Knowledge about the strategies and processes involved in writing, from pre-writing activities to final proofreading.
Text-level choices (linguistic):	Knowledge about structural and text-level features and their effects.
Language choices (linguistic):	Knowledge about language choices and their effects.

Being an author (social):	Knowledge about the personal resources and intentions that authors bring to their writing.
Reader–writer relationship (social):	Knowledge about the interaction between reader and writer, and the ways in which readers become engaged in or affected by writing.

The framework enables us to move from a rather nebulous advocacy of writing as a craft towards one which begins to articulate more clearly what constitutes that craft. In an interview, children's author, Nicola Davies, explains how she became aware of her own knowledge of the craft of writing through teaching writing: 'I realised that I knew how to write in a way that a potter knows how to shape a bowl or a carpenter knows how to make dovetail joints. Looking at other people's writing and knowing how to fix it made me see that I actually had skills' (Culham, 2014, p. 47). As teachers, if we can be more precise about how to craft writing, then we are helping to induct young writers into the broader community of writers.

SELF-REGULATED STRATEGY DEVELOPMENT AND METACOGNITION

One strand of the framework for the craft of writing is the cognitive strand – 'the writing process' – which relates to knowledge about how we write – how we generate ideas, plan and review our writing and prepare it for publication/marking. Central to this is explicit understanding of how as writers we manage these processes (metacognition) and the strategies we use (self-regulation) – for example, knowing what to do if you get stuck. Metacognition is thinking about your own thinking or more formally 'one's knowledge concerning one's own cognitive processes' (Flavell, 1976, p. 232), while self-regulation is the capacity to be strategic about how a task is approached. So, as an example, if I say to myself while writing, 'I'm stuck again – I will simply keep writing, even if it's rubbish, and revise it later' then I am metacognitively aware of the problem of being stuck, and self-regulating how I solve the problem with a strategy. The Education Endowment Foundation (EEF) have judged metacognition to be an important resource for enhancing achievement (2018b), and a skill which can be taught – although a later review by the EEF (Muijs and Bokhove, 2020) is more cautious about some of these claims. Research also suggests that different home backgrounds develop metacognition in lesser or greater ways (Veenman et al., 2006) with more middle-class backgrounds appearing to have greatest influence on metacognition, though Muijs and Bokhove (2020, p. 16) describe this as a 'modest' effect, and Leutwyler and Maag-Merki (2009) found that differences within schools was a more significant factor.

Without doubt, the most substantial body of evidence on the positive impacts of metacognition in writing relates to Self-Regulated Strategy Instruction (SRSD), and particularly the work of Steve Graham and Karen Harris (e.g. Harris et al., 2008; Graham et al., 2012; Harris and Graham, 2016). Their application of SRSD to the teaching of writing is based on six steps, which themselves draw on research about effective metacognitive teaching:

1. Activate background knowledge: exploring the genre, using text models, and teaching students to set goals.

2. Discuss it: using graphic organisers and reviewing exemplar texts to stimulate discussion about the text.

3. Model it: teacher modelling or collaborative modelling through thinking aloud.

4. Memorize it: memorising the self-regulating steps, sometimes with mnemonics.

5. Support it: teacher scaffolding of writing tasks to give greater responsibility to the writer, including for monitoring and goal setting.

6. Independent Performance: more independent use of self-regulation strategies without being so overt about them, as they become part of how they write.

(For more detail about each of these steps, see SRSD, 2017).

The approach involves explicit teaching about the expectations of the genre, alongside the use of self-regulating tools and strategies, and teacher modelling of planning, drafting and reviewing written text. Many of the studies use SRSD with students who have learning difficulties, with positive effects and strong claims are made for the benefits of SRSD with all groups of learners. However, Slavin et al. (2019) critique the rigour of these claims, arguing that 'most SRSD evaluations took place in special education settings, did not meet the sample size or duration requirements, lacked control groups, or otherwise did not meet inclusion standards' (p. 13). However, other studies from different researchers do provide some evidence for positive claims. Coker and Erwin (2011) reported that SRSD combined with collaborative reasoning supported students in a low-income school in the United States: however, their findings are based on students' reporting their views of the intervention not whether their writing improved. More robust evidence was found in Salas et al. (2021), where use of SRSD improved writing for students from all groups. In England, EEF (2018c) evaluated the IPEELL programme, an SRSD programme, securing very positive results for an initial trial, but when scaled up, the results were less conclusive. Improvement in writing was paralleled by a drop in attainment in mathematics, spelling and reading, suggesting that more time may have been allocated to the teaching of writing.

Overall, however, despite some uncertainties about the strength of the evidence, there does seem to be merit in using self-regulation strategies in the teaching of writing. It does also link with the value of teaching metacognitive comprehension strategies for reading, as discussed in Chapter 4, underlining the educational value of metacognition.

METALINGUISTIC UNDERSTANDING

A parallel concept to metacognition is *metalinguistic understanding*: indeed, metalinguistic understanding is often seen as a subset component of metacognition (Gombert, 1992). Just as metacognition represents those moments when learners are aware of and are monitoring their cognitive processes, so metalinguistic understanding is when learners are aware of their linguistic processes. Instead of language simply being the tool of communication, metalinguistic understanding makes it the focus of thinking and reflection. In the context of being a writer, metalinguistic understanding is fundamentally about language and textual choices, and being able to recognise the subtle ways different language choices evoke meaning in different ways. This would include reflection on the appropriacy of imagery used, the connotations of vocabulary choices, and the shaping of sentences, clauses, paragraphs and texts. So metalinguistic understanding does not have to involve discussion of grammar, but it often does.

Although the idea of grammar being important in the teaching of writing is traditionally seen as a *sine qua non*, since obviously writing needs to be grammatically accurate, you will be aware that it is a hugely controversial topic. We will not discuss this debate here as it has been much discussed elsewhere (Hudson, 2004; Locke, 2009; Myhill, 2021), but a focus on grammar solely for accuracy misses the rich potential of grammar in enabling developing writers to understand the implications of their language choices on how they relate to their readers and express their ideas. A growing body of international research, including our own, is showing that teaching students about language choices – in other words, facilitating their meta-linguistic understanding of writing – serves to develop their thinking about writing, being a writer, and authorial decision-making (Myhill et al., 2012; Macken-Horarik et al., 2015; Denham, 2020). This is not about formulaic teaching of what grammatical forms should be in a piece of writing in order to achieve good marks, but in generating understanding of the possibilities and effects of different choices. Or put another way, we are less interested in whether students use fronted adverbials, than whether students understand and can articulate what a fronted adverbial might be accomplishing in a particular sentence.

Common to this more recent research addressing grammar as a creative tool for meaning-making is reinforcing the symbiotic relationship between reading and writing, and between being a reader and being a writer. An active reader 'reads what the writer is doing. The active reader reconstructs the overall design, both the writer's purpose and the techniques used to realize that purpose' (Bazerman, 2010, p. 104). So reading is not simply about ideas but also about how the writer has expressed those ideas, and how we as readers respond to them. Although this might be viewed as a reading skill, it draws on our experiences as a writer: indeed, Smith (1983, p. 565) maintained that 'to read like writers they must see themselves as writers'. Consequently, teaching writing through the lens of metalinguistic understanding involves exploring how published texts are communicating to readers (Humphrey et al., 2012), using these texts as mentor texts (Dorfman and Capelli, 2017; Myhill, 2018), and reading and discussing students' own writing from the perspective of a reader.

Using texts, both published and students' own writing, opens up the possibility for close analysis of the language choices made by the author in relation to a particular writing goal, such as creating a character, developing an emotive argument, or explaining information clearly. This close analysis is best achieved through dialogic talk, as discussed in Chapter 3, which is exploratory and allows space for subjective responses, but sharply oriented to the ways different language choices can create different effects (Myhill and Newman, 2016; Watson and Newman, 2017; Newman and Watson, 2020). To illustrate this, look at the text examples below. In both cases, the first is taken from Michael Morpurgo's children's story, *Arthur, High King of Britain*, and the second is an alternative re-arrangement:

a. *Her fingers, long, white and dancing…*

b. *Her long, white and dancing fingers…*

a. *In the doorway stood a huge knight, his armour the colour of flaming fire, his beard a burning gold.*

b. *A huge knight, his armour the colour of flaming fire, his beard a burning gold, stood in the doorway.*

In both cases, the language is grammatically accurate, so dialogic discussion might focus on how in the first one the position of the adjectives after the noun draws attention to this description of what her fingers were like; and in the second, dialogic discussion might explore how moving the adverbial from the front of the sentence to the back alters what is foregrounded, or how the subject-verb reversal in the first example makes the reader wait to discover what is standing in the doorway, creating anticipation and perhaps suspense. Approaching the teaching of writing in this way, with close attention to examples in texts and how they establish meaning, supported by rich dialogic talk helps to develop metalinguistic understanding for writing, 'explicit knowledge about language that can be brought to conscious awareness, articulated, and used reflexively as a cognitive tool to construct knowledge about language' (Gebhard et al., 2014, p. 107).

HANDWRITING AND SPELLING

We conclude this section outlining the research on effective practices to improve students' writing by considering handwriting and spelling, aspects of writing which are often overlooked in terms of proactive classroom strategies to support improvement. One important skill which underpins development in writing is writing fluency – that is, the capacity to write legibly with accuracy and speed. Teachers in Early Years settings or Key Stage 1 will be very aware of the effort that young writers have to invest in handwriting – securing the fine motor skills that allow them to manipulate a pencil, shape letters and write in straight lines, at the same time as generating the words and sentences needed to express ideas in written form. Children who do not gain this writing fluency face a real challenge as they mature as writers because they expend so much mental effort on the act of getting words onto the page. As a consequence, they have little capacity for thinking about composition or revision. For secondary school teachers, it is worth considering the writing fluency of those children who seem to struggle most with writing: this is not an issue exclusively for younger writers, but writing fluency in secondary schools is rarely addressed.

Research, however, does suggest that focused interventions to support writing fluency can be successful, and typically these interventions involve explicit writing instruction (Santangelo and Graham, 2016) and opportunities to practise. The EEF Guidance report for Key Stage 2 (2021a) recommends that teachers 'monitor pupils' handwriting to ensure accurate letter formation habits, providing effective feedback to promote efficient and fluent handwriting'. The research also shows that teaching strategies which help to secure writing fluency have beneficial impacts on other aspects of writing. Zemlock et al. (2018) found an inter-relationship between developing handwriting and knowledge of letters; Limpo et al. (2018) found that a handwriting fluency intervention had additional benefits on writing composition and how good students felt about themselves as writers; and Graham et al. (2018) developed an intervention for students falling behind their peers which was successful in addressing handwriting and spelling together.

Indeed, handwriting and spelling are perhaps surprisingly inter-related (Caravolas et al., 2020): in practice, they co-occur as we simultaneously manage the decision about what letters comprise a given word and the act of shaping those letters. The first is a cognitive process, whereas the second is a psychomotor process (another reminder of the complexity of the act of writing). It is easier to handwrite fluently if spelling is proficient, but also if handwriting is fluent, spelling can be automatised. Most mature writers do not consciously think about spelling as they write, unless they hit a 'problem' spelling, and even young children quickly automatise the movements to spell their own name and common sight words. So improving spelling and improving handwriting are mutually supportive.

Teaching spelling is largely dependent on understanding spelling development and how students learn spelling. It is a linguistic skill (Robinson-Kooi and Hammond, 2020) needing understanding of phoneme-grapheme correspondences and of morphology (how words are built), and in the case of English especially, recognition of the irregularity of English spelling. But it is also a visual skill, including both the ability to visually discriminate between letters and notice patterns and visual memory. And there is an element of memorisation involved, particularly with irregular spellings. Spelling development tends to proceed in a series of stages from initial *pre-communicative* mark-making, through to *phonetic* spelling which draws only on phonological knowledge, through to *transitional* spelling, where there is greater awareness of morphology, word families and irregular words until the final stage of *correct* spelling (Gentry, 1982). Because students are likely to be at different stages in this developmental trajectory, and because they may have strong visual skills but poor linguistics skills, or vice versa, the teaching of spelling needs to be differentiated to match learners' needs. In a study of the effectiveness of different kinds of spelling strategies, McCurdy et al. (2016) found that different spelling interventions benefitted different students, a finding which is likely to reflect the learners' differing needs.

CRITICAL QUESTIONS

- How does what you have read here (about the craft of writing, metacognition and self-regulation, metalinguistic understanding, and spelling and handwriting) chime with your own professional observations in the classroom?

- Why do you think reading research seems to be prioritised over writing research?

IN THE CLASSROOM

The summary of research above is perhaps, first and foremost, a reminder of just what a challenge the act of writing is, in terms of the physical, cognitive, linguistic and social demands it makes. And one area that we have not addressed is motivation – unless we feel motivated to write, it is very hard to engage with the complex demands of writing. For students who have a low sense of competence as writers, motivation can be particularly poor and writing seen as a pointless and boring activity. The realities in many classrooms will be that learners may not be particularly interested in handwriting or spelling practice, or in revising their writing, or in writing a story. So in the sections which follow, we try to pick up on the findings from research about effective strategies for teaching writing but in ways which attempt to create space for enjoyment and engagement in writing and being a writer.

CRAFTING AND CREATING

Writing, at its heart, is fundamentally a creative act – and not just when it is 'creative' writing. Constructing a convincing argument, explaining a concept, reflecting on your experiences, and even more transactional tasks such as writing an email to complain, all require creative thinking about message and audience and purpose. They also require creative thinking about how to craft the text in terms of structure, layout and language choices. Every piece of writing (even my shopping list!) is a unique combination of words. It is important, therefore, that the writing classroom is established as a community of writers sharing in this process of crafting and creating. As a teacher, you are central to this as a writer yourself – a teacher who writes as well as a teacher who teaches writing. Brandt (2019) argues that teaching writing needs 'teachers who are not custodians of the canon and not even model readers, but rather practicing, engaged writers, teachers who participate in the craft of writing and can perform and demonstrate it to students' (p. 45) because this allows them to 'expose the writing act for what it is: messy, difficult, multi-faceted, and in need of a writer's full engagement' (p. 46).

Clear evidence for a direct benefit on writing outcomes from teachers being writers themselves is inconclusive, including in our own research (Cremin and Oliver, 2017; Cremin et al., 2020), but we have conducted two research projects with Arvon, a creative writing charity, which focused on giving teachers an intensive residential writing experience, and transferring their learning into how they teach writing. One striking effect of these projects was the strong effect it had on students' enjoyment of and engagement with writing – the voices below in Figure 6.1 represent some of the students' reflections on what they had enjoyed about the project.

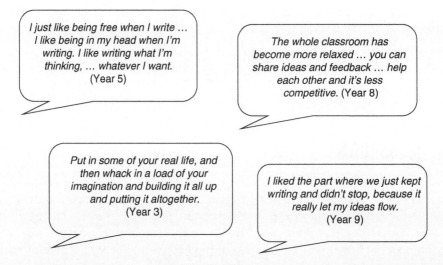

Figure 6.1   Student reflections

You might like to try some of the teaching strategies which generated this increase in motivation and enjoyment. They include:

- **Just Write**: this is freewriting, where you just write, without evaluation, for a burst of time letting your ideas flow onto the page. It is a strategy for generating ideas and thoughts, which can later be developed into a piece of writing, or not. This writing is not assessed.

- **Writing Notebooks/Messy Books**: the teachers distinguished between the notebooks which could be messy and more formal writing which is likely to be published or assessed.

- **Starting Points for Writing**: using starting points for writing which were varied and engaged the imagination, using artefacts, images, one-line starters, the outdoors…

- **Writing Together**: the teacher wrote while the children wrote and shared her writing or work-in-progress with students.

- **Sharing Writing**: the teachers created frequent opportunities for sharing each other's writing, including the teachers' own writing, and for reflective and critical comment.

- **Publishing Writing**: the teachers found ways to give the students' writing an audience through publishing, including for example, creating an anthology, publishing on a website, creating a display of writing in school, creating a booklet to send home to parents.

ACTION POINT

- Download and read the Resource Pack from the *Teachers as Writers* projects at http://social-sciences.exeter.ac.uk/education/research/centres/writing/grammar-teacher-resources/crea-tivewriting/.

- Plan a writing lesson which draws on one or more of the Craft of Writing Framework strands.

- Look at the Starting Points for Writing, and test some out with your class, adapting them to suit their needs and interests.

- Test out some of the strategies used by the project teachers, listed above, in your own classroom, and consider embedding these routinely into your practice.

GOING META

Given the evidence that metacognition in general, and metacognition related to writing in particular, seem to be beneficial for students' learning, it makes sense to consider how your teaching of writing creates space for metacognitive thinking, and for self-regulation. In other words, are you giving children the strategies they need to develop as writers? One reason that 'Writing Process' became a strand of the *Craft of Writing Framework* was because our interviews with professional writers on the *Teachers as Writers* project had highlighted how acutely aware of their own writing processes, and the strategies they used to write successfully. The volume of research on Self-Regulated Strategy Development (SRSD) certainly suggests it is worth trying in the classroom as a way to heighten metacognitive knowledge and the use of appropriate strategies. This approach is not restricted to older writers – working with 5- to 7-year-olds, we created a poster to support these emergent and developing writers in thinking strategically about their writing (Fisher et al. 2010, p. xii). For example, to encourage the use of oral rehearsal to hear 'written' text before committing it to paper, we had a speech bubble which said 'Say it, write it', with a reflective question underneath: 'What does my writing sound like?' The young children involved were well able to use our poster, with teacher scaffolding, to support their emergent writing. Table 6.1 below takes the seven recommendations from the EEF (2018) Guidance Report on metacognition, and gives examples which apply this to writing.

Table 6.1   Metacognition exemplified in the writing classroom

General recommendation	Example for teaching writing
Teachers should acquire the professional understanding and skills to develop their pupils' metacognitive knowledge	Reflect on yourself as a writer and the strategies that you use to manage your own writing process; and find out more about SRSD strategies.
Explicitly teach pupils metacognitive strategies, including how to plan, monitor and evaluate their learning	Teach students to pause regularly as they write to re-read what they have written, sometimes just the paragraph they are writing, sometimes the whole text.
Model your own thinking to help pupils develop their metacognitive and cognitive skills	Model how you respond to a writing task, and think about what the task is asking you to do, for what purpose, and for which audience.
Set an appropriate level of challenge to develop pupils' self-regulation and metacognition	For a class struggling with writing coherent arguments, use a graphic organiser to introduce students to a strategy for gathering points and evidence before writing an argument.
Promote and develop metacognitive talk in the classroom	Use the think, pair and share strategy to explore what students know about writing information texts.
Explicitly teach pupils how to organise, and effectively manage, their learning independently	When beginning a particular writing task, work collaboratively with the class to create a timeplan through to completion, with discrete manageable stages.
Schools should support teachers to develop their knowledge of these approaches and expect them to be applied appropriately	Consider whether as a school or an English department you might benefit from specific professional development on SRSD in writing.

In tandem with heightening attention to self-regulation in your writing lessons, you might complement this with an emphasis on metalinguistic understanding, drawing on our research on grammar as choice. We have generated, and refined over successive studies, a set of pedagogical principles (LEAD principles) to inform planning and teaching of writing, which embeds grammar purposefully. These are outlined below:

The **LEAD** Principles

Link	Make a link between the grammar being introduced and how it works in the writing being taught
Example	Explain the grammar through examples, not lengthy explanations
Authentic text	Use examples from authentic texts to links writers to the broader community of writers
Discussion	Build in dialogic metalinguistic discussion about grammar and its effects

Over our successive studies, we have been able to evidence the efficacy of this approach (Myhill et al., 2012, 2018), but also to understand how different ways it is implemented can limit or enhance its effectiveness, particularly in relation teachers' grammatical subject knowledge (Myhill et al., 2013) and teacher management of metalinguistic talk (Myhill and Newman, 2016; Watson and Newman, 2017; Newman and Watson, 2020). An EEF evaluation at scale (Tracey et al., 2019) which did not find an impact on writing outcomes also highlighted lesser teacher confidence with metalinguistic talk. In the classroom example below, discussion is embedded through the lesson, and bold print is used to highlight where the teaching draws on a LEAD principle.

A Classroom Example, using the LEAD Principles.

Writing context:	Persuasive writing
Learning focus:	Creating an emotional hook as a persuasive opening
Grammar link:	The use of present tense to create a sense of immediacy and heighten the emotion; the choice of descriptions which make the reader sympathise with the tiger family.
Focus text:	From a World Wildlife Fund campaign leaflet (**AUTHENTIC TEXT**)

Inside the forest, a majestic tiger stirs. Stretching and yawning, she emerges from her resting place and pads silently down to the riverbank to drink. Her two young cubs follow, wrestling each other in a stripey tumble as they reach the water's edge. A pair of sarus cranes take flight at the sudden disturbance.

Dusk falls. The tiger is hungry. Days ago she killed a cow and dragged its carcass to a hiding-place. Tonight she will return, unaware that angry villagers have found and poisoned it, in fear of any further attacks. This tiger is about to eat her last meal.

Introduction:	*(Whole class).* Briefly share what students know about tigers and where they live. Read the opening two paragraphs of the text, and as a whole class **discuss** how it makes them feel. What do they think of the tiger? What is going to happen next?
Development:	*(In pairs).* Read the paragraphs again and **discuss** together how the writer tries to make us sympathetic to the tiger **(LINK)**. Highlight in colour the descriptions which make us feel like this (**EXAMPLES**).
	(Whole class). The teacher takes feedback from the pairs, collating their ideas as annotations round the two paragraphs. (Draw out: *a majestic tiger; her two young cubs*; the tiger is at ease in her world, *'stretching and yawning'*, padding silently. The cubs are playful *'wrestling…in a stripey tumble'*.) (**EXAMPLES**)

(Continued)

(Continued)

	(Individual). The teacher asks students to think on their own for one minute about why the writer might have chosen to include the cubs in this text. Hear students' thoughts as a buzz session (everyone quickly shares their thoughts) with no comment on answers. **(LINK)**
	(Whole class). The teacher shows the text with all the present tense verbs highlighted in colour (**EXAMPLES**), and then reads the two paragraphs aloud – once as written, and then in the past tense. Invite table group **discussion** of why the writer might have chosen to write this in present tense rather than as a narrative past tense **(LINK)**. (Draw out – the present tense creates a sense of immediacy, that this is happening now; we are viewers of this scene, drawn into the story as it unfolds; does it make us feel we could intervene to stop the tiger eating the poisoned meat?)
Plenary:	*(Whole class).* Consolidate the learning – ask students to jot down quickly what they have learned in today's lesson about writing a persuasive opening. Hear a selection of responses, and explain that one choice writers sometimes make is to begin a persuasive text with an emotional appeal to the reader, before moving on to the logical argument. In this text, the writer does this by using present tense to create a sense of immediacy and heighten the emotion; and choosing descriptions which make us sympathise with the tiger family.

REFLECTION POINT

Because the teaching of writing is comprised of a number of different elements including, for example, composition and the writing process, self-regulation strategies, spelling, different written forms and genres, and grammar, it makes a high demand on teacher subject knowledge. Reflect on the strength of your own subject knowledge using the prompts below to stimulate your reflection.

- Knowledge of the writing process: planning; drafting, reviewing and its non-linear, recursive nature;

- Knowledge of the phonology and morphology related to spelling: spelling patterns; how children's spelling develops; teaching strategies to support learning spelling;

- Knowledge of metacognition and self-regulation: self-regulation strategies for writing;

- Knowledge of grammar: knowledge of how grammatical choices shape meaning in different texts.

CONCLUSION

What is evident from the points discussed in this chapter is that there is an urgent need for more research which directly considers the needs and characteristics of socially disadvantaged learners as writers. At the same time, the review of research also highlights that evidence of effective practices for teaching writing is often inconclusive, particularly when evaluated at scale. This may be because writing is such a complex skill that clear-cut 'best practice' is elusive. A study focusing on spelling, or creative writing, or self-regulation strategies is always focusing in one aspect, and thus not looking at other aspects of writing; but it is not really possible to design rigorous intervention studies which include all aspects. But it may also be a reminder that every teacher and every classroom is unique, and the real skill in teaching writing well is strong subject knowledge which allows you to select the appropriate approach for your students.

At the same time, there do seem to be two cross-cutting, recurrent themes in the research. Firstly, there is a clear role for both explicit instruction and targeted intervention in the teaching of writing, making sure that we are precise and clear about the process of composing – managing the recursive skills of planning, drafting and reviewing; and that we are clear about the written text itself – the expectations of the genre, how language and imagery choices evoke meaning, and audience and purpose. Secondly, this direct instruction needs to be grounded within a classroom where there is a positive and vibrant sense of community as writers, which encourages enjoyment in writing and being a writer, which creates space for students' own choices as writers and allows them to grow as agentic, engaged and independent authors.

7
ENRICHING LITERACY WITH DIGITAL RESOURCES

INTRODUCTION

It is well documented that the contexts within which children become literate extend beyond classrooms and involve more than paper-based books and resources (Hull and Schultz, 2001; Dyson, 2018). Children's literacies – and the skills and attitudes that form and inform them – develop in relation to the full range of social and cultural experiences and resources with which they engage. As scholars of the New Literacy Studies argue, literacies are plural practices (Street, 2001, p. 11). This means that opportunities to become literate will vary for learners, despite the provision of standardised curricula and access to formal education. Increasingly, these opportunities involve digital resources (Ofcom, 2021), both in and beyond educational settings.

Burnett first reviewed the research literature on digital technologies in literacy contexts between 2003 and 2009, to identify three main areas of research:

- How technology is used as deliverer of literacy (teacher-led, to develop literacy skills);

- How technology impacts interaction around texts (focusing on the talk and collaboration afforded);

- How technology serves as a medium for meaning-making (involving the comprehension and creation of digital textual forms)

(Burnett, 2010, p. 254).

As digital resources and possibilities for their use have evolved, research orientations have developed to be more far-reaching. Topics include the affordances of the resources; considerations of how digital resources impact the processes of reading and writing/text-making; the role of the teacher while working with digital resources; and considerations of the learner, where attainment and engagement in reading and writing activities, access, equity and inequity are explored. An associated strand involves issues of safety and criticality, where for all children, the skills deemed necessary for engaging in digital contexts safely continues to be a subject of research interest.

This chapter will consider how you might acknowledge the role of digital resources in children's literacy learning, and how they can be used to complement and enrich your classroom literacy practice, in order to fruitfully build on the expansive 'communication repertoires' (Burnett and Merchant, 2018, p. 2) that young literacy learners bring to their formal education. In order to do this, an understanding of issues relating to children's access to and experiences with digital resources, along with a sense of existing perspectives about the use of digital resources to promote literacy learning, for all children, needs to be established.

UNDERSTANDING THE RESEARCH

DIGITAL LITERACY, DIGITAL LITERACIES AND LITERACY WITH DIGITAL RESOURCES

The terminology involved in a consideration of how digital resources can promote literacy is complex. The term 'digital literacy' is an overarching, all-encompassing term, that is used in many developmental frameworks that aim to promote specific digital skills and ways of 'being digital' in a digital communication landscape. A good example is the UNESCO *Global Framework of Reference on Digital Literacy Skills* (DLGF) (2018), which outlines competences relating to a broad range of areas including information and data literacy, communication and collaboration, digital content creation, safety and problem-solving. The 'literacy' processes of reading and writing are invoked by this document, but are not explicitly articulated.

From a literacy perspective, Sefton-Green et al. (2016, p. 15) define digital literacy as 'a social practice that involves reading, writing and multimodal meaning-making through the use of a range of technologies'. This definition clearly expands understandings of literacy beyond the acts of reading and writing, as outlined in the national curriculum English Programmes of Study (DfE, 2014); and reflects the diverse and changing multiple practices of learners with digital resources (Lankshear and Knobel, 2015, p. 12). Accordingly, the plural form 'digital literacies' allows the full diversity of children's experiences, where their skills and techniques for reading and writing are embedded in diverse sites of social practices, to be accepted. These may involve accessing a story or phonics game using a phone, tablet, e-reader or traditional storybook; they might involve contributing to a fan-fiction website, a wiki or writing in an exercise book; or they may involve writing for a class blog, making a TikTok video, or writing a formal letter of complaint.

The term 'digital literacies' is therefore more useful when considering the range of reading and writing opportunities available to children today. It is grounded in the theoretical frame offered by the new literacies studies and multiliteracies pedagogy (New London Group, 1996; Cope and Kalantzis, 2009). Current research involves accounts of the impact of digital texts and digitally mediated communication on literacy practices, and the responsive pedagogies being developed as a result of them. These accounts are often aligned with an increased recognition of the place of multimodality in contemporary communication (Kress, 2010) as afforded especially by the use of the screen for reading and writing, in children's literacy; and the opportunities to make connections to children's playful and informal literacies that take place beyond as well as within the school context. For an example of the early work in this area, see Carrington and Robinson (2009), or more recently, accounts of the use of new media in the classroom (Burnett and Merchant, 2018; Erstad et al., 2020; Dowdall and Burnett, 2021). In these volumes, examples of how creative teachers integrate children's every day and digitally mediated experiences with digital resources to acknowledge literacies in their widest sense are presented. As Burnett and Merchant articulate, access to digital resources facilitates new possibilities for meaning making, broadening a child's 'communication repertoire' and involving 'creative, collaborative and experimental meaning making' (2018, p. 2). In this chapter, this pluralistic and expansive view is adopted to explore the possibilities for literacy with digital resources.

ACCESS TO DIGITAL RESOURCES

A key issue for educators is the issue of enabling access to resources that will support literacy development. We know that children use digital resources prolifically, beyond the classroom. As the most recent Ofcom survey of children and parents' media use shows, nearly all children in England went online in 2020, with seven in ten (of these children) using laptops, tablets and mobile devices. However, we also know that while these data imply that online access is a possibility for most learners, children's experiences in relation to digital resources cannot be described as 'equitable', particularly in relation to literacy learning. In their survey, Ofcom found that despite targeted support from the Department for Education (2021), one in five children did not have access to an appropriate device to support home-schooling; and that two per cent of school age children relied on a smart phone alone to access the internet during the first COVID lockdown (Ofcom, 2021, p. 2).

For educators, this inequity of access is concerning and significant. As the Children's Commissioner for England [CCE] recently reported, access to good quality devices is a necessity for play, socialising and learning, facilitating engagement with educational public resources, such as the Oak National Academy and BBC Bitesize, however this may not be equally accessible to all (2020). This view has intensified during the recent lockdown period, with observations about disadvantaged children's access to digital resources and their relatively low attainment being made. According to the Primary Literacy Research Collective [PLRC] rapid review briefing paper (2021), the Education Endowment Fund has noted that this group of children have achieved less well in standardised reading test scores, than their more 'advantaged' peers. However, as well as observing that that these claims have not been systematically reviewed, the PLRC noted some positive accounts of children's literacy learning at this time of school closure, where children were observed to write for expression and read for pleasure, with and without access to digital resources (Clark et al., 2020; Clark and Picton, 2020). This is an important observation as it moderates the claim that children without access are automatically disadvantaged in their literacy learning.

This brief introduction therefore seeks to make it clear that access to digital resources is a complex topic that may not simply correlate with higher literacy attainment. Well-worn phrases such as the 'Digital Divide' set up binaries that oversimplify the complex issues around access to literacy learning in a digital world. This situation has been neatly theorised by Talaee and Noroozi (2019) who claim that we should move beyond simplified understandings of a relationship between access and life chances to argue that the *'social envelope'* that surrounds learners is more important (p. 33). This means that while some children have access to digital resources, the family's use of these resources (e.g. the way that a smartphone is used to communicate) is as important as the access itself, to educational success. Their view aligns with Rizk and Davies (2021) who describe a second digital divide, where differences in the *nature* of engagement with digital resources and contingent implications for learning, rather than access alone, are recognised.

Rizk and Davies take a positive view about the use of digital resources, proposing that they can bridge the reported engagement gap for learners with varying Socio-Economic Status (SES) (2021, p. 1). They argue that while engagement and attainment overall has been correlated with access to print literacy practices in the home and school, the introduction of digital resources can lessen the engagement 'gap' traditionally associated with literacies involving print literacy. Their study spanning 10 Ontario School Boards in Canada involving learners from Kindergarten to Grade 8 found no marked difference in the engagement of children from a range of SES backgrounds, when digital resources were introduced, supporting the notion that the use of digital resources may help to balance opportunities for engagement – and therefore learning.

Educators have long been working with the notion that children are 'growing up' digital (Palfrey and Gasser, 2008). Current initiatives in this area continue to research, promote and protect the rights of children in a digital world – see, for example, in Australia, *The Centre of Excellence for the Digital Child* and in the United Kingdom, the Children's Commissioner's project *Growing Up Digital*. Along with issues of access to and use of digital resources, this notion of 'being digital' is a concept that needs continual recalibration, as the resources that educators and learners have access to continually change and develop (Sefton-Green et al., 2016, p. 1). Educators and learners are not 'digital beings' in a static sense. This is evident if we think about how educators have had to adapt their practice to introduce tablet technology in the last 10 years, and how this may vary from one educator to another. Moving forward, it is clear that newer technologies, for example, Virtual Reality headsets, will impact classroom practice and involve the need for new teacher expertise. Introducing new digital resources into classroom pedagogies is an ongoing challenge for teachers, and the need for proper teacher support has been noted (Children's Commissioner, 2020). It cannot be presumed that all children experience the same opportunities to learn be literate with digital resources; or that all teachers are equally confident to work with them, as they evolve (Picton, 2019). Based on all of these observations, it is evident that children are likely to be inducted variously into a range of ways of being literate with digital resources by their families, caregivers, teachers and wider social networks. Consequently there will be implications for their formal literacy learning.

For educators, digital literacies are practices that can work with and beyond formal education, and that can enrich and evolve the possibilities for curricula, pedagogy and classroom practice. These practices involve possessing the knowledge and skills required to participate in a society that is mediated increasingly digitally. Formal literacy education can involve digital resources and digitally mediated ways of communicating, along with paper- and print-orientated practices. It is to the idea of literacy with digital resources that we now turn.

DIGITAL RESOURCES FOR LITERACY LEARNING IN SCHOOLS AND PRE-SCHOOLS

Teachers have always had to work with the resources available to them and these resources have changed along with policy and technological developments. The National Literacy Trust recently surveyed over 200 teachers to identify their formal technology use (Picton, 2019) and noted the following items:

- Ipads
- Laptops
- Desktop computers
- Tablets
- Chromebooks
- (Bring your) own device (BYOD)
- e-readers, e.g. Kindle and Kobo
- VR headsets

Clearly, this list is not comprehensive, and is context specific; however, it reflects the range of hardware widely available, and illustrates that there may be marked differences between the types of hardware that can be accessed by teachers and learners of different ages and stages. For example, it may be common practice in some settings for learners to use personal (BYOD) phones to research a website nominated by the teacher; while in others, children may share a small number of tablets, under the control of the teacher to play a phonics game, or read a digital version of a storybook. Overall, Picton's survey reports that access to contemporary hardware in UK classrooms (tablets, laptops and desk top computers) remains surprisingly low, with less than 50% of the surveyed teachers agreeing that learners had access to these resources. Only 43.8% of the teachers agreed that they used technology regularly to support literacy, and 20.1% said they rarely or never used technology for this purpose (Picton, 2019, p. 4). This is clearly likely to have changed given the recent pandemic situation, with teachers' access to resources and pedagogies having developed at pace and out of necessity, during this time. Nevertheless, more recent data indicate that equity of access to literacy learning involving digital resources in formal settings cannot be assured.

Along with this list of hardware, teachers are likely to have access to a whole plethora of free and commercially available software. These may be provided by a setting and mandated for use, or accessed by individual teachers to support their own aims and learners' needs. These software have developed exponentially, given the pandemic situation, to include charitable 'resource hubs' (see Oak National Academy website), that provide wholescale didactic curriculum, planning and associated resources for literacy (and all other curriculum areas). Equally, commercial software may be acquired by settings at an institutional level to support professional teaching activities (assessment, record keeping, behaviour tracking), for example, *Accelerated Reader*. Individual teachers may also access everyday websites and screen-based texts, including YouTube videos, podcasts, and social media platforms and any other multimodal textual form that can be used for reading, writing and communication practices. These may include digital resources from public service and independent broadcasters with an educational remit (e.g. BBC programmes designed to promote early reading, such as *CBeebies Alphablocks*); as well as independently produced and curated 'freely' available educational YouTube channels (e.g. *Mr Thorne's Phonics channel, with Geraldine the Giraffe*). What is significant is that all these different forms of software have the potential to impact literacy education as spaces for online reading, storytelling and composition activities (Dowdall, 2020). Teachers may also use web-based digital adaptations of established resources, such as 'read-alouds' of children's classic books, that are freely available on YouTube (see *The Very Hungry Caterpillar* with over 160 million views); or the commercial editions of digital story toys and read-alongs, that are based on original print versions of texts (Dowdall and Burnett, 2021).

In contrast to these digital adaptations, Kucirkova et al. (2016) consider digital books to be a special type of resource, 'encompassing the various kinds of digital texts available for young readers, including ebooks, ibooks, storyapps, bookapps and LeapReader books' (p. 68). Digital books commonly share features of interactivity, including hyperlinks or the possibility of customised reading. In this way, they differ from digital versions of stories, or audiobooks that are simply narrated and presented for readers to listen to, watch or read along with.

CRITICAL QUESTIONS

- What are the literacy practices you want to enrich with digital resources?
- Where and when can these enriched literacy practices happen?
- What do you need to be able to introduce digital resources?
- What aspects of your literacy pedagogy can be enriched with digital resources?
- How can children's critical digital literacy and safe practice be ensured?
- What are the barriers that may prevent the introduction of digital resources to promote literacy learning?

IN THE CLASSROOM

PEDAGOGIES FOR LITERACY TEACHING AND LEARNING WITH DIGITAL RESOURCES

Along with access to a wide range of hardware and software that can be adopted for literacy education, teachers have access to a range of evolving recommendations for working with digital resources and developing literacy pedagogy. Nearly 20 years ago, the Qualifications and Curriculum Authority (QCA) developed materials entitled *More than Words* to promote approaches to reading and writing that involved multimodal understanding of how image, screen, sound and movement work in picture book and film texts (2004, 2005). Key ideas from these materials have more recently been articulated to promote the incorporation of multimodal texts into literacy pedagogy (Bearne and Reedy, 2018). In these recommendations, the processes of reading on screen and with film, and composing in screen-based multimodal environments, are described in relation to the development of narrative understanding, navigation pathways and handling skills; along with awareness of different modes, content, structure and the use of technical features for effect that are required. These ideas are not new. Researchers and educators have long advocated for the introduction of multimodal pedagogies and digital resources to literacy pedagogy (Bearne and Wolstencroft, 2007; Bulman, 2017; Burnett and Merchant, 2018; Carrington and Robinson, 2009). Their work aligns with that of subject associations such as the United Kingdom Literacy Association (UKLA), and commercial and charitable organisations, (including the British Film Institute and The Literacy Shed), who provide free and paid for online resources to support literacy educators to work with digital resources.

Bhojwani and Wilkie (2018) have particularly explored the use of digital and multi-modal resources with a group of children recognised as 'disadvantaged' (looked after children), in relation to their literacies. In their account they present the '**SWIM**' diagram as a tool to support learners to consider how four modes interplay in texts as a way of building critical analysis of how multi-modal texts are composed and communicate meaning (2018, p. 14).

- **S**ound

- **W**riting

- **I**mage and

- **M**ovement

They present a teaching sequence that moves through five stages (2018, p. 16) of *discovery, exploration, responding and analysis, developing and transposing, creating and translating*. This stage-model echoes the integrated model for planning children's progression from reading into writing originally articulated in Bearne (2002) and adopted by the Primary National Strategy in 2004 as presented in the UKLA publication (2004), *Raising Boys' Achievements in Writing*. Common to these models are a practical approach to text analysis and subsequent production, where digital technologies mediate traditional paper-based reading and writing processes and familiar screen-based materials. In this way, learners engage in digital literacy practices which are inclusive and engaging. This is exemplified in the classroom example below, where children collaborate in digital story-making.

A CLASSROOM EXAMPLE

In a year one classroom, a teacher uses a school edition of an app called *Puppet Pals* to scaffold the children as they learn to recount the well-loved story *Owl Babies*. Using a tablet, the teacher photographs and imports some key images from the picture book into the app, creating a silent cartoon-style version of the story. Having read and enjoyed the picture book in small teaching groups with their teacher, the children take it in turns to recount the story using the cartoon of images in the app to help them recall the events. As they take turns to narrate their own version of the story to accompany the screen-based images, they are recorded in the app, creating a new, collaborative multi-modal and digital version of the story. The engagement and delight of the children is captured in the digital recording, as they take control of the composing practice. The app frees the children to focus on recalling the events and to enter the role of the narrator, without being hampered by the transcriptional demands that a paper-based composing activity would require.

The teacher explains how this activity promotes their children's independence and confidence as authors. Children experience success as story makers, using the original text from their memory of the shared reading from the story book – but also embellishing and adapting the text providing evidence of their sophisticated understandings of the story and the owl babies' characters. The children delight in watching their digital version back, providing opportunities for discussion and learning about many strands of their literacy: their understanding of the story; their vocabulary choices, the use of their spoken language and performance. Their digital texts can be shared with parents, and also re-viewed by the teacher as they assess the children's development as readers and writers.

(Bulman et al., n.d.)

Working internationally, Burnett and Merchant (2018) have built on the work of scholars to articulate *The Charter for 21st Century Literacies*. This Charter aims to expand understandings of children's literacies beyond curricula that foregrounds print and text. Its aim is to support learners' confident and discerning engagement with the new media forms that they will encounter in their everyday lives. As such, it is a far reach from the skills-based, print-orientated curriculum (DfE, 2014) that teachers in England currently work with. *The Charter for 21st Century Literacies* includes nine principles for educators, arguing that they should:

- *Acknowledge the changing nature of meaning making*

- *Recognise and build on children's linguistic, social and cultural repertoires*

- *Acknowledge diverse modes and media*

- *Recognise the affective, embodied and material dimensions of meaning making*

- *Encourage improvisation and meaning making*

- *Use playful pedagogies*

- *Create opportunities to work with the provisionality of digital media*

- *Provide contexts that facilitate criticality*

- *Promote collaboration around and through texts in negotiating meaning.*

(Burnett and Merchant, 2018, pp. 3–5)

What these principles and previous examples illustrate is that educators have a range of opportunities for introducing new media and digital resources into their practice, and while support for teachers to enrich children's literacy learning and communicative practices with digital resources exists, it has not been consistently mandated in policy for literacy (Dowdall and Burnett, 2021, p. 8). This has implications for the development of pedagogy and supportive professional development, and may offer you a helpful way to think about the extent to which you are encouraged and supported to incorporate digital resources into your teaching of literacy.

ACTION POINT

- Consider your literacy curriculum. How fully does it reflect the possibilities for digital resources in communication, reading and writing?

- Read the UNESCO Digital Literacy Global Framework (DLGF) (2018), noting implications for your own literacy curriculum.

- Consider the features of three digital resources, e.g. an app, a website and an ebook. Compare making meaning with these resources to the skills involved in reading and writing in more traditional print-based formats.

TEACHERS' KNOWLEDGE

Your own proficiency with digital resources for literacy learning is likely to be variable, despite the turn to technology necessitated by the pandemic. Winter et al. (2021) recently surveyed 38 teachers in Ireland about their use of technology and the impact of COVID-19. They found that while many used technology skilfully, some still lacked confidence and avoided using it; calling for further in-school training and support. In 2006, Mishra and Koehler, building on Shulman's articulation of teacher 'pedagogic content knowledge', outlined the *Technological Pedagogical Content Knowledge* (TPCK) framework to support educators to integrate technological knowledge with pedagogical and content knowledge, noting the complexity of this challenge and the situated and dynamic nature of it (Mishra and Koehler, 2006, p. 1021). The (now named) TPACK framework has been cited as a useful tool for noting individual capabilities with technology (Stoilescu, 2015). However, it has also been the subject of much criticism (Mishra, 2019), with Mishra calling for the addition of contextual knowledge to the frame, and other researchers noting that it is not practically useful (Willermark, 2018). These challenges strengthen observations that the introduction of digital resources into literacy education is neither simple, nor straightforward. It is not a question of simply providing access to new resources and requiring educators to adjust their planning accordingly. Account has to be taken of statutory requirements in the light of the affordances of the new technologies, the variation in access to hardware and software, the implementation of local policy, the variable requirements and experiences of the learners and the confidence and expertise of the educators. It also requires educators to consider what children's literacy is, what it involves, where it can be done, and who it can be done with, reminding us that for children labelled as 'disadvantaged', this disadvantage may extend to their opportunities to become fully literate in the digital contexts of the 21st century.

READING WITH DIGITAL RESOURCES

Tablet technology has been widely introduced into educational settings in industrialised and less 'developed' countries to impact learning (Truncano, 2015). A strong body of literacy research investigates reading with tablets, e-reading, and using digital book formats. Findings are mainly framed positively, with benefits and growth for the reading practices of less engaged and struggling readers noted in particular (Clark and Picton, 2019; Picton, 2019). Oakley et al. (2020) recently reviewed the research literature for tablet use, reporting specific positive effects:

- as tools that enhance learning and pleasure;

- as tools that are enabling for the widest range of learners;

- as tools that that complement child-centred 'playful' pedagogies;

- as tools that that stimulate talk, social interaction and problem-solving; and

- as tools with benefits involving the development of positive attitudes towards literacy in general.

(pp. 658–659)

With tablet use, the interplay between the teacher, learner and technology has been of interest in recent research. Oakley et al. (2020) investigated how tablets may support literacy learning in a sample of Australian schools. The teachers in their study reported that the guided use of tablets (to support rather than replace the teacher) resulted in improvements in early reading, writing and oracy (pp. 671–674). Kucirkova and Cremin (2018) draw attention to how the role of the professionals who support children's reading development (teachers and librarians) is changed by digital resources, rendering their roles as mere curators and monitors of children's reading in the presence of digital resources; rather than as listeners and co-readers and mentors. In this same study they recommend that serious consideration be given to how teachers are positioned in relation to digital reading practices in order that pedagogies to build reading for pleasure can be developed and supported, in the light of digital resources. Both these studies draw our attention to the idea that tablets can be used as part of active literacy teaching, where the teacher, learner and resource interplay to create affective and effective literacy practice.

Shifting the focus to how teachers may mediate the use of ebooks for reading, Lee (2019) provides a compelling account of how ebook reading can support children via the use pre-recorded teacher audio-book narration and animated images to support word learning. Working with children described as having low SES in schools in one US State, Lee argues that ebook reading can be a positive strategy for developing comprehension and word learning, particularly when audio-narration is provided by the teacher, prior to reading. Lee's (2019) study resonates with the argument made by Kucirkova and Cremin

(2018) regarding a shift in the role of the teacher in the presence of the digital resource. Lee notes that while ebook reading generally benefits word learning, the role of the teacher in the presence of e-readers differs from when they are working with traditional print-based text. Traditional 'book' reading promotes teacher–learner dialogue that is focused on book content; while ebook reading promotes dialogue that centres on the learner's behaviour with the technology (Lee, 2019, p. 696).

Reich et al. (2019), working with 200 pre-schoolers in the United States, compared the reading behaviours of young children reading with an auto-narrated ebook (with an adult present) to reading a print-book with an adult. This study found that children's reading with a print book and adult together yielded better recall of story sequence than with the auto-narrated the ebook. In addition, and resonating with Lee (2019), the children reading with an e-reader talked more about use of the device, than the content.

Based on these observations, it may be beneficial for you to consider your aims when using tablets and e-readers and question the way that these resources can be put to work. Of equal importance is the consideration of how the digital resource may impact children's reading identity and sense of community. Reading involving digital resources amongst older youth has been explored by Merga (2021), who has investigated the use of #Booktok on the social media platform TikTok for its potential to build reading community and reader identity, as contributors share responses to reading. Merga found that, while only a small number of authors featured in the 116 TikTok videos that used the hashtag #BookTok, the contributors were using the digital platform to share their emotional reading responses, build communities of reading and forge a reader identity. Taken together, these accounts from research suggest that, when thinking about introducing ebooks in your classroom, you might think about how you could focus learners' attention on the content being read, rather than the use of the resource itself; and how you could support the learner's sense of reader identity and community, as they engage with these digital forms.

In their study of reading for pleasure and digital texts, Kucirkova et al. (2016, pp. 71–72) present six inter-related dimensions of reading for pleasure that can be used to evaluate children's engagement with digital books. They provide a useful rubric for considering the child reader's behaviour in the presence of reading on screen, and also the ways in which educators work with learners to promote meaningful reading experiences. These dimensions involve the extent to which reading engagement is *sustained, shared, interactive, affective, creative and personalised*. While these facets are derived from a consideration of digital books specifically, they may be used along with the suggestions above to orientate educators towards planning reading activities that begin with reader enjoyment and engagement, and that will benefit from the specific affordances described in this section.

WRITING AND DIGITAL RESOURCES

Kucirkova et al. (2019) note that less is reported about the process of writing than reading on screen, and its effect on attainment and engagement, as was noted in Chapter 6. Based on a thematic analysis of available studies, they make five observations that raise a number of issues:

- Accounts of writing on screen tend to be drawn from either socio-cultural or cognitive perspectives, failing to allow for a rich analysis of the processes involved.

- Existing studies frame composing as an activity that is subject to caregiver control, rather than focusing on the child as agent.

- Existing research is not sufficiently detailed in terms of understanding the applications used and children's writing process stages.

- The social and individual nature of screen-based writing has not been sufficiently explored by research.

- The experiences of children of different ages have not been systematically considered.

(Kucirkova et al., 2019)

These observations, while not providing answers, can be used to direct attention to how screen-based writing activities may be incorporated to give young writers agency, to incorporate ways of working that develop audience and collaborator awareness, and to explore how children of different ages may use different sorts of digital resources to support their writing process. In particular, you might consider how greater use of digital resources can support both learning and motivation in writing for disaffected writers, and those from more disadvantaged backgrounds.

Schmier (2021), working in the United States, has explored digital storytelling as a way of engaging less willing writers to tell their own stories in what is described as a 'turn-around pedagogy' (Kamler and Comber, 2005). From this perspective, the teacher's focus is shifted from addressing 'gaps' in attainment, to building from the learner's interests and repositioning them in relation to what they can, rather than cannot achieve. This is a clear example of how digital resources might be used to build writer agency and engagement. Schmier uses a multimodal theoretical lens to recognise that writing in digital contexts (making TikTok – style videos); or inspired by digital texts (creating anime), enables the representation of complex ideas and understandings in new ways. She notes the benefits associated with bringing digital storytelling practices in to school – drawing from her own and others' research. These include the development of teacher awareness about student experience; student voice, sense of self and agency as learners, engagement with writing; practice that values diversity and positions learners as designers of meaningful texts. The understandings of the pre-service teachers described in her account shift from regarding the learners as passive recipients to being active creators of content, and Schmier makes recommendations for the introduction of digital storytelling alongside existing literacy activities to promote more inclusive practice for all learners.

While Schmier's study is located in the school, research into screen-based writing has long reported the potential for digital resources to support older children's literacies in informal contexts (Davis et al., 2017; Dowdall, 2009; Connolly and Burn, 2019). These studies regard young people's composition from an asset perspective, identifying the young writers' use of social and cultural resources in their writing processes. Building on these claims, Tan and Kim (2019) more recently note that adolescents' use of social media, e.g. Facebook, in Asian contexts, can support the development of 'personal trajectories for learning', that can be harnessed as 'personal pedagogies' that promote learners' awareness of what works for them as text makers. In turn, they argue that educators must acknowledge these personal pedagogies to promote adolescent agency in their literacy learning in more formal contexts.

A CLASSROOM EXAMPLE

A Year 10 class are revising *Macbeth* in readiness for their GCSE English Literature examination. Rather than making revision notes, the teacher allocates small groups one of the key characters to work with. Their task is to write a blog from the perspective of their character, presenting the character's view of the events in the play, revealing their inner thinking and embedding direct quotations from the play. After this, new groups are created, and each is given a study theme (e.g. ambition; imagery; social and historical context etc.) and they prepare and write a webpage on that theme, thus creating collaboratively a revision website for the whole class.

However, it can be observed that there is a tension for educators who, in an attempt to build agency, seek to harness informal and multimodal text production processes in more formal education contexts. Mills and Exley (2014), working in an Australian school with a case study approach, note how teachers working with 8–9-year-olds experience the disconnect between what is expected in schooled writing practice – as mandated by curriculum and accountability measures, and involving requirements for assessment of grammar, spelling and punctuation; and the broader composing and design practice afforded by the everyday multimodal texts and contexts that children can learn and play with. They note the challenge for educators, as they try to introduce digital text production practices involving multimodal grammars from broader experiences into the highly regulated writing classroom.

CRITICAL DIGITAL LITERACY

This chapter has considered the role that digital literacies play in children's literacy learning and some ways in which digital resources can be harnessed to promote inclusive and expansive practice, in order to support all learners. As children access digital resources, the need for renewed attention to critical digital literacy has been noted (Burnett and Merchant, 2019). In the digital age, the nature of texts produced and read is quite different. Digital texts have a very different multi-modal design grammar (Kress, 2010; Sefton-Green et al., 2016, p. 13). In addition to words, they may involve images (still and/or moving), sound, icons, emojis, dynamic layouts, hyperlinks and more. Children may find themselves viewing the text, from within the text as an avatar, or even embodying the world of the story – using a VR headset, for example. The conventions for communicating and meaning making in these multi-modal spaces may involve users learning new rules and ways of being, in order to successfully and safely participate and achieve their intentions – whether that includes being able to buy a game pass for a console; to produce and upload a TikTok video; or to understand how to read critically in a 'post-truth' world (Harrison, 2018).

Research in this area has evolved from accounts that explored the perceived risks and opportunities for learners (Byron, 2008; Livingstone and Haddon, 2009); to more recent theoretical considerations of how criticality in digital contexts involves the design, as well as consumption (meaning-making) of texts – as reading and writing practices are blended by the affordances of the media being used (Pangrazio, 2016). Newer conceptual models for critical digital literacy move beyond concern for the nature of the text itself to argue that the socio-material practices of individuals and groups as they compose across time and space should be considered relationally. In this way, understandings will more fully reflect the ways that being and doing with digital resources inflect the reading and writing processes.

To support educators as they plan, Burnett and Merchant raise three questions with the intention of broadening understandings of critical literacies in the presence of digital resources.

*   Who's making what, and with who and with what?

*   What are the ethics of production? (What's made? Who and what else is implicated? Whose interests are served?)

*   How do the different layers of making interface?

(Burnett and Merchant, 2019, p. 266)

These questions can be used as an overarching frame to 'check' plans for the introduction of digital resources to promote schooled reading and writing. They may help you to consider not just the text being 'written' or 'read', but the relations around the text, given the possibilities and affordances of digital resources. They also invoke the full complexity of what children's literacy with digital resources can involve, including the sense that the processes of reading and writing are deepened and expanded by the possibilities of interaction and engagement.

REFLECTION POINT

*   How do you use digital resources to promote literacy engagement and learning?

*   How is your role affected by the use of digital resources in relation to supporting children to become and develop as speakers, readers and writers?

*   How do you support readers to make deep meaning when reading with digital resources?

*   How can digital resources be used to promote inclusive literacy communities?

*   How can digital resources be used to promote positive reading and writing identities for all learners?

CONCLUSION

The research informing this chapter makes it clear that children's school-based literacy activities can be enriched using digital resources, and this can impact the experiences of all learners positively. This chapter has attempted to demonstrate how the introduction of digital resources can support those learners labelled as being 'disadvantaged' to gain access to ways of learning that may promote their attainment and engagement, from the perspective of formal literacy education. For all families and learners, but especially those described as experiencing social disadvantage, educators are uniquely positioned to be able to provide access to schooled literacy activities that involve digital resources, for the development of children's reading and writing. In so doing, educators may help children to build connections from their formal learning to the everyday, authentic, relevant literacies that they may experience in their wider social worlds, as they engage in everyday communicative practices that are increasingly digitally mediated. This promotion of schooled literacy as part of a more wide-ranging notion of 'digital literacies' will help to ensure that learners have opportunities to become 'digitally literate' and prepared for citizenship in its fullest sense. Of most significance is the potential for the use of digital resources to promote engagement in school literacy activities.

Additionally, literacy practices with digital resources in the classroom can become part of an expanded communication repertoire that involves formal and informal experiences and competences with digital literacies. These digital literacies may involve reading an e-reader with a teacher, or uploading a video made with friends to TikTok. They are a subset of an overarching ability to be literate and digitally literate – and participate fully and competently in contexts that continue to be mediated increasingly in relation to digital resources and practices in the 21st-century textual landscape.

8
CONCLUSION

UNDERSTANDING THE RESEARCH

It is clear from the research synthesised for this book that there is a strong and persistent link between social disadvantage and educational outcomes, both in the United Kingdom and internationally. There is also evidence that the problem is more pronounced in the United Kingdom than elsewhere, and that the group labelled 'white working-class' seem to be the group most strongly affected by this relationship, although some ethnic groups are also prone to lower educational outcomes. In general, however, research is better at identifying that there is a problem than it is at explaining and addressing the problem, and it is crucially important to remember that correlation is not causation. Large statistical analyses are hugely helpful in drawing attention to different patterns of performance but they should not be seen as determinants of future success, nor be used to regard any group of students as homogeneous. Group labels may be useful but they can inadvertently lead to social stereotyping and are blind to the fact to the considerable variation that exists *within* groups as well as *between* groups.

There is less research which specifically addresses the relationship between literacy and disadvantage, particularly beyond the Early Years, and in terms of how teachers can intervene to address the imbalance. There is a strong body of evidence about the importance of early language development as the foundation for literacy, fostered by a home environment where parents and caregivers engage and interact with their children in everyday situations, and where books and storytelling are part of the home routines. The chapters in this book spotlight how these early language experiences shape later spoken language development, reading comprehension, vocabulary and writing. But it is all too easy to locate the issue of differential outcomes for different students as a problem outside the school – remember that, despite the powerful influence of what child bring into school from home, the gap in attainment increases as children progress through their education. A gloomy way to express this would be that school seems to amplify the effect of social disadvantage. But the much more positive picture is that schools have successfully broken the link between social disadvantage and educational outcomes, especially for some ethnic minority groups. What you do in your classroom really does matter!

At the same time, it is important to acknowledge the limitations and gaps in the research, and what research can and cannot do. There is sometimes a tendency to view research as the place where a solution lies, waiting to be uncovered and shared. Even in hard science this rarely happens: breakthroughs and discoveries are regularly re-written as more evidence or theories are developed. Consider, for example, the discovery of Pluto as a ninth planet in our solar system and its more recent reclassification as a dwarf planet. Researching anything that involves humans and behaviour, as education does, is even more 'uncertain' as we are not investigating fundamental laws of nature but highly complex systems of interaction, influence and individuals. The research on literacy and disadvantage reveals conflicting positions and theories or the promotion of simplistic quick-fix solutions. This is most evident in research which tries to determine 'what works' in school. This body of research is important because it tests out particular interventions for their effectiveness, thus potentially providing valuable evidence to inform your decisions. But they can be reported in rather black-and-white ways, not taking account of the diversity of teachers, classrooms and contexts. What works in one research context may not work for you, with your students, in your school – or it may be significantly more effective in your context. In some ways, we have all learned a lot about research through the experience of COVID. The vaccine for COVID is a classic example of 'what works' research – and yet, as we have seen, there is not one vaccine but a range of vaccines with differing kinds of effectiveness. And although, in general, the vaccine works, there are people for whom it is less effective, or even dangerous. So educational research needs careful interpretation: research-informed teaching of literacy draws on your professional understanding of your students and context as well as good understanding of how to read research.

BEING CRITICAL

Understanding how to read research demands criticality. Throughout this book we have tried, very deliberately, to present conflicting evidence, including concerning our own research, and each chapter has critical questions to provoke this kind of thinking. We have highlighted where there have been criticisms of the methodology used in particular studies, and we have explained what statistical analyses can and cannot do. But at the heart of reading research evidence is adopting a critical stance: for example, about the nature of the participants and how typical they are of the general population; about how the evidence was gathered; how the findings are evidenced by the data; and how the final claims are expressed. For example, in Chapter 6, we discussed the EEF evaluation of the IPEELL programme. The report summary explicitly states that 'these writing results are not statistically significant' and that 'IPEELL is no longer listed as a promising project' (EEF, 2018b), but it is listed on the EEF Toolkit as an intervention which generates two months progress. A critical reader should note the tension inherent in this (in fact, two months progress is probably just 'noise', neither here nor there, but it does seem a little misleading).

Equally important is to be critical of qualitative research – this is not about privileging one type of research over another, but about questioning how a study arrived at its results. Qualitative research can be hugely valuable in providing in-depth understanding of why certain things happen in education: there is a natural complement between statistical analyses which foreground patterns of differential achievement and qualitative studies which seek to explain why this is so. But qualitative research can be very selective about what it chooses to present – for example, cherry-picking the data to support a particular line of argument or not presenting counter-evidence. It can also be prone to make generalised or over-stated claims from a small data set, or making claims which the data cannot support. For example, a common issue here is making claims about how effective an intervention is based on teachers' or students' reports of how good it is, rather than evidence of improvement from students' work.

But being critical is not simply about questioning research claims and arguments, but it is also about your own stance towards your professional practice. Are you inclined to privilege research which supports your existing professional beliefs and ideology (this is, of course, what governments tend to do!) or do you allow the research to challenge what you think and do? Do you look critically at the individuals in your classes to consider whether the teaching strategies you are using are leading to better understanding or better engagement? Do you understand the principles or theories behind a teaching strategy, such as using word banks, shared reading or the use of digital literacy resources? The risk otherwise is that schools treat research like a fashion, with fads which come and go – think, for example, about VAK (visual, auditory, kinaesthetic learning) and Brain Gym.

A RICH LITERACY ENVIRONMENT

So having come to the end of this book, what can you take from it for your own practice, other than recognising the need to be critical in reading the research and in reflecting on your own practice? A theme that does resonate through the book is the importance of a rich literacy environment, not just at home but also in school. It is a sad phenomenon that many children are being put off reading and writing by the experiences of learning in both primary and secondary schools, and that English departments at university are increasingly concerned about the falling number of students applying to take English degrees. We know that the current curriculum and assessment requirements, and the high-stakes accountability regime are a factor in this, but we would challenge you to reflect on how your students experience literacy in your classes. While, obviously, you need to abide by your statutory responsibilities, re-imagine what is possible and what could be transformed in your classrooms to make literacy a richer, more engaging and more rewarding learning experience.

There are many ideas in this book which might help you think about the environment you create, but at their core is the foregrounding of talking, reading and writing as engaging activities, which relate to learners' interests, choices and experiences, and the communities in which they live. Within this, there is space for explicit teaching, focused feedback and careful monitoring – but this can be imaginatively located in an environment where there is time and space for writing creatively, opportunities to share books, collaborative talk and the use of digital literacy resources which enhance learning. You might also draw on external resources to make your classroom a dynamic, vibrant place to learn – for example, by having a writer work alongside the class in developing their writing. It is hard to thrive as a learner, perhaps especially if you are already struggling with literacy, if your experience of literacy/English is tedious and over-focused on test or examination preparation.

Finally, recall the key messages noted in the introduction and reinforced through the research syntheses and practical ideas in subsequent chapters. The link between social disadvantage and literacy outcomes can be broken by what schools and teachers do: there are no quick fix solutions, but a need for constant reflection on the quality of teaching you provide, including the literacy environment you establish. This includes avoiding adopting deficit beliefs and attitudes towards socially disadvantaged students and acknowledging every learner as a unique individual within a community which embraces diversity and difference.

SOURCES OF ADDITIONAL SUPPORT

The list below is just an example of the wide range of organisations who support literacy in different ways. They offer many ways to support literacy in schools, including free resources and projects involving schools. It is also a good idea to investigate whether there are any local literacy charities and build relationships with these.

PROFESSIONAL LITERACY/ENGLISH ASSOCIATIONS

It is well worth joining a professional subject association to be part of a literacy/English network and to gain access to a range of opportunities, such as national and regional activities, resources for teachers and an annual International conference.

United Kingdom Literacy Association (UKLA): https://ukla.org/

National Association for the Teaching of English (NATE): https://www.nate.org.uk/

THE CAMBRIDGE UNIVERSITY THINKING TOGETHER WEBSITE

Practical resources to support spoken language and dialogic teaching and access to relevant publications.

https://thinkingtogether.educ.cam.ac.uk/

SEDA

If you'd like to investigate talk in your own classroom or school, you might find the Scheme for Dialogue Analysis (SEDA) resource pack helpful.

https://www.educ.cam.ac.uk/research/projects/tseda/index.html

I CAN

A children's communication charity, focused on how to support children's speech and language in school. A wealth of information and research evidence on talk and communication, including resources specifically for teachers.

https://ican.org.uk/

https://ican.org.uk/i-cans-talking-point/professionals/primary-and-secondary-school-teachers/

DAVID HEATHFIELD

A storyteller active in schools but also with a YouTube channel with many recorded stories. You may also like to investigate if there is a local storyteller with whom you and your school could build a relationship.

https://davidheathfieldblog.wordpress.com/

CENTRE FOR LITERACY IN PRIMARY EDUCATION (CLPE)

A literacy charity for primary schools, with a rich range of resources, projects and professional development, including work with socially disadvantaged children.

https://clpe.org.uk/

ENGLISH AND MEDIA CENTRE

A charity serving the needs of secondary and FE English teachers in particular, with teaching resources and professional development courses which can be trusted to represent best practice.

https://www.englishandmedia.co.uk/

NATIONAL LITERACY TRUST

A national charity interested in all aspects of literacy and a particular mission to work with disadvantaged children and young people.

https://literacytrust.org.uk/

ARVON

A creative writing charity for anyone interested in writing, but specifically, they run writing residentials for teachers and for students.

https://www.arvon.org/

FIRST STORY

A writing charity focused on working with secondary schools, including bringing writers into residence in schools serving disadvantaged communities.

https://firststory.org.uk/

BOOKTRUST

A national reading charity, committed to generating a love of reading and to supporting parents, teachers and children through a wide range of activities and resources.

https://www.booktrust.org.uk/

DIGITAL LITERACY APPS MENTIONED IN CHAPTER 7

Puppet Pals HD: https://apps.apple.com/gb/app/puppet-pals-hd/id342076546

Mr T's Phonics with Geraldine the Giraffe: https://www.youtube.com/channel/UC7sW4j8p7k9D_qRR MUsGqyw

CBeebies Alphablocks: https://www.bbc.co.uk/cbeebies/shows/alphablocks

REFERENCES

Aikens, N. L., & Barbarin, O. (2008). Socioeconomic differences in reading trajectories: The contribution of family, neighborhood, and school contexts. *Journal of Educational Psychology*, 100, 235–251. http://dx.doi.org/10.1037/0022-0663.100.2.235

Alexander, R. (2018). Developing dialogic teaching: Genesis, process, trial. *Research Papers in Education*, 33(5), 561–598. https://doi.org/10.1080/02671522.2018.1481140

Alexander, R. (2019). Whose discourse? Dialogic pedagogy for a post-truth world. *Dialogic Pedagogy: An International Online Journal*, 7.

Alexander, R. (2020). *A dialogic teaching companion*. Routledge.

Allen, R., & Sims, S. (2018). Do pupils from low-income families get low-quality teachers? Indirect evidence from English schools. *Oxford Review of Education*, 44(4), 441–458. https://doi.org/10.1080/03054985.2017.1421152

Allington, R., & Gabriel, R. (2012). Every child, every day. *Educational Leadership*, 69(6).

Allington, R. L., McGill-Franzen, A., Camilli, G., Williams, L., Graff, J., Zeig, J., Zmach, C., & Nowak, R. (2010). Addressing summer reading setback among economically disadvantaged elementary students. *Reading Psychology*, 31(5), 411–427. https://doi.org/10.1080/02702711.2010.505165

Anderson, J., Anderson, A., Friedrich, N., & Kim, J. E. (2010). Taking stock of family literacy: Some contemporary perspectives. *Journal of Early Childhood Literacy*, 10(1), 33–53. https://doi.org/10.1177/1468798409357387

Andrews, J., Robinson, D., & Hutchinson, J. (2016). *Closing the gap? Trends in educational attainment and disadvantage*. Education Policy Institute. https://epi.org.uk/publications-and-research/closing-gap-trends-educational-attainment-disadvantage/

Askew, S., & Ross, C. (1988). *Boys don't cry: Boys and sexism in education*. Open University Press.

Au, K. (2013). *Multicultural issues and literacy achievement*. Routledge.

Avineri, N., Johnson, E., Brice-Heath, S., McCarty, T., Ochs, E., Kremer-Sadlik, T., Blum, S., Zentella, A. C., Rosa, J., Flores, D., & Paris, D. (2015). Invited forum: Bridging the 'language gap'. *Journal of Linguistic Anthropology*, 25(1), 66–86. https://doi.org/10.1111/Jola.12071

Bakhtin, M. M. (1986). *Speech genres and other late essays*. University of Texas Press.

Barbarin, O. A., & Aikens, N. (2015). Overcoming the educational disadvantages of poor children: How much do teacher preparation, workload, and expectations matter. *American Journal of Orthopsychiatry*, 85(2), 101–105. https://doi.org/10.1037/ort0000060

Barg, K. (2013). The influence of students' social background and parental involvement on teachers' school track choices: Reasons and consequences. *European Sociological Review*, 29(3), 565–579. https://doi.org/10.1093/esr/jcr104

Barnes, D. (2008). Exploratory talk for learning. In N. Mercer & S. Hodgkinson (Eds.), *Exploring talk in school* (pp. 1–16). SAGE.

Barrs, M., & Cork, V. (2001). *The reader in the writer*. CLPE.

Baugh, J. (2017). Meaning-less differences: Exposing fallacies and flaws in 'the word gap' hypothesis that conceal a dangerous 'language trap' for low-income American families and their children. *International Multilingual Research Journal*, 11(1), 39–51. https://doi.org/10.1080/19313152.2016.1258189

Bazerman, C. (2010). *The informed writer: Using sources in the disciplines*. The WAC Clearinghouse.

Bearne, E. (2002). *Making progress in writing*. RoutledgeFalmer.

Bearne, E., & Grainger, T. (2004). Research in progress – raising boys' achievements in writing: Joint PNS/UKLA pilot research project. *Literacy*, 38(3), 156–158. https://doi.org/10.1111/j.1741-4350.2004.00388.x

Bearne, E., & Reedy, D. (2018). *Teaching primary English*. Routledge.

Bearne, E., & Wolstencroft, H. (2007). *Visual approaches to teaching writing: Multimodal literacy 5–7*. SAGE.

Beck, I. L., McKeown, M. G., & Kucan, L. (2013). *Bringing words to life: Robust vocabulary instruction*. Guilford Press.

Bercow, J. (2008). *The Bercow report: A review of services for children and young people (0–19) with speech, language and communication needs*. Department for Schools, Children and Families. Original-bercow-report.pdf (rcslt.org)

Bergen, E., Zuijen, T., Bishop, D., & Jong, P. F. (2016). Why are home literacy environment and children's reading skills associated? What parental skills reveal. *Reading Research Quarterly*, 52(2), 147–160. https://doi.org/10.1002/rrq.160

Bernstein, B. (1971). *Class, codes and control volume I theoretical studies towards a sociology of language*. Routledge.

Best, E. (2020). *Audiobooks and literacy. A rapid review of the literature*. National Literacy Trust. https://files.eric.ed.gov/fulltext/ED607775.pdf

Best, E., Clark, C., & Picton, I. (2020). *Children, young people and audiobooks before and during lockdown*. National Literacy Trust. https://files.eric.ed.gov/fulltext/ED607856.pdf

Bhattacharya, A. (2010). Children and adolescents from poverty and reading development: A research review. *Reading & Writing Quarterly*, 26(2), 115–139. https://doi.org/10.1080/10573560903547445

Bhojwani, P., & Wilkie, C. (2018). *Power-up literacy: Technology and multimodality within the extended classroom*. UKLA.

Bibby, T., Lupton, R., & Raffo, C. (2017). *Responding to poverty and disadvantage in schools*. Palgrave Macmillan.

Blackburn, S. W. (n.d). *Philosophy of language*. Encyclopedia Britannica. https://www.britannica.com/topic/philosophy-of-language

Boaler, J., Wiliam, D., & Brown, M. (2000). Students' experiences of ability grouping – disaffection, polarisation and the construction of failure. *British Educational Research Journal*, 26(5), 631–648. https://doi.org/10.1080/713651583

Bourdieu, P. (1986). The forms of capital. In J. G. Richardson (Ed.), *Handbook of theory and research for the sociology of education* (pp. 241–258). Greenwood Press.

Bowyer-Crane, C., Bonetti, S., Compton, S., Nielsen, D., D'Apice, K., & Tracey, L. (2021). *The impact of Covid-19 on school starters: Interim briefing 1: Parent and school concerns about children starting school*. Education Endowment Foundation. https://educationendowmentfoundation.org.uk/public/files/Impact_of_Covid19_on_School_Starters_-_Interim_Briefing_1_-_April_2021_-_Final.Pdf

Boyd, M., & Markarian, W. (2015). Dialogic teaching and dialogic stance: Moving beyond interactional form. *Research in the Teaching of English*, 49(3), 272–296.

Bradley, R. H., Corwyn, R. F., McAdoo, H. P., & García Coll, C. (2001). The home environments of children in the United States part I: Variations by age, ethnicity, and poverty status. *Child Development*, 72, 1844–1867. https://doi.org/10.1111/1467-8624.t01-1-00382

Brandt, D. (2019). The problem of writing in mass education. *Utbildning & Demokrati*, 28(2), 37–53. https://doi.org/10.48059/uod.v28i2.1120

Breitenstein, S. M., & Gross, D. (2013). Web-based delivery of a preventive parent training intervention: A feasibility study. *Journal of Child and Adolescent Psychiatric Nursing*, 26(2), 149–157. https://doi.org/10.1111/jcap.12031

British Medical Association [BMA]. (2017). *Health at a price: Reducing the impact of poverty*. British Medical Association. https://www.bma.org.uk/media/2084/health-at-a-price-2017.pdf

Britton, J. (1970). *Language and learning*. Penguin Books.

Brooker, L. (2002). *Starting school – young children learning cultures*. Open University Press.

Brooks, G., & Hutchinson, D. (2002). *Family numeracy adds on*. Basic Skills Agency.

Bruner, J. S. (1975). The ontogenesis of speech acts. *Journal of Child Language*, 2(1), 1–19. https://doi.org/10.1017/S0305000900000866

Buckingham, J., Wheldall, K., & Beaman-Wheldall, R. (2013). Why poor children are more likely to become poor readers: The school years. *Australian Journal of Education*, 57(3), 190–213. https://doi.org/10.1177/0004944113495500

Bulman, J. H. (2017). *Children's reading of film and visual literacy in the primary curriculum*. Palgrave Macmillan.

Bulman, J., Burnett, B., Dowdall, C., Colvert, A., Erricker, K., Harrison, A., Parry, B., Tarling, G., & Wheatcroft, L. (n.d.). Classroom example. In *UKLA viewpoints – digital literacies* (p. 5). UKLA. https://ukla.org/wp-content/uploads/View_Digital_Literacies.pdf

Burgess, S., & Greaves, E. (2013). Test scores, subjective assessment, and stereotyping of ethnic minorities. *Journal of Labor Economics*, 31(3), 535–576. http://dx.doi.org/10.1086/669340

Burnett, C. (2010). Technology and literacy in early childhood educational settings: A review of research. -*Journal of Early Childhood Literacy*, 10(3), 247–270. https://doi.org/10.1177/1468798410372154

Burnett, C., & Merchant, G. (2018). *New media in the classroom: Rethinking primary literacy*. SAGE.

Burnett, C., & Merchant, G. (2019). Revisiting critical literacy in the digital age. *The Reading Teacher*, 73(3), 263–266. https://doi.org/10.1002/trtr.1858

Byron, T. (2008). *Byron review: Safer children in a digital world*. DCSF. https://webarchive.nationalarchives.gov.uk/ukgwa/20130401151715/http:/www.education.gov.uk/publications/eOrderingDownload/DCSF-00334-2008.pdf

Cain, K., & Oakhill, J. (2011). Matthew effects in young readers: Reading comprehension and reading experience aid vocabulary development. *Journal of Learning Disabilities*, 44(5), 431–443. https://doi.org/10.1177/0022219411410042

Cain, K., & Oakhill, J. (2014). Reading comprehension and vocabulary: Is vocabulary more important for some aspects of comprehension? *L'Annee Psychologique*, 114(4), 647–662. https://doi.org/10.4074/S0003503314004035

Camilli, G., Vargas, S., & Yurecko, M. (2003). Teaching children to read: The fragile link between science and federal education policy. *Analysis Archives*, 11(15). http://epaa.asu.edu/ojs/article/view/243

Canfield, C., Seerya, A., Weisleder, A., Workman, C., Brockmeyer-Cates, C., Roby, E., Payne, R., Levine, S., Mogilner, L., Dreyer, B., & Mendelsohn, A. (2018). Encouraging parent–child book sharing: Potential additive benefits of literacy promotion in health care and the community. *Early Childhood Research Quarterly*, 50(2020), 221–229. https://doi.org/10.1016/j.ecresq.2018.11.002

Caravolas, M., Downing, C., Hadden, C. L., & Wynne, C. (2020). Handwriting legibility and its relationship to spelling ability and age: Evidence from monolingual and bilingual children. *Frontiers in Psychology*, 11, 1097. https://doi.org/10.3389/fpsyg.2020.01097

Carpentieri, J. D., Fairfax-Cholmeley, K., Litster, J., & Vorhaus, J. (2011). *Family literacy in Europe: Using parental support initiatives to enhance early literacy eevelopment*. National Research and Development Centre for Adult Literacy and Numeracy, Institute of Education.

Carrington, V. & Robinson, M. (Eds.) (2009). *Digital literacies, social learning and classroom practices*. SAGE.

Cassen, R., & Kingdon, G. (2007). *Tackling low educational achievement*. Joseph Rowntree Foundation. https://www.jrf.org.uk/sites/default/files/jrf/migrated/files/2063-education-schools-achievement.pdf

Centre for Literacy in Primary Education [CLPE]. (2015). *Reading for pleasure: What we know works*. Centre for Literacy in Primary Education [CLPE]. https://clpe.org.uk/research/reading-pleasure-what-we-know-works

Centre for Literacy in Primary Education [CLPE]. (2018). *Reflecting realities*. Centre for Literacy in Primary Education [CLPE]. https://clpe.org.uk/system/files/CLPE%20Reflecting%20Realities%20Report%20July%202018.pdf

Centre for Literacy in Primary Education [CLPE]. (2021). *Reading for pleasure in 2020*. Centre for Literacy in Primary Education [CLPE]. https://clpe.org.uk/system/files/CLPE%20Reading%20for%20Pleasure%202021_0.pdf

Chatzitheochari, S., & Platt, L. (2018). Disability differentials in educational attainment in England: Primary and secondary effects. *British Journal of Sociology*, 70(2), 502–525. http://eprints.lse.ac.uk/87373/

Children's Commissioner for England. (2020). *Children without Internet access during lockdown*. Children's Commissioner for England. https://www.childrenscommissioner.gov.uk/2020/08/18/children-without-internet-access-during-lockdown/

Clark, C. (2007). *Why it is important to involve parents in their children's literacy development – a brief research summary*. National Literacy Trust. https://files.eric.ed.gov/fulltext/ED496346.pdf

Clark, C., & Akerman, R. (2006). *Social inclusion and reading: An exploration*. National Literacy Trust. https://files.eric.ed.gov/fulltext/ED496345.pdf

Clark, C., & Picton, I. (2019). *Children, young people and digital reading: National literacy trust research report*. National Literacy Trust.

Clark, C., & Picton, I. (2020). *Children and young people's reading in 2020 before and during lockdown*. National Literacy Trust. https://literacytrust.org.uk/research-services/research-reports/children-and-young-peoples-reading-in-2020-before-and-during-the-covid-19-lockdown/

Clark, C., Picton, I., & Lant, F. (2020). *'More time on my hands': Children and young people's writing during the COVID-19 lockdown in 2020*. National Literacy Trust. https://files.eric.ed.gov/fulltext/ED607968.pdf

Classick, R., Gambhir, G., Liht, J., Sharp, C., & Wheater, R. (2021). *PISA 2018 additional analyses: What differentiates disadvantaged pupils who do well in PISA from Rhose who do not?* National Foundation for Educational Research (NFER). https://www.nfer.ac.uk/pisa-2018-additional-analyses-what-differentiates-disadvantaged-pupils-who-do-well-in-pisa-from-those-who-do-not/

Clay, M. (1966). *Emergent reading behaviour*. Unpublished doctoral thesis. University of Auckland.

Clotfelter, C. T., Ladd, H. F., & Vigdor, J. L. (2006). Teacher-student matching and the assessment of teacher effectiveness. *Journal of Human Resources*, 41, 778–820. https://doi.org/10.3368/jhr.xli.4.778

Coker, D. (2006). Impact of first-grade factors on the growth and outcomes of urban schoolchildren's primary-grade writing. *Journal of Educational Psychology*, 98(3), 471. https://doi.org/10.1037/0022-0663.98.3.471

Coker, D. L., Jr, & Erwin, E. (2011). Teaching academic argument in an urban middle school: A case study of two approaches. *Urban Education*, 46(2), 120–140. https://doi.org/10.1177/00420.85910.37742.6

Comber, B. (2016). *Literacy, place, and pedagogies of possibility*. Routledge.

Connelly, R., Sullivan, A., & Jerrim, J. (2014). *Primary and secondary education and poverty review*. Centre for Longitudinal Studies [CLS]. https://www.basw.co.uk/system/files/resources/basw_11434-4_0.pdf

Connolly, S., & Burn, A. (2019). *The story engine*: Offering an online platform for making 'unofficial' creative writing work. *Literacy*, 53, 30–38. https://doi.org/10.1111/lit.12138

Cope, B., & Kalantzis, M. (2009). 'Multiliteracies': New literacies, new learning. *Pedagogies: An International Journal*, 4(3), 164–195. https://doi.org/10.1080/15544800903076044

Coughlan, S. (2021a, August 11). *A-levels: Warning over private and state school gap*. https://www.bbc.co.uk/news/education-58172292

Coughlan, S. (2021b, July 29). *Richer parents pressure teachers on exam grades*. https://www.bbc.co.uk/news/education-57999790

Crampton, A., & Hall, J. (2017). Unpacking socio-economic risks for reading and academic self-concept in primary school: Differential effects and the role of the preschool home learning environment. *British Journal of Educational Psychology*, 7, 365–382. https://doi.org/10.1111/bjep.12154

Cremin, T., Mottram, M., Safford, K., Collins, F. M., & Powell, S. (2014). *Building communities of engaged readers: Reading for pleasure*. Routledge.

Cremin, T., & Myhill, D. (2013). *Writing voices: Creating communities of writers*. Routledge.

Cremin, T., Myhill, D., Eyres, I., Nash, T., Oliver, L., & Wilson, A. (2020). Teachers as writers: Learning together with others. *Literacy*, 54(2), 49–59. https://doi.org/10.1111/lit.12201

Cremin, T., & Oliver, L. (2017). Teachers as writers: A systematic review. *Research Papers in Education*, 32(3), 269–295. https://doi.org/10.1080/02671522.2016.1187664

Crenna-Jennings, W. (2018). *Key drivers of the disadvantage gap, a literature review*. Education Policy Institute. https://epi.org.uk/wp-content/uploads/2018/07/EPI-Annual-Report-2018-Lit-review.pdf

Culham, R. (2014). *The writing thief: Using mentor texts to teach the craft of writing*. Stenhouse Publishers.

Cunningham, A. E., & Stanovich, K. E. (1997). Early reading acquisition and its relation to reading experience and ability 10 years later. *Developmental Psychology*, 33, 934–945. https://doi.org/10.1037/0012-1649.33.6.934

Cushing, I. (2020). Policy mechanisms of the standard language ideology in England's education system. *Journal of Language, Identity & Education*, 1–15. https://doi.org/10.1080/15348458.2021.1877542

Cushing, I. (2021a). 'Say it like the Queen': The standard language ideology and language policy making in English primary schools. *Language, Culture and Curriculum*, 1–16. https://doi.org/10.1080/07908318.2020.1840578

Cushing, I. (2021b). Language, discipline and 'teaching like a champion'. *British Educational Research Journal*, 47(1), 23–41. https://doi.org/10.1002/berj.3696

Davis, K., Ambrose, M., & Orand, M. (2017). Identity and agency in school and afterschool settings: Investigating digital media's supporting role. *Digital Culture and Education*, 9(1), 31–47.

Deem, R. (Ed.) (1980). *Schooling for women's work*. Routledge. https://doi.org/10.4324/9780203803677

Denham, K. (2020). Positioning students as linguistic and social experts: Teaching grammar and linguistics in the United States. *L1-Educational Studies in Language and Literature*, 1–16. https://doi.org/10.17239/L1ESLL-2020.20.03.02

Department for Children, Schools and Families. (2008). *A review of services for children and young people (0–19) with speech, language and communication needs (the Bercow Report)*. DCSF.

Department for Education. (2014). *The National curriculum for England: English programmes of study*. [Online]. https://www.gov.uk/government/publications/national-curriculum-in-england-english-programmes-of-study/national-curriculum-in-england-english-programmes-of-study

Department for Education. (2015). *Supporting the attainment of disadvantaged pupils: Articulating success and good practice.* https://assets.publishing.service.gov.uk/government/uploads/system/uploads/attachment_data/file/473974/DFE-RR411_Supporting_the_attainment_of_disadvantaged_pupils.pdf

Department for Education. (2019). *National curriculum assessments at key stage 2, 2019,* (revised). www.gov.uk/government/statistics/national-curriculum-assessments-key-stage-2-2019-revised

Department for Education. (2020). *Key stage 4 performance, 2019,* (revised). https://assets.publishing.service.gov.uk/government/uploads/system/uploads/attachment_data/file/863815/2019_KS4_revised_text.pdf

Department for Education. (2021). *Laptops and tablets data week 28, 2021.* https://explore-education-statistics.service.gov.uk/find-statistics/laptops-and-tablets-data/2021-week-28

Department for Education [DfE]. (2013). *Teachers' standards.* https://assets.publishing.service.gov.uk/government/uploads/system/uploads/attachment_data/file/1040274/Teachers__Standards_Dec_2021.pdf

Department for Education [DfE]. (2014). *The National curriculum for England.* Her Majesty's Stationery Office (HMSO).

Department for Education [DfE]. (2017). *Statutory framework for the early years foundation stage.* https://www.foundationyears.org.uk/files/2017/03/EYFS_STATUTORY_FRAMEWORK_2017.pdf

Department for Education [DfE]. (2021). *Statutory framework for the early years foundation stage.* https://assets.publishing.service.gov.uk/government/uploads/system/uploads/attachment_data/file/974907/EYFS_framework_-_March_2021.pdf

Department for Education and Skills. (2006). *Independent review of the teaching of early reading: Final report by Jim Rose.* DfES.

Department for Schools, Children and Families [DCSF]. (2008). *Getting going: Generating, shaping and developing ideas in writing.* https://www.sgsts.org.uk/SchoolSupport/EnglishCurriculum/Shared%20Documents/Generating%20and%20Developing%20Ideas%20in%20Writing.pdf

Dodur, H. M. S., Kumaş, O. A., & Yüzbaşioğlu, Y. (2021). How socioeconomic status, verbal memory, rapid naming and receptive language contribute to phonological awareness in Turkish preschool children. *Education,* 3–13. https://doi.org/10.1080/03004279.2021.1958894

Dolean, D., Melby-Lervåg, M., Tincas, I., Damsa, C., & Lervåg, A. (2019). Achievement gap: Socioeconomic status affects reading development beyond language and cognition in children facing poverty. *Learning and Instruction,* 63, 101218. https://doi.org/10.1016/j.learninstruc.2019.101218

Dorfman, L., & Capelli, R. (2017). *Mentor texts: Teaching writing through children's literature.* Stenhouse Publishers.

Douglas, W. B., Ross, J. M., & Simpson, H. R. (1968). *All our future: A longitudinal study of secondary education.* Peter Davies.

Dowdall, C. (2009). Impressions, improvisations and compositions: Reframing children's text production in social networking sites. *Literacy,* 43(2), 91–99.

Dowdall, C. (2020). Teaching writing in digital times: Stories from the early years. In H. Chen, D. Myhill & H. Lewis (Eds.), *Growing into writing: Developing writers across primary and secondary school years.* Taylor and Francis.

Dowdall, C., & Burnett, C. (2021). *Digital literacies in education.* United Kingdom Literacy Association.

Duin, A. H., & Graves, M. F. (1987). Intensive vocabulary instruction as a prewriting technique. *Reading Research Quarterly,* 22(3), 311–330. https://doi.org/10.2307/747971

Durrant, P., & Brenchley, M. (2019). Development of vocabulary sophistication across genres in English children's writing. *Reading and Writing,* 32(8), 1927–1953. https://doi.org/10.1007/s11145-018-9932-8

Durrant, P., & Durrant, A. (2022). Appropriateness as an aspect of lexical richness: What do quantitative measures tell us about children's writing? *Assessing Writing*, 51, 100596. https://doi.org/10.1016/j.asw.2021.100596

Dutro, E. (2010). What 'hard times' means: Mandated curricula, class-privileged assumptions, and the lives of poor children. *Research in the Teaching of English*, 44(3), 255–291. https://eric.ed.gov/?id=EJ879573

Dyson, A. H. (2009). Writing childhood worlds. In R. Beard, D. Myhill, J. Riley & M. Nystrand (Eds.), *The SAGE handbook of writing development* (pp. 233–245). SAGE.

Dyson, A. H. (2018). A sense of belonging: Writing (righting) inclusion and equity in a child's transition to school. *Research in the Teaching of English*, 52(3), 236–261. http://www.jstor.org/stable/44821302

Early, E., Miller, S., Dunne, L., Thurston, A., & Filiz, M. (2020). The influence of socio-economic background and gender on school attainment in the United Kingdom: a systematic review. *Review of Education*, 8(1), 120–152. https://doi.org/10.1002/rev3.3175

Education Endowment Foundation [EEF]. (2017). *Challenge the gap: Evaluation report and executive summary*. https://files.eric.ed.gov/fulltext/ED581102.pdf

Education Endowment Foundation [EEFa]. (n.d.). *Improving literacy in key stage 2: Guidance report*. https://d2tic4wvo1iusb.cloudfront.net/eef-guidance-reports/literacy-ks2/EEF-Improving-literacy-in-key-stage-2-report-Second-edition.pdf

Education Endowment Foundation [EEFb]. (n.d.). *Improving literacy in secondary schools*. https://d2tic4wvo1iusb.cloudfront.net/eef-guidance-reports/literacy-ks3-ks4/EEF_KS3_KS4_LITERACY_GUIDANCE.pdf

Education Endowment Foundation [EEFc]. (n.d.). *Reading comprehension strategies*. https://educationendowmentfoundation.org.uk/education-evidence/teaching-learning-toolkit/reading-comprehension-strategies

Education Endowment Foundation [EEF]. (2018a). *Metacognition and self-regulation: A guidance report*. https://d2tic4wvo1iusb.cloudfront.net/eef-guidance-reports/metacognition/EEF_Metacognition_and_self-regulated_learning.pdf

Education Endowment Foundation [EEF]. (2018b). *Testing a scalable model of a programme that uses 'self-regulated strategy development' and memorable experiences to improve pupils' writing*. https://educationendowmentfoundation.org.uk/projects-and-evaluation/projects/ipeell

Education Endowment Foundation [EEF]. (2018c). *The attainment gap 2017*. https://educationendowmentfoundation.org.uk/public/files/Annual_Reports/EEF_Attainment_Gap_Report_2018.pdf

Education Endowment Foundation [EEF]. (2018d). *Preparing for literacy: Improving communication, language and literacy in the early years guidance report*. [online]. https://d2tic4wvo1iusb.cloudfront.net/eef-guidance-reports/literacy-early-years/Preparing_Literacy_Guidance_2018.pdf

Education Endowment Foundation [EEF]. (2021). *Improving literacy in key stage 2*. https://educationendowmentfoundation.org.uk/education-evidence/guidance-reports/literacy-ks2

Education Endowment Foundation [EEF]. (2021a). *Parental engagement*. https://educationendowmentfoundation.org.uk/education-evidence/early-years-toolkit/parental-engagement

Education Endowment Foundation [EEF]. (2021b). *Early years toolkit: Early literacy approaches*. https://educationendowmentfoundation.org.uk/education-evidence/early-years-toolkit/early-literacy-approaches

Education Endowment Fund. (2018). *Preparing for literacy: Seven recommendations*. [online]. https://educationendowmentfoundation.org.uk/education-evidence/guidance-reports/literacy-early-years

Elleman, A. M., Lindo, E. J., Morphy, P., & Compton, D. L. (2009). The impact of vocabulary instruction on passage-level comprehension of school-age children: A meta-analysis. *Journal of Research on Educational Effectiveness*, 2(1), 1–44. https://doi.org/10.1080/19345740802539200

Elliot Major, L. (2020). *Submission to the house of commons education committee – left behind white pupils from disadvantaged backgrounds*. https://committees.parliament.uk/writtenevidence/9116/pdf/

Elliot Major, L., & Higgins, S. (2019). *What works? Research and evidence for successful teaching*. Bloomsbury Education.

Elliot Major, L., & Machin, S. (2018). *Social mobility and its enemies*. Pelican. https://doi.org/10.1080/02601370.2019.1659563

Elliot, V., Nelson-Addy, L., Chantiluke, R., & Courtney, M. (2021). *Lit in colour: Diversity in literature in English schools*. Penguin and Runnymede. https://litincolour.penguin.co.uk

Erstad, O., Flewitt, R., Kummerling-Meibauer, B., & Pereira, I. (2020). The emerging field of digital literacies in early childhood. In O. Erstad, R. Flewitt, B. Kummerling-Meibauer & I. Pereira (Eds.) *The Routledge handbook of digital literacies in early childhood* (pp. 1–16). Routledge.

Erstad, O., Flewitt, R., Kümmerling-Meibauer, B. & Pereira, I. (Eds.) (2020). *The Routledge handbook of digital literacies in early childhood*. Routledge.

European Centre for Reading Recovery. (2012). *Standards and guidelines: For the implementation of reading recovery in Europe*. University College London. https://www.ucl.ac.uk/reading-recovery-europe/sites/reading-recovery-europe/files/standards_guidelines_reduce_file_size_2012.pdf

Fairfax, J., & Moat, J. (1998). *The way to write*. Penguin.

Feinstein, L., & Bynner, J. (2004). The importance of cognitive development in middle childhood for adulthood socioeconomic status, mental health, and problem behaviour. *Child Development*, 75(5), 1329–1339. https://doi.org/10.1111/j.1467-8624.2004.00743.x

Fergusson, D. M., Horwood, L. J., & Boden, J. M. (2008). The transmission of social inequality: Examination of the linkages between family socioeconomic status in childhood and educational achievement in young adulthood. *Research in Social Stratification and Mobility*, 26(3), 277–295. https://doi.org/10.1016/j.rssm.2008.05.001

Ferreiro, E., & Teberosky, A. (1982). *Literacy before schooling*. Heinemann.

Field, F. (2010). *The foundation years: Preventing poor children becoming poor adults*. The Report of the Review on Poverty and Life Chances. https://webarchive.nationalarchives.gov.uk/ukgwa/20110120090128/http://povertyreview.independent.gov.uk/media/20254/poverty-report.pdf

Fisher, D., & Frey, N. (2018). Raise reading volume through access, choice, discussion, and book talks. *The Reading Teacher*, 72(1), 89–97. https://doi.org/10.1002/trtr.1691

Fisher, R., Jones, S., Larkin, S., & Myhill, D. (2010). *Using talk to support writing*. SAGE.

Flavell, J. (1976). Metacognitive aspects of problem-solving. In L. B. Resnick (Ed.), *The nature of intelligence* (pp. 231–235). Erlbaum.

Flewitt, R. (2013). *Occasional paper 3: Early literacy: A broader vision*. TACTYC Association for Professional Development in Early Years. https://eprints.ncrm.ac.uk/id/eprint/3132/1/flewitt_occasional-paper3.pdf

Floud, J. H., Halsey, A. H., & Martin, F. M. (1957). *Social class and educational opportunity*. Heinemann.

Francis, B. (2017). Government policies in practice: Response 1. In T. Bibby, R. Lupton & C. Raffo (Eds.), *Responding to poverty and disadvantage in schools* (pp. 100–101). Palgrave Macmillan.

Francis, B., Archer, L., Hodgen, J., Pepper, D., Taylor, B., & Travers, M.-C. (2017). Exploring the relative lack of impact of research on 'ability grouping' in England: A discourse analytic account. *Cambridge Journal of Education*, 47(1), 1–18. https://doi.org/10.1080/0305764X.2015.1093095

Francis, B., Craig, N., Hodgen, J., Taylor, B., Tereshenko, A., Connolly, B., & Archer, L. (2020). The impact of tracking by attainment on pupil self-confidence over time: Demonstrating the accumulative impact of self-fulfilling prophecy. *British Journal of Sociology of Education*, 41(5), 626–642. https://doi.org/10.1080/01425692.2020.1763162

Fraumeni-McBride, J. P. (2017). The effects of choice on reading engagement and comprehension for second- and third-grade students: An action research report. *Journal of Montessori Research*, 3(2), 19–38.

Freire, P. (1985). Reading the world and reading the word: An interview with Paolo Freire. *Language Arts*, 62(1), 15–21.

Freire, P., & Macedo, D. P. (1987). *Literacy: Reading the word and the World*. Bergin and Garvey Publishers.

Friedman, S., Macmillan, L., & Maurison, D. (2017). *Social mobility, the class pay gap and intergenerational worklessness: New insights from the labour force survey*. Social Mobility Commission. http://dera.ioe.ac.uk/id/eprint/28474

Gadotti, M. (1994). *Reading Paolo Freire: His life and work*. State University of New York Press.

Gao, J., Brooks, C., Xu, Y., & Kitto, E. (2020). *What makes an effective early childhood parenting programme: A systematic review of reviews and meta-analyses*. Centre for Teacher and Early Years Education, UCL.

Gazeley, L. (2019). Unpacking 'disadvantage' and 'potential' in the context of fair access policies in England. *Educational Review*, 71(6), 673–690.

Gebhard, M., Chen, I.-A., Britton, L., & Graham, H. (2014). 'Miss, nominalization is a nominalization': English language learners' use of SFL metalanguage and their literacy practices. *Linguistics in Education*, 26, 106–125. https://doi.org/10.1016/j.linged.2014.01.003

Gentry, J. R. (1982). An analysis of developmental spelling in GNYS AT WRK. *The Reading Teacher*, 36, 192–200.

Geven, S., Batruch, A., & van de Werfhorst, H. (2018). *Inequality in teacher judgements, expectations and track recommendations: A review study*. University of Amsterdam. https://hdl.handle.net/11245.1/72d4594e-9518-4e19-9839-73a3264efac4

Gewirtz, S. (2001). Cloning the Blairs: New labour's programme for the re-socialization of working-class parents. *Journal of Educational Policy*, 16(4), 365–378. https://doi.org/10.1080/02680930110054353

Gilkerson, J., Richards, J. A., Warren, S. F., Montgomery, J. K., Greenwood, C. R., Kimbrough Oller, D., Hansen, J. H. L., & Paul, T. D. (2017). Mapping the early language environment using all-day recordings and automated analysis. *American Journal of Speech-Language Pathology*, 26(2), 248–265. https://doi.org/10.1044/2016_AJSLP-15-0169

Gillborn, D., & Mirza, H. (2000). *Educational inequality: Mapping race, class and gender*. Ofsted. https://dera.ioe.ac.uk/4428/2/Educational_inequality_mapping_race,_class_and_gender_(PDF_format).pdf

Gillen, J., & Hall, N. (2012). The emergence of early childhood literacy. In J. Larson & J. Marsh (Eds.), *The SAGE handbook of early childhood literacy* (2nd ed., pp. 3–17). SAGE Publications.

Golinkoff, R. M., Hoff, E., Rowe, M. L., Tamis-LeMonda, C. S., & Hirsh-Pasek, K. (2019). Language matters: Denying the existence of the 30-million-word gap has serious consequences. *Child Development*, 90(3), 985–992. https://doi.org/10.1111/cdev.13128

Golos, D. B., & Moses, A. M. (2011). Representations of deaf characters in children's picture books. *American Annals of the Deaf*, 156(3), 270–282.

Goodall, J., & Vorhaus, J. (2010). *Review of best practice in parental engagement*. Department for Education. https://assets.publishing.service.gov.uk/government/uploads/system/uploads/attachment_data/file/182508/DFE-RR156.pdf

Gorard, S., & Huat See, B. (2013). *Do parental involvement interventions increase attainment? A review of the evidence*. Nuffield Foundation.

Gore, J., Jaremus, F., & Miller, A. (2021). Do disadvantaged schools have poorer teachers? Rethinking assumptions about the relationship between teaching quality and school-level advantage. *The Australian Educational Researcher*. https://doi.org/10.1007/s13384-021-00460-w

Gombert, E. J. (1992). *Metalinguistic development*. Harvester Wheatsheaf.

Graham, S., & Harris, K. (2018). An examination of the design principles underlying a self-regulated strategy development study. *Journal of Writing Research*, 10(2), 139–187. https://doi.org/10.17239/jowr-2018.10.02.02

Graham, S., Harris, K. R., & Adkins, M. (2018). The impact of supplemental handwriting and spelling instruction with first grade students who do not acquire transcription skills as rapidly as peers: A randomized control trial. *Reading and Writing*, 31, 1273–1294. https://doi.org/10.1007/s11145-018-9822-0

Graham, S., McKeown, D., Kiuhara, S., & Harris, K. (2012). A meta-analysis of writing instruction for students in the elementary grades. *Journal of Educational Psychology*, 104(4), 879–896. https://doi.org/10.1037/a0029185

Graves, M. F., & Philippot, R. A. (2002). High-interest, easy reading: An important resource for struggling readers. *Preventing School Failure: Alternative Education for Children and Youth*, 46(4), 179–182. https://doi.org/10.1080/10459880209604419

Gritter, K., van Duinen, D. V., Montgomery, K., Blowers, D., & Bishop, D. (2017). Boy troubles? Male literacy depictions in children's choices picture books. *Reading Teacher*, 70(5), 571–581. https://doi.org/10.1002/trtr.1559

Guthrie, J. T., Hoa, A. L. W., Wigfield, A., Tonks, S. M., Humenick, N. M., & Littles, E. (2007). Reading motivation and reading comprehension growth in the later elementary years. *Contemporary Educational Psychology*, 32(3), 282–313. https://doi.org/10.1016/j.cedpsych.2006.05.004

Guthrie, J., & Humenick, N. (2004). Motivating students to read: Evidence of classroom practices that increase motivation and achievement. In P. McCardle & V. Chabra (Eds.), *The voice of evidence in reading research* (pp. 329–374). Paul H. Brookes.

Hall, N. (1987). *The emergence of literacy: Young children's developing understanding of reading and writing*. Hodder and Stoughton.

Halliday, M. A. (1993). Towards a language-based theory of learning. *Linguistics and Education*, 5(2), 93–116. https://doi.org/10.1016/0898-5898(93)90026-7

Halsey, A. H., Heath, A. F., & Ridge, J. M. (1980). *Origins and destinations*. Clarendon Press.

Hammett, R. F., & Sanford, K. (2008). *Boys, girls, and the myths of literacies and learning*. Canadian Scholars Press.

Hannon, P., & Nutbrown, C. (1997). Teachers' use of a conceptual framework for early literacy education involving parents. *Teacher Development*, 1(3), 405–420. https://doi.org/10.1080/13664539700200031

Hannon, P., Nutbrown, N., & Morgan, A. (2020). Effects of extending disadvantaged families' teaching of emergent literacy. *Research Papers in Education*, 35(3), 310–336. https://doi.org/10.1080/02671522.2019.1568531

Hansen, K., & Vignobles, A. (2005). The United Kingdom education system in a comparative context. In S. Machin & A. Vignobles (Eds.), *What's the good of education?* (pp. 13–34). Princeton University Press. https://doi.org/10.1515/9780691188652

Harris, K. R., & Graham, S. (2016). SRSD in writing for students with learning disabilities and their normally achieving peers: Policy implications of an evidence-based practice. *Policy Insights from Behavioral and Brain Sciences*, 3, 77–84. https://doi.org/10.1177/2372732215624216

Harrison, C. (2018). Defining and seeking to identify critical internet literacy: A discourse analysis of fifth-graders' internet search and evaluation activity. *Literacy*, 52, 153–160. https://doi.org/10.1111/lit.12136

Harris, K., Santangelo, T., & Graham, S. (2008). Self-regulated strategy development in writing: Going beyond NLEs to a more balanced approach. *Instructional Science*, 36(3), 395–408. https://doi.org/10.1007/s11251-008-9062-9

Hartley, D., & Platt, L. (2016). *Social advantage and disadvantage*. Oxford University Press.

Hart, B., & Risley, T. R. (1992). American parenting of language-learning children: Persisting differences in family-child interactions observed in natural home environments. *Developmental Psychology*, 28(6), 1096. https://doi.org/10.1037/0012-1649.28.6.1096

Hart, B., & Risley, T. R. (1995). *Meaningful differences in the everyday experience of young American children*. Paul H Brookes Publishing.

Hattie, J. A. C. (2009). *Visible learning*. Routledge.

Hay, I., & Fielding-Barnsley, R. (2009). Competencies that underpin children's transition into early literacy. *Australian Journal of Language and Literacy*, 32(2), 148–162. https://search.informit.org/doi/10.3316/ielapa.801882271625265

Heath, S. B. (1982). What no bedtime story means: Narrative skills at home and school. *Language in Society*, 11(1), 49–76. https://doi.org/10.1017/S0047404500009039

Heath, S. B. (1983). *Ways with words: Language, life and work in communities and classrooms*. Cambridge University Press.

Heidlage, J. K., Cunningham, J. E., Kaiser, A. P., Trivette, C. M., Barton, E. E., Frey, J. R., & Roberts, M. Y. (2020). The effects of parent-implemented language interventions on child linguistic outcomes: A meta-analysis. *Early Childhood Research Quarterly*, 50(2020), 6–23. https://doi.org/10.1016/j.ecresq.2018.12.006

Hempel-Jorgensen, A., Cremin, T., Harris, D., & Chamberlain, L. (2018). Pedagogy for reading for pleasure in low socio-economic primary schools: Beyond 'pedagogy of poverty'? *Literacy*, 52(2), 86–94. https://doi.org/10.1111/lit.12157

Hennessy, S., Calcagni, E., Leung, A., & Mercer, N. (2021). An analysis of the forms of teacher-student dialogue that are most productive for learning. *Language and Education*, 1–26. https://doi.org/10.1080/09500782.2021.1956943

Henning, C., McIntosh, B., Arnott, W., & Dodd, B. (2010). Long-term outcome of oral language and phonological awareness intervention with socially disadvantaged preschoolers: The impact on language and literacy. *Journal of Research in Reading*, 33(3), 231–246. https://doi.org/10.1111/j.1467-9817.2009.01410.x

Hingle, M., O'Connor, T., Dave, J., & Baranowski, T. (2010). Parental involvement in interventions to improve child dietary intake: A systematic review. *Preventive Medicine*, 51, 103–111. https://doi.org/10.1016/j.ypmed.2010.04.014

Hirsh-Pasek, K., Adamson, L. B., Bakeman, R., Owen, M. T., Golinkoff, R. M., Pace, A., Yust, P. K. S., & Suma, K. (2015). The contribution of early communication quality to low-income children's language success. *Psychological Sciences*, 26(7), 1071–1083. https://doi.org/10.1177/0956797615581493

Hoff, E. (2013). Interpreting the early language trajectories of children from low-SES and language minority homes: Implications for closing achievement gaps. *Developmental Psychology*, 49(1), 4. https://doi.org/10.1037/a0027238

Holmes, V. R. (2019). *Supporting school readiness through home instruction for parents of preschool youngsters (HIPPY) and the Texas maternal, infant and early childhood home visiting (MIECHV) programs in HISD, 2018–2019*. Research Educational Program Report. https://web.s.ebscohost.com/ehost/detail/detail?vid=3&sid=68f3217c-3019-44d8-bccd-739e0ff98123%40redis&bdata=JnNpdGU9ZWhvc3QtbGl2ZQ%3d%3d#AN=ED603815&db=eric

House of Commons Education Committee. (2021). *The forgotten: How white working-class pupils have been let down, and how to change it. First report of session 2021–22*. House of Commons Education Committee. https://publications.parliament.uk/pa/cm5802/cmselect/cmeduc/85/8502.htm

House of Commons Education Committee [HCEC]. (2014). *Underachievement in education by white working class children*. https://publications.parliament.uk/pa/cm201415/cmselect/cmeduc/142/142.pdf

Howe, C., Hennessy, S., Mercer, N., Vrikki, M., & Wheatley, L. (2019). Teacher–student dialogue during classroom teaching: Does it really impact on student outcomes? *Journal of the Learning Sciences*, 28(4–5), 462–512. https://doi.org/10.1080/10508406.2019.1573730

Hudson, R. (2004). Why education needs linguistics. *Journal of Linguistics*, 40(1), 105–130. https://doi.org/10.1017/S0022226703002342

Hughes, J., & Cao, Q. (2017). Trajectories of teacher-student warmth and conflict at the transition to middle school: Effects on academic engagement and achievement. *Journal of School Psychology*, 67, 148–162. https://doi.org/10.1016/j.jsp.2017.10.003

Hull, G., & Schultz, K. (2001). Literacy and learning out of school: A review of theory and research. *Review of Educational Research*, 71(4), 575–611. https://doi.org/10.3102/00346543071004575

Humphrey, S., Droga, L., Feez, S., & Primary English Teaching Association. (2012). *Grammar and meaning*. PETAA.

Husbands, D., & Pearce, J. (2012). *What makes great pedagogy? Nine claims from research*. National College for School Leadership. https://www.researchgate.net/publication/309384091_What_makes_great_pedagogy_Nine_claims_from_research

Hutchings, M., Francis, B., & De Vries, R. (2014). *Chain effects: The impact of academy chains on low-income students*. The Sutton Trust. https://www.suttontrust.com/wp-content/uploads/2019/12/Chain-Effects-2018.pdf

Hutchinson, J., Reader, M., & Akhal, A. (2020). *Education in England: Annual report*. Education Policy Institute. https://epi.org.uk/publications-and-research/education-in-england-annual-report-2020/

I CAN, The Communication Charity. (n.d). *Sentence trouble*. sentence-trouble.1294933642.pdf (the-dyslexia-spldtrust.org.uk).

ICAN, & RCSLT. (2018). *Bercow ten years on: An independent review of provision for children and young people with speech, language and communication needs in England*. https://www.bercow10yearson.com/

Ireson, J., & Hallam, S. (2001). *Ability grouping in education*. Chapman.

Ivinson, G., Beckett, L., Thompson, I., Wrigley, T., Egan, D., Leitch, R., & McKinney, S. (2017). *The research commission on poverty and policy advocacy*. British Educational Research Association. https://www.bera.ac.uk/project/poverty-and-policy-advocacy

Jæger, M. M., & Møllegaard, S. (2017). Cultural capital, teacher bias, and educational success: New evidence from monozygotic twins. *Social Science Research*, 65, 130–144. https://doi.org/10.1016/j.ssresearch.2017.04.003

Jay, T., Willis, B., Thomas, P., Taylor, R., Moore, N., Burnett, C., & Stevens, A. (2017). *Dialogic teaching: Evaluation report and executive summary.* https://educationendowmentfoundation.org.uk/projects-and-evaluation/projects/dialogic-teaching

Jenkins, S. P., Micklewright, J., & Schnepf, S. V. (2006). *Social segregation in secondary schools: How does England compare with other countries?* IZA Discussion Papers, No. 1959. Institute for the Study of Labor (IZA).

Jerrim, J., & Moss, G. (2019). The link between fiction and teenagers' reading skills: International evidence from the OECD PISA study. *British Educational Research Journal*, 45(1), 181–200. https://doi.org/10.1002/berj.3498

Jerrim, J., & Sims, S. (2019). Why do so few low- and middle-income children attend a grammar school? New evidence from the millennium cohort study. *British Educational Research Journal*, 45(3), 425–457. https://doi.org/10.1002/berj.3502

Johns, L. (2011, August 16). *Ghetto grammar Robs the young of a proper voice.* Evening Standard.

Johnson, E. J. (2015). Debunking the 'language gap'. *Journal for Multicultural Education*, 9(1), 42–50. https://doi.org/10.1108/JME-12-2014-0044

Jones, S. (2008). Grass houses: Representations and reinventions of social class through children's literature. *Journal of Language and Literacy Education*, 4(2), 40–58.

Jones, D. (2017). Talking about talk: Reviewing Oracy in English primary education. *Early Child Development and Care*, 187(3–4), 498–508. https://doi.org/10.1080/03004430.2016.1211125

Joo, Y. S., Magnuson, K., Duncan, G. J., Schindler, H. S., Yoshikawu, H., & Ziol-Guest, K. M. (2020). What works in early childhood education programs? A meta-analysis of preschool enhancement programs. *Early Education and Development*, 31(1), 1–26. http://dx.doi.org/10.1080/10409289.2019.1624146

Kalil, A., & Ryan, R. (2020). Parenting practices and socioeconomic gaps in childhood outcomes. *The Future of Children*, 30(2020), 29–54.

Kamler, B., & Comber, B. (2005). Turn-around pedagogies: Literacy interventions for at-risk students. *Improving Schools*, 8(2), 121–131. https://doi.org/10.1177/1365480205057702

Kellogg, R. T. (2008). Training writing skills: A cognitive developmental perspective. *Journal of Writing Research*, 1(1), 1–26. https://doi.org/10.17239/jowr-2008.01.01.1

Kennedy, E. (2018). Engaging children as readers and writers in high-poverty contexts. *Journal of Research in Reading*, 41(4), 716–731. https://doi.org/10.1111/1467-9817.12261

King, S. (2012). *On writing: A memoir of the craft.* Hodder.

Klauda, S. L., & Guthrie, J. T. (2008). Relationships of three components of reading fluency to reading comprehension. *Journal of Educational Psychology*, 100(2), 310–321. https://doi.org/10.1037/0022-0663.100.2.310

Knowles, E., & Evans, H. (2012). *PISA 2009: How does the social attainment gap in England compare with countries internationally?* Department for Education. https://assets.publishing.service.gov.uk/government/uploads/system/uploads/attachment_data/file/198957/DFE-RB206.pdf

Kolb, K. J., & Jussim, L. (1994). Teacher expectations and underachieving gifted children. *Roeper Review*, 17(1), 26–30. https://doi.org/10.1080/02783199409553613

Kress, G. (2010). *Multimodality: A social semiotic theory.* Routledge.

Kuchirko, Y. (2019). On differences and deficits: A critique of the theoretical and methodological underpinnings of the word gap. *Journal of Early Childhood Literacy*, 19(4), 533–562. https://doi.org/10.1177/1468798417747029

Kucirkova, N., & Cremin, T. (2018). Personalised reading for pleasure with digital libraries: Towards a pedagogy of practice and design. *Cambridge Journal of Education*, 48(5), 571–589. https://doi.org/10.1080/0305764X.2017.1375458

Kucirkova, N., Littleton, K., & Cremin, T. (2016). Young children's reading for pleasure with digital books: Six key facets of engagement. *Cambridge Journal of Education*, 47(1), 67–84. https://doi.org/10.1080/0305764X.2015.1118441

Kucirkova, N., Littleton, K., & Cremin, T. (2017). Young children's reading for pleasure with digital books: Six key facets of engagement. *Cambridge Journal of Education*, 47(1), 67–84. https://doi.org/10.1080/0305764X.2015.1118441

Kucirkova, N., Wells Rowe, D., Oliver, L., & Piestrzynski, L. E. (2019). Systematic review of young children's writing on screen: What do we know and what do we need to know. *Literacy*, 53, 216–225. https://doi.org/10.1111/lit.12173

Kuhl, P. K., Conboy, B. T., Padden, D., Nelson, T., & Pruitt, J. (2005). Early speech perception and later language development: Implications for the 'critical period'. *Language Learning and Development*, 1(3–4), 237–264. https://doi.org/10.1080/15475441.2005.9671948

Labov, W. (1973). The logic of nonstandard English. In N. Keddie (Ed.), *The Myth of cultural deprivation* (pp. 21–66). Penguin.

Ladson-Billings, G. (1995). But that's just good teaching! The case for culturally relevant pedagogy. *Theory Into Practice*, 34(3), 159–165. https://doi.org/10.1080/00405849509543675

Lampert, J., Wilkinson, J., Kaukko, M., & Garcia-Carron, R. (forthcoming). *Disadvantage: Keywords in teacher education*. Bloomsbury.

Lancaster, L. (2013). Moving into literacy: How it all begins. In J. Larson & J. Marsh (Eds.), *The SAGE handbook of early childhood literacy* (2nd ed., pp. 313–328). SAGE Publications.

Lankshear, C., & Knobel, M. (2015). Digital literacy and digital literacies: Policy, pedagogy and research considerations for education. *Nordic Journal of Digital Literacy*, 10, 8–20. https://doi.org/10.18261/ISSN1891-943X-2015-Jubileumsnummer-02

Lareau, A. (2011). *Unequal childhoods: Class, race and family life* (2nd ed.). University of California Press.

Le Guin, U. (2015). *Steering the craft: A twenty-first-century guide to sailing the sea of story*. Mariner Books.

Lee, S. H. (2019). Learning vocabulary from e-book reading and recorded word explanation for low-income elementary students with and without reading difficulties. *Reading and Writing*, 33, 691–717. https://doi.org/10.1007/s11145-019-09983-2

Lefstein, A., & Snell, J. (2013). *Better than best practice: Developing teaching and learning through dialogue*. Routledge.

Leung, C., Hernandez, M., & Suskind, D. (2018). Enriching home language environment among families from low-SES backgrounds: A randomized controlled trial of a home visiting curriculum. *Early Childhood Research Quarterly*, 50(2020), 24–35. https://doi.org/10.1016/j.ecresq.2018.12.005

Leutwyler, B., & Maag Merki, K. (2009). School effects on students' self-regulated learning. *Journal for Educational Research Online*, 1, 197–223. https://doi.org/10.25656/01:4562

Lewis, J., Ream, R., Bocian, K., Fast, L., Cardullo, R., & Hammond, K. (2012). Con Cariño: Teacher caring, math self-efficacy and math achievement among Hispanic English learners. *Teachers College Record*, 114(7), 1–42. https://doi: 10.1177/016146811211400701

Limpo, T., Parente, N., & Alves, R. A. (2018). Promoting handwriting fluency in fifth graders with slow handwriting: A single-subject design study. *Reading and Writing*, 31, 1343–1366. https://doi.org/10.1007/s11145-017-9814-5

Lindsay, G., & Strand, S. (2013). Evaluation of the national roll-out of parenting programmes across England: The parenting early intervention programme (PEIP). *BMC Public Health*, 13, 972. https://doi.org/10.1186/1471-2458-13-972

Livingstone, S., & Haddon, L. (2009). *EU kids online final report.* https://eucpn.org/sites/default/files/document/files/5._eu_kids_online_-_final_report.pdf

Locke, A., Ginsborg, J., & Peers, I. (2002). Development and disadvantage: Implications for the early school years and beyond. *International Journal of Language & Communication Disorders*, 37(1), 3–15. https://doi.org/10.1080/13682820110089911

Locke, T. (2009). Grammar and writing: The international debate. In R. Beard, D. Myhill, M. Nystrand & J. Riley (Eds.), *The SAGE handbook of writing development* (pp. 182–193). SAGE.

Long, J., Lawrie, E., Richardson, H., & Coughlan, S. (2021, August 12). *GCSE results 2021: Record passes and top grades.* https://www.bbc.co.uk/news/education-58174253

Lubliner, S., & Smetana, L. (2005). The effects of comprehensive vocabulary instruction on students' metacognitive word-learning skills and reading comprehension. *Journal of Literacy Research*, 37(2), 163–200. https://doi.org/10.1207/s15548430jlr3702_3

Lundberg, I., Larsman, P., & Strid, A. (2012). Development of phonological awareness during the pre-school year: The influence of gender and socio-economic status. *Reading and Writing*, 25, 305–320. https://doi.org/10.1007/s11145-010-9269-4

Lupton, R. (2005). Social justice and school improvement: Improving the quality of schooling in the poorest neighbourhoods. *British Educational Research Journal*, 31(5), 589–604. https://doi.org/10.1080/01411920500240759

Machin, S., McNally, S., & Viarengo, M. (2018). Changing how literacy is taught: Evidence on synthetic phonics. *American Economic Journal: Economic Policy*, 10(2), 217–241. https://doi.org/10.1257/pol.20160514

Macken-Horarik, M., Sandiford, C., Love, K., & Unsworth, L. (2015). New ways of working 'with grammar in mind' in school English: Insights from systemic functional grammatics. *Linguistics and Education*, 31, 145–158. https://doi.org/10.1016/j.linged.2015.07.004

Mackey, M. (2021). *Social justice for young readers: Advocating for access, choice and time to read.* Literacy. http://doi.org/10.1111/lit.12264

Macleod, S., Sharp, C., Bernardinelli, D., Skipp, A., & Higgins, S. (2015). *Supporting the attainment of disadvantaged pupils: Articulating success and good practice.* Research Report. Department of Education. https://assets.publishing.service.gov.uk/government/uploads/system/uploads/attachment_data/file/473975/DFE-RB411_Supporting_the_attainment_of_disadvantaged_pupils_brief.pdf

Maine, F. (2015). *Dialogic readers: Children talking and thinking together about visual texts.* Routledge.

Malouff, J., & Thorsteinsson, E. (2016). Bias in grading: A meta-analysis of experimental research findings. *Australian Journal of Education*, 60(3), 245–256. https://doi.org/10.1177/0004944116664618

Mantei, J., & Kervin, L. (2014). Interpreting the images in a picture book: Students make connections to themselves, their lives and experience. *English Teaching: Practice and Critique*, 13(2), 76–92.

Manz, P. H., Hughes, C., Barnabas, E., Bracaliello, C., & Ginsburg-Block, M. (2010). A descriptive review and meta-analysis of family-based emergent literacy interventions: To what extent is the research applicable to low-income, ethnic-minority or linguistically-diverse young children? *Early Childhood Research Quarterly*, 25(4), 409–431. https://doi.org/10.1016/j.ecresq.2010.03.002

Marsh, J., Lahmar, J., Plowman, L., Yamada-Rice, D., Bishop, J., & Scott, F. (2021). Under threes' play with tablets. *Journal of Early Childhood Research*, 19(3), 283–297. https://doi.org/10.1177/1476718X20966688

Marsh, J., & Richards, C. (2013). Play, media and children's playground cultures. In R. Willett, C. Richards, J. Marsh, A. Burn & J. C. Bishop (Eds.), *Children, media and playground cultures. Studies in childhood and youth* (pp. 1–20). Palgrave Macmillan. https://doi.org/10.1057/9781137318077_1

Martino, W. (2001). Boys and reading: Investigating the impact of masculinities on boys' reading preferences and involvement in literacy. *Australian Journal of Language and Literacy*, 24(1), 61–74.

McCurdy, M., Clure, L. F., & Bleck, A. A. (2016). Identifying effective spelling interventions: Using a brief experimental analysis and extended analysis. *Journal of Applied School Psychology*, 32(1), 46–65. https://doi.org/10.1080/15377903.2015.1121193

McDowell, K. D., Lonigan, C. J., & Goldstein, H. (2007). Relations among socioeconomic status, age, and predictors of phonological awareness. *Journal of Speech, Language, and Hearing Research*, 50(4), 1079–1092. https://doi.org/10.1044/1092-4388(2007/075)

McGaw, B. (2008). The role of the OECD in international comparative studies of achievement. *Assessment in Education*, 15(3), 223–243.

McGeown, S. P. (2015). Sex or gender identity? Understanding children's reading choices and motivation. *Journal of Research in Reading*, 38(1), 35–46. https://doi.org/10.1111/j.1467-9817.2012.01546.x

Melhuish, E., Phan, M. B., Sylva, K., Sammons, P., Siraj-Blatchford, I., & Taggart, B. (2008). Effects of the home learning environment and preschool center experience upon literacy and numeracy development in early primary school. *Journal of Social Issues*, 64(1), 95–114. https://doi.org/10.1111/j.1540-4560.2008.00550.x

Mercer, N. (1995). *The guided construction of knowledge: Talk amongst teachers and learners*. Multilingual Matters.

Mercer, N., & Dawes, L. (2008). The value of exploratory talk. In N. Mercer & S. Hodgkinson (Eds.), *Exploring talk in schools* (pp. 55–72). SAGE.

Mercer, N., & Littleton, K. (2007). *Dialogue and the development of children's thinking: A sociocultural approach*. Routledge.

Merga, M. (2021). How can Booktok on TikTok inform readers' advisory services for young people? *Library & Information Science Research*, 43(2), 101091. https://doi.org/10.1016/j.lisr.2021.101091

Mills, K., & Exley, B. (2014). Time, space, and text in the elementary school digital writing classroom. *Written Communication*, 31(4), 434–469. https://doi.org/10.1177/0741088314542757

Mishra, P. (2019). Considering contextual knowledge: The TPACK diagram gets an upgrade. *Journal of Digital Learning in Teacher Education*, 35(2), 76–78. https://doi.org/10.1080/21532974.2019.1588611

Mishra, P., & Koehler, M. J. (2006). Technological pedagogical content knowledge: A framework for teacher knowledge. *Teacher College Record*, 108(6), 1017–1054. http://dx.doi.org/10.1111/j.1467-9620.2006.00684.x

Mol, S. E., Bus, A. G., de Jong, M. T., & Smeets, D. J. (2008). Added value of dialogic parent-child readings: A meta-analysis. *Early Education and Development*, 19(1), 7–26. https://doi.org/10.1080/10409280701838603

Montacute, R., & Cullinane, C. (2018). *Parent power: How parents use financial and cultural resources to boost their children's chances of success*. The Sutton Trust. https://www.suttontrust.com/wp-content/uploads/2019/12/Parent-Power-2018.pdf

Moon, B. R. (2012). Remembering rhetoric: Recalling a tradition of explicit instruction in writing. *English in Australia*, 47(1), 37–52.

Morgan, P. L., & Fuchs, D. (2007). Is there a bidirectional relationship between children's reading skills and reading motivation? *Exceptional Children*, 73(2), 165–183. https://doi.org/10.1177/001440290707300203

Morrison, A. (2019). Contributive justice: Social class and graduate employment in the UK. *Journal of Education and Work*, 32(4), 335–346. https://doi.org/10.1080/13639080.2019.164644

Muijs, D., & Bokhove, C. (2020). *Metacognition and self-regulation: Evidence review*. Education Endowment Foundation. https://educationendowmentfoundation.org.uk/education-evidence/evidence-reviews/metacognition-and-self-regulation

Myhill, D. A., Lines, H., & Jones, S. M. (2018). Texts that teach: Examining the efficacy of using texts as models. *L1-Educational Studies in Language and Literature*, 18, 1–24. https://doi.org/10.17239/L1ESLL-2018.18.03.07

Myhill, D. (2018). Grammar as a meaning-making resource for improving writing. *L1-Educational Studies in Language and Literature*, 18, 1–21. https://doi.org/10.17239/L1ESLL-2018.18.04.04

Myhill, D. A. (2009). Becoming a designer: Trajectories of linguistic development. In R. Beard, D. Myhill, J. Riley & M. Nystrand (Eds.), *The SAGE handbook of writing development* (pp. 402–414). SAGE.

Myhill, D. A. (2021). Grammar Re-imagined. *English in Education*, 55(3), 265–278. https://doi.org/10.1080/04250494.2021.1885975

Myhill, D. A., Cremin, T. M., & Oliver, L. J. (2021). Writing as a craft. *Research Papers in Education*. https://doi.org/10.1080/02671522.2021.1977376

Myhill, D. A., Jones, S. M., Lines, H., & Watson, A. (2012). Re-thinking grammar: The impact of embedded grammar teaching on students' writing and students' metalinguistic understanding. *Research Papers in Education*, 27(2), 139–166. https://doi.org/10.1080/02671522.2011.637640

Myhill, D., Jones, S., Lines, H., & Watson, A. (2016). *Essential primary grammar*. Open University Press.

Myhill, D. A., Jones, S., & Watson, A. (2013). Grammar matters: How teachers' grammatical subject knowledge impacts on the teaching of writing. *Teaching and Teacher Education*, 36, 77–91. http://dx.doi.org/10.1016/j.tate.2013.07.005

Myhill, D. A., & Newman, R. (2016). Metatalk: Enabling metalinguistic discussion about writing. *International Journal of Education Research*, 80, 177–187. https://doi.org/10.1016/j.ijer.2016.07.007

Myhill, D., & Newman, R. (2019). Writing talk – developing metalinguistic understanding through dialogic teaching. In N. Mercer, R. Wegerif & L. Major (Eds.), *International handbook of research on dialogic education* (pp. 360–372). Routledge.

Myhill, D., Newman, R., Watson, A., & Jones, S. (2022). Writing dialogues: Enabling metalinguistic thinking through dialogic talk. In R. Solheim, H. Otnes & M. Riis-Johansen (Eds.), *Samtale, samscrive, samhandle* (pp. 71–93). Universitetsforlaget.

Nash, R. (1990). Bourdieu on education and social and cultural reproduction. *British Journal of Sociology of Education*, 11(4), 431–447. https://doi.org/10.1080/0142569900110405

Nash, H., & Snowling, M. (2006). Teaching new words to children with poor existing vocabulary knowledge: A controlled evaluation of the definition and context methods. *International Journal of Language & Communication Disorders*, 41(3), 335–354.

New London Group. (1996). A pedagogy of multiliteracies: Designing social futures. *Harvard Educational Review*, 66(1), 60–92.

Neuman, S., Kaefer, T., & Pinkham, A. (2017). Improving low-income children's word and world knowledge: The effects of content rich instruction. *Elementary School Journal*, 116(4), 652–674. https://doi.org/10.1086/686463

Neuman, S. B., Kaefer, T., & Pinkham, A. M. (2018). A double dose of disadvantage: Language experiences for low-income children in home and school. *Journal of Educational Psychology*, 110(1), 102.

Neuman, S. B., & Moland, N. (2019). Book deserts: The consequences of income segregation on children's access to print. *Urban Education*, 54(1), 126–147. https://doi.org/10.1177/0042085916654525

New South Wales [NSW] Department of Education and Training. (2010). *Teaching comprehension strategies*. Teaching-Comprehension-Strategies-DEC.pdf (nsw.gov.au).

Newbolt Report. (1921). *The teaching of English in England*. Her Majesty's Stationery Office.

Newman, R. (2016). Working talk: Developing a framework for the teaching of collaborative talk. *Research Papers in Education*, 31(1), 107–131. https://doi.org/10.1080/02671522.2016.1106698

Newman, R., & Watson, A. (2020). Shaping spaces: Teachers' orchestration of metatalk about written text. *Linguistics and Education*, 60. https://doi.org/10.1016/j.linged.2020.100860

Norbury, C., Griffiths, S., Vamvakas, G., Baird, G., Charman, T., Simonoff, E., & Pickles, A. (2021). Socioeconomic disadvantage is associated with prevalence of developmental language disorders, but not rate of language or literacy growth in children from 4 to 11 years: Evidence from the Surrey Communication and Language in Education Study (SCALES). https://ssrn.com/abstract=3814832 or http://dx.doi.org/10.2139/ssrn.3814832

Nuffield Foundation Education Limited. (2021). *Nuffield early language intervention*. https://www.teachneli.org/

Nuffield Foundation News. (2021, April 27). *News*. https://www.nuffieldfoundation.org/news/62000-children-ake-part-in-nuffield-early-language-intervention

Nutbrown, C., & Hannon, P. (2011). *ORIM – a framework for practice*. http://www.real-online.group.shef.ac.uk/wordpress/wp-content/uploads/ORIM-A-Framework-for-Practice.pdf

Nystrand, M., Gamoran, A., Kachur, R., & Prendergast, C. (1997). *Opening dialogue: Understanding the dynamics of language and learning in the English classroom*. Teachers College Press.

Oakhill, J., & Cain, K. (2012). The precursors of reading comprehension and word reading in young readers: Evidence from a four-year longitudinal study. *Scientific Studies of Reading*, 16, 91–121. https://doi.org/10.1080/10888438.2010.529219

Oakley, G., Wildy, H., & Berman, Y. (2020). Multimodal digital text creation using tablets and open-ended creative apps to improve the literacy learning of children in early childhood classrooms. *Journal of Early Childhood Literacy*, 20(4), 655–679. https://doi.org/10.1177/1468798418779171

Ofcom. (2021). *Children and parents: Media use and attitudes report 2020/21*. [Online]. https://www.ofcom.org.uk/__data/assets/pdf_file/0025/217825/children-and-parents-media-use-and-attitudes-report-2020-21.pdf

Ofsted. (2009). *English at the crossroads: An evaluation of English in primary and secondary schools 2005/8*. HMSO.

Ofsted. (2013). *Unseen children: Access and achievement 20 years on*. https://www.gov.uk/government/publications/unseen-children-access-and-achievement-20-years-on

Ofsted. (2016). *Unknown children – Destined for disadvantage?* https://assets.publishing.service.gov.uk/government/uploads/system/uploads/attachment_data/file/541394/Unknown_children_destined_for_disadvantage.pdf

O'Hare, L., Stark, P., Cockerill, M., Lloyd, K., McConnellogue, S., Gildea, A., & Bower, C. (2019). *Reciprocal reading: Evaluation report*. Education Endowment Foundation.

O'Higgins, A., Sebba, J., & Luke, N. (2015). *What is the relationship between being in care and the educational outcomes of children?* University of Oxford. https://www.basw.co.uk/system/files/resources/basw_33005-5_0.pdf

Olinghouse, N. G., & Wilson, J. (2013). The relationship between vocabulary and writing quality in three genres. *Reading and Writing*, 26(1), 45–65.

Oliver, K. (2016). *How to teach vocabulary acquisition*. The English and Media Centre Blog. https://www.englishandmedia.co.uk/blog/how-to-teach-vocabulary-acquisition

Open University. (n.d.). *Reading aloud*. https://ourfp.org/finding/reading-aloud/

Organisation for Economic Cooperation and Development [OECD]. (2002). *Reading for change*. Organisation for Economic Cooperation and Development [OECD]. https://www.oecd.org/education/school/programmeforinternationalstudentassessmentpisa/33690904.pdf

Organisation for Economic Cooperation and Development [OECD]. (2010). *PISA 2009 results: Overcoming social background – equity in learning opportunities and outcomes* (Vol. II). http://dx.doi.org/10.1787/9789264091504-en

Organisation for Economic Cooperation and Development [OECD]. (2019). *PISA 2018 results (volume II): Where all students can succeed*. PISA, OECD Publishing. https://doi.org/10.1787/b5fd1b8f-en

Owen, Z. (2015). The importance of supporting language and communication. *British Journal of School Nursing*, 10(10), 507–509. https://doi.org/10.12968/bjsn.2015.10.10.507

Palfrey, J., & Gasser, U. (2008). *Born digital*. Basic Books.

Palincsar, A. S., & Brown, A. L. (1984). Reciprocal teaching of comprehension-fostering and comprehension-monitoring activities. *Cognition and Instruction*, 1(2), 117–175. https://doi.org/10.1207/s1532690xci0102_1

Pangrazio, L. (2016). Reconceptualising critical digital literacy. *Discourse: Studies in the Cultural Politics of Education*, 37(2), 163–174. https://doi.org/10.1080/01596306.2014.942836

Parodi, G. (2007). Reading-writing connections: Discourse-oriented research. *Reading and Writing*, 20, 225–250. https://doi.org/10.1007/s11145-006-9029-7

Perera, K. (1984). *Children's writing and reading: Analysing classroom language*. Blackwell.

Perfetti, C. (2010). Decoding, vocabulary, and comprehension. The golden triangle of reading skill. In M. G. McKeown & L. Kucan (Eds.), *Bringing reading research to life* (pp. 291–302). Guilford.

Perfetti, C., McKeown, M. G., & Kucan, L. (2010). Decoding, vocabulary, and comprehension. *Bringing Reading Research to Life*, 291–303.

Phillippo, K. (2012). 'You're trying to know me': Students from nondominant groups respond to teacher personalism. *The Urban Review*, 44(4), 441–467. https://doi.org/10.1007/s11256-011-0195-9

Picton, I. (2019). *Teachers' use of technology to support literacy in 2018*. National Literacy Trust.

Picton, I., & Clark, C. (2015). *The impact of ebooks on the reading motivation and reading skills of children and young people: A study of schools using RM books*. National Literacy Trust.

Pressley, M., & Harris, K. R. (2006). Cognitive strategy instruction: From basic research to classroom instruction. In P. A. Alexander & P. Winne (Eds.), *Handbook of educational psychology* (2nd ed., pp. 265–286). Erlbaum.

Pribesh, S., Gavigan, K., & Dickinson, G. (2011). The access gap: Poverty and characteristics of school library media centers. *The Library Quarterly*, 81(2), 143–160. https://doi.org/10.1086/658868

Prior, P. (2006). A sociocultural theory of writing. In C. Macarthur, S. Graham & J. Fitzgerald (Eds.), *Handbook of writing research* (pp. 54–66). Guilford Press.

PNS/UKLA. (2004). *Raising boys' achievements in writing*. Primary National Strategy and United Kingdom Literacy Association. https://dera.ioe.ac.uk/5400/1/RR636.pdf

Primary Literacy Research Collective. (2021). *Briefing: Experiences of literacy in lockdown: What can we learn?* https://ukla.org/wp-content/uploads/PLRC-Research_Briefing-1.pdf

Pruzinsky, T. (2014). Read books. Every day. Mostly for pleasure. *English Journal*, 103(4), 25–30.

Public Health England. (2020). *Best start in speech, language and communication: Guidance to support local commissioners and service leads best start in speech, language and communication: Guidance to support local commissioners and service leads.* publishing.service.gov.uk

QCA/UKLA. (2004). *More than words 1: Creating stories on page and screen.* https://www.open.edu/open-learncreate/pluginfile.php/5762/mod_resource/content/1/1847210724.pdf

QCA/UKLA. (2005). *More than words 2: Multimodal texts in the classroom.* http://www.suehorner.com/resources/7_More_than_words_(2004).pdf

Qualifications and Curriculum Authority [QCA]. (2004). *Introducing the grammar of talk.* QCA.

Quigley, A. (2018). *Closing the vocabulary gap.* Routledge.

Quigley, A., & Coleman, R. (2019). *Improving literacy in secondary schools. Guidance report.* Education Endowment Foundation.

Rampton Report. (1981). *West Indian children in our schools, interim report of the committee of inquiry into the education of children from ethnic minority groups.* HM Stationery Office.

Raz, I., & Bryant, P. (1990). Social background, phonological awareness and children's reading. *Developmental Psychology,* 8(3), 209–225. https://doi.org/10.1111/j.2044-835X.1990.tb00837.x

Reay, D. (2008). Tony Blair, the promotion of the 'active' educational citizen, and middle-class hegemony. *Oxford Review of Education,* 34(6), 639–650. https://doi.org/10.1080/03054980802518821

Reay, D. (2017). *Miseducation: Inequality, education and the working classes.* Policy Press.

Reedy, D., & Bearne, E. (2021). *Talk for teaching and learning: The dialogic classroom.* UKLA.

Reich, S., Yau, C. Y., Xu, Y., Muskat, T., Uvalle, J., & Cannata, D. (2019) Digital or print? A comparison of pre-schoolers' comprehension, vocabulary, and engagement from a print book and an e-book. *AERA Open,* 5(3), 1–16. https://doi.org/10.1177/2332858419878389

Resnick, L., Asterhan, C., & Clarke, S. (2015). *Socializing intelligence through academic talk and dialogue.* American Educational Research Association.

Reynolds, D. (2007). *Schools learning from their best.* National College for School Leadership.

Riley, J. (2006). *Language and literacy 3–7.* SAGE.

Rizk, J., & Davies, S. (2021). Can digital technology bridge the classroom engagement gap? Findings from a qualitative study of K-8 classrooms in 10 Ontario school boards. *Social Sciences,* 10(1), 12. http://dx.doi.org/10.3390/socsci10010012

Robinson-Kooi, S., & Hammond, L. (2020). The spelling detective project: A year 2 explicit instruction spelling intervention. *Australian Journal of Teacher Education,* 45(3). http://dx.doi.org/10.14221/ajte.2020v45n3.5

Romeo, R. R., Leonard, J. A., Robinson, S. T., West, M. R., Mackey, A. P., Rowe, M. L., & Gabrieli, J. D. (2018). Beyond the 30-million-word gap: Children's conversational exposure is associated with language-related brain function. *Psychological Science,* 29(5), 700–710. https://doi.org/10.1177/0956797617742725

Roorda, D. L., Koomen, H., Spilt, J. L., & Oort, F. J. (2011). The influence of affective teacher-student relationships on students' school engagement and achievement: A meta-analytic approach. *Review of Educational Research,* 81(4), 493–529. https://doi.org/10.3102/0034654311421793

Rose, J. (2006). *Independent review of the teaching of early reading.* DfES.

Rosen, M. (2019, March 9). Why reading aloud is a vital bridge to literacy. *The Guardian.*

Rowe, M. L. (2018). Understanding socioeconomic differences in parents' speech to children. *Child Development Perspectives,* 12(2), 122–127. https://doi.org/10.1111/cdep.12271

Rowe, M. L., Pan, B. A., & Ayoub, C. (2005) Predictors of variation in maternal talk to children: A longitudinal study of low-income families. *Parenting Science and Practice,* 5(3), 259–283. https://doi.org/10.1207/s15327922par0503_3

Roy, P., Chiat, S., & Dodd, B. (2014). *Language and socioeconomic disadvantage: From research to practice*. City University London. https://openaccess.city.ac.uk/id/eprint/4989/

Salas, N., Birello, M., & Ribas, T. (2021). Effectiveness of an SRSD writing intervention for low- and high-SES children. *Reading and Writing*, 34, 1653–1680. https://doi.org/10.1007/s11145-020-10103-8

Santangelo, T., & Graham, S. (2016). A comprehensive meta-analysis of handwriting instruction. *Educational Psychology Review*, 28(2), 225–265. https://doi.org/10.1007/s1064 8-015-9335-1

Scales, P., Pekel, K., Sethi, J., Chamberlain, R., & Van Boekel, M. (2020). Academic year changes in student teacher developmental relationships and their linkage to middle and high school students' motivation: A mixed methods study. *Journal of Early Adolescence*, 40(4), 499–536. https://doi.org/10.1177/0272431619858414

Scarborough, H. S. (2001). Connecting early language and literacy to later reading (dis)abilities: Evidence, theory, and practice. In S. Neuman & D. Dickinson (Eds.), *Handbook for research in early literacy* (pp. 97–110). Guilford Press.

Schiefele, U., Schaffner, E., Möller, J., & Wigfield, A. (2012). Dimensions of reading motivation and their relation to reading behavior and competence. *Reading Research Quarterly*, 47(4), 427–463. https://doi.org/10.1002/RRQ.030

Schleppegrell, M. J. (2013). The role of metalanguage in supporting academic language development. *Language Learning*, 63, 153–170. https://doi.org/10.1111/j.1467-9922.2012.00742.x

Schmier, S. A. (2021). Using digital storytelling as a turn-around pedagogy. *Literacy*, 55, 172–180. https://doi.org/10.1111/lit.12250

Scholes, L. (2019). Working-class boys' relationships with reading: Contextual systems that support working-class boys' engagement with, and enjoyment of, reading. *Gender and Education*, 31(3), 344–361. https://doi.org/10.1080/09540253.2018.1533921

Scott, F., & Marsh, J. (2018). *Digital literacies in early childhood*. Oxford Research Encyclopedia of Education. https://oxfordre.com/education/view/10.1093/acrefore/9780190264093.001.0001/acrefore-9780190264093-e-97

Sefton-Green, J., Marsh, J., Erstad, O., & Flewitt, R. (2016). *Establishing a research agenda for the digital literacy practices of young children: A white paper for COST action IS1410*. COST European Cooperation in Science and Technology. http://digilitey.eu

Shanahan, T. (2006). Relations among oral language, reading and writing. In C. MacArthur, S. Graham, & J. Fitzgerald (Eds.), *Handbook of writing research* (pp. 171–186). Guilford Press.

Shanahan, T. (2018). *Is there really a 30 million-word gap?* http://shanahanonliteracy.com/blog/is-there-really-a-30-million-word-gap#sthash.V1A4A5RB.dpbs

Shannon, P. (1985). Reading instruction and social class. *Language Arts*, 62(6), 604–613. http://www.jstor.org/stable/41405328

Sharples, J., Slavin, R., Chambers, B., & Sharp, C. (2011). *Effective classroom strategies for closing the gap in educational achievement for children and young people living in poverty, including white working-class boys*. Centre for Excellence and Outcomes in Children and Young People's Services. https://www.york.ac.uk/media/iee/documents/Closing%20the%20Gap.pdf

Sibieta, L., Kotecha, M., & Skipp, A. (2016). *Nuffield early language intervention evaluation report and executive summary*. Education Endowment Fund. https://files.eric.ed.gov/fulltext/ED581138.pdf

Siraj-Blatchford, I. (2004). Educational disadvantage in the early years: How do we overcome it? Some lessons from research. *European Early Childhood Education Research Journal*, 12(2), 5–20. https://doi.org/10.1080/13502930485209391

Siraj-Blatchford, I., Mayo, A., Melhuish, E., Taggart, B., Sammons, P., & Sylva, K. (2011). *Performing against the odds: Developmental trajectories of children in the EPPSE 3–16 study*. Research Report DFE-RR128. Department for Education.

Siraj, I., & Mayo, A. (2014). *Social class and educational inequality*. Cambridge University Press.

Slavin, E. R., Lake, C., Inns, A., Baye, A., Dachet, D., & Haslam, J. (2019). *A quantitative synthesis of research on writing approaches in years 3 to 13*. Education Endowment Foundation. https://educationendowmentfoundation.org.uk/public/files/Writing_Approaches_in_Years_3_to_13_Evidence_Review.pdf

Smit, R. (2012). Towards a clearer understanding of student disadvantage in higher education: Problematising deficit thinking. *Higher Education Research and Development*, 31(3), 369–380.

Smith, F. (1983). Reading like a writer. *Language Arts*, 60(5), 558–567.

Snell, J., & Lefstein, A. (2018). 'Low ability', participation, and identity in dialogic pedagogy. *American Educational Research Journal*, 55(1), 40–78. https://doi.org/10.3102/0002831217730010

Social Mobility Commission [SMC]. (2020a). *Monitoring social mobility*. https://assets.publishing.service.gov.uk/government/uploads/system/uploads/attachment_data/file/891155/Monitoring_report_2013-2020_-Web_version.pdf

Social Mobility Commission [SMC]. (2020b). *The long shadow of deprivation*. https://assets.publishing.service.gov.uk/government/uploads/system/uploads/attachment_data/file/923623/SMC_Long_shadow_of_deprivation_MAIN_REPORT_Accessible.pdf

Social Mobility Commission [SMC]. (2021). *State of the nation 2020–2021*. https://assets.publishing.service.gov.uk/government/uploads/system/uploads/attachment_data/file/1003977/State_of_the_nation_2021_-_Social_mobility_and_the_pandemic.pdf

Sperry, D. E., Sperry, L. L., & Miller, P. J. (2019). Reexamining the verbal environments of children from different socioeconomic backgrounds. *Child Development*, 90(4), 1303–1318. https://doi.org/10.1111/cdev.13072

SRSD. (2017). *Each step of SRSD*. Literacy on Demand. https://srsdonline.org/each-step-of-srsd/

Stevenson, J., O'Mahoney, J., Khan, O., Ghaffar, F., & Stiell, B. (2019). *Understanding and overcoming the challenges of targeting students from under-represented and disadvantaged ethnic backgrounds*. Office for Students. https://www.officeforstudents.org.uk/media/d21cb263-526d-401c-bc74-299c748e9ecd/ethnicity-targeting-research-report.pdf

Stiles, M. (2013). 'Do we make ourselves clear?' Developing a social, emotional and behavioural difficulties (SEBD) support service's effectiveness in detecting and supporting children experiencing speech, language and communication difficulties (SLCD). *Emotional and Behavioural Difficulties*, 18(2), 213–232. https://doi.org/10.1080/13632752.2012.716573

Stoilescu, D. (2015). A critical examination of the technological pedagogical content knowledge framework: Secondary school mathematics teachers integrating technology. *Journal of Educational Computing Research*, 52(4), 514–547. https://doi.org/10.1177/0735633115572285

Stone, C. A. (1998). The metaphor of scaffolding: Its utility for the field of learning disabilities. *Journal of Learning Disabilities*, 31(4), 344–364. https://doi.org/10.1177/002221949803100404

Strand, S. (2021). *Ethnic, socio-economic and sex inequalities in educational achievement at age 16: An analysis of the second longitudinal study of young people in England (LSYPE2)*. Commission on Race and Ethnic Disparities. https://www.gov.uk/government/publications/the-report-of-the-commission-on-race-and-ethnic-disparities-supporting-research/ethnic-socio-economic-and-sex-inequalities-in-educational-achievement-at-age-16-by-professor-steve-strand

Street, B. (2001). *Literacy and development: Ethnographic perspectives*. Routledge.

Sullivan, A., & Brown, M. (2015). Reading for pleasure and progress in reading and mathematics. *British Educational Research Journal*, 41(6), 971–991. https://doi.org/10.1002/berj.3180

Swann Report. (1985). *Education for all. Report of the committee of enquiry into the education of children from ethnic minority groups*. Her Majesty's Stationery Office.

Sylva, K., Melhuish, E., Sammons, P., Siraj-Blatchford, I., & Taggart, B. (2004). *The effective provision of pre-school education (EPPE) project: Findings from pre-school to end of key stage 1*. Sure Start/DFES. https://dera.ioe.ac.uk/18189/2/SSU-SF-2004-01.pdf

Sylva, K., Scott, S., & Vasiliki, T. (2008). Training parents to help their children read: A randomised controlled trial. *British Journal of Educational Psychology*, 78(3), 435–455. http://dx.doi.org/10.1348/000709907X255718

Taggart, B., Sylva, K., Melhuish, E., Sammons, P., & Siraj, I. (2015a) *Effective pre-school, primary and secondary education project (EPPSE 3-16+) department for education*. https://assets.publishing.service.gov.uk/government/uploads/system/uploads/attachment_data/file/455670/RB455_Effective_pre-school_primary_and_secondary_education_project.pdf.pdf

Taggart, B., Sylva, K., Melhuish, E., Sammons, P., & Siraj, I. (2015b). *How pre-school influences children and young people's attainment and developmental outcomes over time research brief*. Department for Education. https://assets.publishing.service.gov.uk/government/uploads/system/uploads/attachment_data/file/455670/RB455_Effective_pre-school_primary_and_secondary_education_project.pdf.pdf

Talaee, E., & Noroozi, O. (2019). Re-conceptualization of 'digital divide' among primary school children in an era of saturated access to technology. *International Electronic Journal of Elementary Education*, 12(1), 27–35. https://doi.org/10.26822/iejee.2019155334

Tamis-LeMonda, C. S., Luo, R., McFadden, K. E., Bandel, E. T., & Vallotton, C. (2019). Early home learning environment predicts children's 5th grade academic skills. *Applied Developmental Science*, 23(2), 153–169. https://doi.org/10.1080/10888691.2017.1345634

Tan, L., & Kim, B. (2019). Adolescents' agentic work on developing personal pedagogies on social media. *Literacy*, 53, 196–205. https://doi.org/10.1111/lit.12180

Teale, W. H., & Sulzby, E. (1986). *Emergent literacy as a perspective for examining how young children become writers and readers*. Ablex.

Teale, W. H., Whittingham, C. E., & Hoffman, E. B. (2020). Early literacy research, 2006–2015: A decade of measured progress. *Journal of Early Childhood Literacy*, 20(2), 169–222. https://doi.org/10.1177/1468798418754939

The Sutton Trust. (2011). *Improving the impact of teachers on pupil achievement in the UK*. The Sutton Trust. https://dera.ioe.ac.uk//30348/

Thurston, A., Cockerill, M., Chaing, T.-H., Taylor, A., & O'Keefe, J. (2020). An efficacy randomized controlled trial of reciprocal reading in secondary schools. *International Journal of Educational Research*, 104, 101626. https://doi.org/10.1016/j.ijer.2020.101626

Tizard, B., & Hughes, M. (2002). *Young children learning* (2nd ed.). Blackwell.

Torppa, M., Niemi, P., Vasalampi, K., Lerkkanen, M. K., Tolvanen, A., & Poikkeus, A. M. (2020). Leisure reading (but not any kind) and reading comprehension support each other – a longitudinal study across grades 1 and 9. *Child Development*, 91(3), 876–900. https://doi.org/10.1111/cdev.13241

Tracey, L., Boehnke, J. R., Elliott, L., Thorley, K., Ellison, S., & Bowyer-Crane, C. (2019). *Grammar for writing: Evaluation report and executive summary*. Education Endowment Foundation.

Travers, M.-C. (2016). *Success against the odds! An analysis of the influences involved in accessing, experiencing and completing an undergraduate degree for white working class men*. Unpublished PhD. King's College London. https://kclpure.kcl.ac.uk/portal/en/theses/success-against-the-odds(f80c0f73-54c0-4d89-a29e-3834a013b9c7).html

Trudgill, P. (2011). Standard English: What it isn't. In T. Bex & R. J. Watts (Eds.), *Standard English: The widening debate* (pp. 117–128). Routledge.

Truncano, M. (2015). *Tablets in education*. EduTech. https://blogs.worldbank.org/edutech/tablets-education

Tunmer, W. E., & Chapman, J. W. (2012). The simple view of reading redux: Vocabulary knowledge and the independent components hypothesis. *Journal of Learning Disabilities*, 45(5), 453–466. https://doi.org/10.1177/0022219411432685

Twiselton, S. (2006). The problem with English: The exploration and development of student teachers' English subject knowledge in primary classrooms. *Literacy*, 40(2), 88–96. https://doi.org/10.1111/j.1467-9345.2006.00437.x

Twist, L., Schagan, I., & Hogson, C. (2007). *Progress in international reading literacy study (PIRLS): Reader and reading national report for England 2006*. NFER and DCSF.

UNESCO. (2018). *Global framework of reference on digital literacy skills*. http://uis.unesco.org/sites/default/files/documents/ip51-global-framework-reference-digital-literacy-skills-2018-en.pdf

UNICEF. (2019). *A world ready to learn: Prioritizing quality early childhood education*. https://www.unicef.org/media/57926/file/Aworld-ready-to-learn-advocacy-brief-2019.pdf

United Nations. (1948). *Universal declaration of human rights*.

United Nations. (n.d.). *Sustainable development goals – 4 quality education*. https://www.un.org/sustainabledevelopment/education/

Van Steensel, R., McElvany, N., Kurvers, J., & Herppich, S. (2011). How effective are family literacy programs?: Results of a meta-analysis. *Review of Educational Research*, 81(1), 69–96. https://doi.org/10.3102/0034654310388819

Veenman, M. V. J., Van Hout-Wolters, B. H. A. M., & Afflerbach, P. (2006). Metacognition and learning: Conceptual and methodological considerations. *Metacognition Learning*, 1, 3–14. https://doi.org/10.1007/s11409-006-6893-0

Vincent, C., Braun, A., & Ball, S. (2008). 'It's like saying "coloured"': Understanding and analysing the urban working classes. *The Sociological Review*, 56(1), 61–77. https://doi.org/10.1111/j.1467-954X.2008.00777.x

Vincent, C., Braun, A., & Ball, S. (2008). Childcare, choice and social class: Caring for young children in the UK. *Critical Social Policy*, 28(1), 5–26. https://doi.org/10.1177/0261018307085505

Vinopal, K., & Morrisey, T. (2020). Neighborhood disadvantage and children's cognitive skill trajectories. *Children and Youth Services Review*, 116, 105231. https://doi.org/10.1016/j.childyouth.2020.105231

Vygotsky, L. S. (1986). *Thought and language*, translated revised and edited by A. Kozulin. MIT Press.

Vygotsky, L. S., & Cole, M. (1978). *Mind in society: Development of higher psychological processes*. Harvard University Press.

Waes, V. L., Leijten, M., Roeser, J., Olive, T., & Grabowski, J. (2021). Measuring and assessing typing skills in writing research. *Journal of Writing Research*, 13(1), 107–153. https://doi.org/10.17239/jowr-2021.13.01.04

Walker, B. J. (2003). The cultivation of student self-efficacy in reading and writing. *Reading &Writing Quarterly*, 19(2), 173–187. https://doi.org/10.1080/10573560308217

Watson, A. M., & Newman, R. M. C. (2017). Talking grammatically: L1 adolescent metalinguistic reflection on writing. *Language Awareness*, 26(4), 381–398. https://doi.org/10.1080/09658416.2017.1410554

Wegerif, R. (2007). *Dialogic education and technology: Expanding the space of learning.* Springer.

Weisleder, A., & Fernald, A. (2013). Talking to children matters early language experience strengthens processing and builds vocabulary. *Psychological Science*, 24(11), 2143–2152. https://doi.org/10.1177/0956797613488145

Westbrook, J., Sutherland, J., Oakhill, J., & Sullivan, S. (2019). 'Just reading': The impact of a faster pace of reading narratives on the comprehension of poorer adolescent readers in English classrooms. *Literacy*, 56(2), 60–68.

Wiliam, D. (2019). *Dylan Wiliam: Teaching not a research-based profession.* Times Educational Supplement. https://www.tes.com/news/dylan-wiliam-teaching-not-research-based-profession

Wilkinson, A. (1965). *Spoken English. Educational review (occasional publications, No 2).* University of Birmingham.

Wilkinson, I. A., Soter, A. O., Murphy, P. K., & Lightner, S. C. (2019). Dialogue-intensive pedagogies for promoting literate thinking. In N. Mercer, R. Wegerif & L. Major (Eds.), *International handbook of research on dialogic education* (pp. 320–335). Routledge.

Willermark, S. (2018). Technological pedagogical and content knowledge: A review of empirical studies published from 2011 to 2016. *Journal of Educational Computing Research*, 56(3), 315–343. https://doi.org/10.1177/0735633117713114

Winter, E., Costello, A., O'Brien, M., & Hickey, G. (2021). Teachers' use of technology and the impact of Covid-19. *Irish Educational Studies*, 40(2), 235–246. https://doi.org/10.1080/03323315.2021.1916559

Wood, D., Bruner, J. S., & Ross, G. (1976). The role of tutoring in problem solving. *Journal of Child Psychology and Psychiatry*, 17(2), 89–100. https://doi.org/10.1111/j.1469-7610.1976.tb00381.x

Wood, C., Clark, C., Teravainen-Goff, A., Rudkin, G., & Vardy, E. (2020). Exploring the literacy-related behaviours and feelings of pupils eligible for free school meals in relation to their use of and access to school libraries. *School Library Research*, 23. http://irep.ntu.ac.uk/id/eprint/40185

Wright, T. S., & Cervetti, G. N. (2017). A systematic review of the research on vocabulary instruction that impacts text comprehension. *Reading Research Quarterly*, 52(2), 203–226. https://doi.org/10.1002/rrq.163

Wyse, D., Jones, R., Bradford, H., & Wolpert, M. (2018). *Teaching English, language and literacy* (4th ed.). Routledge.

Zemlock, D., Vinci-Booher, S., & James, K. H. (2018). Visual–motor symbol production facilitates letter recognition in young children. *Reading and Writing*, 31, 1255–1271. https://doi.org/10.1007/s11145-018-9831-z

Zentella, A. C. (2005). *Building on strength: Language and literacy in Latino families and communities.* Teachers College Press.

INDEX